Wilderness Mission

Wilderness Mission

Preliminary Studies

OF THE

Texas Catholic Historical Society

II

TEXAS CATHOLIC HISTORICAL SOCIETY
STUDIES IN SOUTHWESTERN CATHOLIC HISTORY
NUMBER 2

Jesús F. de la Teja
General Editor

Austin, Texas
1999

First Edition

Some chapters originally appeared in other publications:
Peter P. Forrestal, "The Venerable Padre Fray Antonio Margil de Jesús," *Mid-America* 3, 4 (April 1932); Paul J. Foik, "Early Plans for the German Catholic Colonization in Texas," *Mid-America* 5, 4 (1934); published courtesy *Mid-America*, Department of History, Loyola University Chicago, 6525 North Sheridan Road, Chicago, Illinois 60626.

Francis Borgia Steck, "Forerunners of Captain De León's Expedition to Texas, 1670–1675," *The Southwestern Historical Quarterly* 36, 1 (July 1932); Carlos E. Castañeda, "Silent Years in Texas History," *The Southwestern Historical Quarterly* 38, 2 (Oct. 1934); published courtesy the Texas State Historical Association, 2.306 Richardson Hall, University Station, Austin, Texas 78712.

Peter P. Forrestal, "Peña's Diary of the Aguayo Expedition," *Records and Studies of the United States Catholic Historical Society* 24 (Oct. 1934); published courtesy The United States Catholic Historical Society, The Catholic University of America, Washington, D.C. 20064.

ISBN 0–9660966–1–4

Cover. 1935 stamp issued by the bishop of Guadalajara, Francisco Orozco y Jiménez, in commemoration of the death of the Venerable Fr. Antonio Margil de Jesús.

CONTENTS

FOREWORD

Heading into the 1936 Texas Centennial, Father Paul J. Foik, C.S.C., president of the Texas Catholic Historical Society and chairman of the Knights of Columbus Historical Commission, had acquired statewide status. He was a member of a state commission charged with how the centennial should be commemorated and with determining what historical projects should be funded. He had an opportunity to promote a positive view of the state's Catholic heritage and he ran with it.

Foik and those he enlisted into the service of promoting a positive view of Texas's Catholic past had a lot of work to do. Although Herbert E. Bolton and some of his students had revealed the extent and complexity of Spain's frontier history, a regional response to the Turnerian frontier thesis that America's political and social institutions were a product of westward expansion, their emphasis was not exactly what Foik and fellow Catholic scholars had in mind. While Bolton looked at the missions as an arm of imperial government and the missionizing process as an instrument for the extension of royal control, Catholic writers wished to emphasize the religious and civilizing project of the Franciscans. For them, Catholicism was the first form of Christianity to enter Texas and the instrument by which the region began to be carved from the wilderness. The Texas centennial could not become a celebration solely of the previous century of Texas history which, after all, had been dominated by the largely Protestant Anglo-American migration so closely tied to Manifest Destiny.

The stories on which Foik chose to focus during the second volume's run of the *Preliminary Studies* reflect a two-fold agenda. First, the heroic efforts of Franciscan explorer-missionaries to seek out and begin the Christianization process among the native peoples of Texas. These pioneer tales are told mostly in the form of *entrada* diaries of the late-seventeenth and early eighteenth centuries—the Terán de los Ríos, Ramón, and Aguayo expeditions—or articles documenting related activities for which diaries were not available—Steck on Fray Larios and companions, Castañeda on St. Denis. These writings placed Catholic pioneers on the same footing with later Anglo-American explorers and frontiersmen. The religious and their secular counterparts were involved in the same process of bringing civilization to the wilderness that Stephen F. Austin and his compatriots were heir to over a century later. A point further illustrated in Foik's own article on Catholic-German colonization efforts.

The second agenda was to counter the anti-Catholic rhetoric that was still popular in the 1930s, although much reduced from its Klan directed heyday in the 1920s. In this view early Spanish-Catholic activities were integral to an understanding of Texas history and part-and-parcel of the state's patriotic heritage. Carlos Castañeda's 1932 Columbus Day address to the Knights of Columbus, titled "The Six Flags of Texas," admirably carried the weight. It concludes:

> it is significant that the pioneers in the real beginnings of civilization in the state were the humble and pious Franciscan missionaries who almost three centuries ago, when there were no material incentives to stimulate interest in the country, braved the hardships of the wilderness, risked their lives, and gave the best they had in them to save the souls of the natives and to implant the seeds of Christian civilization in Texas, the land of God's special predilection. May the Stars and Stripes wave over the state forever, a guarantee of justice and liberty!

Foik was determined to prove that Catholics could be both good Americans and Texans **and** good Roman Catholics. The ironies in Foik's efforts cannot be overlooked. He was Canadian-born, and arrived in Texas in 1924, a forty-four year-old Holy Cross priest charged with directing the library at what was then St. Edward's College in Austin. His most important collaborator and the man he entrusted to carry the message of Catholic-American patriotism was Castañeda, a Mexican-born fellow librarian-historian, who was in charge of the precursor to the Nettie Lee Benson Latin American Collection at the University of Texas at Austin. By the time Castañeda's piece appeared as volume 2, number 4, of the *Preliminary Studies* in January 1933, plans had already been launched for what became the two men's most significant collaboration and the latter's magnum opus, *Our Catholic Heritage in Texas*, the inclusive philosophy behind which the title makes abundantly clear.

Although the included studies have begun to show their age— outmoded style, culturally unfashionable or unacceptable attitudes—they remain an important body of evidence, both historically and historiographically. They attest to a rich documentary legacy that remains one of the few windows on the world of the Texas Indians, before, during, and after subjugation. Just as important, they document the early struggle to make a large portion of the state's population confident in its place in Texas and American history. That they remain useful instruments in the Texas social science tool chest, attests to their enduring contribution to the study of Texas history.

JESÚS F. DE LA TEJA

GENERAL EDITOR'S NOTE

As was the case with its predecessor, preparation of volume two of the *Preliminary Studies of the Texas Catholic Historical Society* for publication in a new edition has entailed work on both the text and the notes. As far as possible, given the lack of a uniform style in the original series, an effort has been made to standardize citations to primary and secondary sources according to current standards as represented by the Chicago *Manual of Style*, 13th edition. The text has been altered minimally to achieve some consistency of usage in matters of capitalization and punctuation. Every effort has been made to leave the author's original wording in place. Where absolutely necessary for clarity, explanatory notes have been introduced, clearly set off from the original notes by remaining unnumbered. To assist researchers in following the trails of the authors, a three-part select bibliography has again been included. Part I focuses on the location of the primary material used in the text. Part II lists all the secondary sources cited throughout the volume. Part III lists other secondary sources regarding the subject matter of the essays in the volume, including newer works and alternative translations of documents.

The reader should consider that the works included in this volume are products of their time. A late twentieth-century audience will necessarily find some of the language used insensitive or offensive, and some of the ideas expressed therein equally disturbing. Nevertheless, in putting before the public the fruits of research into Texas's early history, the authors' services to the historical community and the state's population in general deserve recognition and attention.

THE EXPEDITION OF DON DOMINGO TERÁN DE LOS RÍOS INTO TEXAS

TRANSLATED BY
Mattie Austin Hatcher*

FOREWORD

Here is presented for the first time in English, a complete translation of the principal documents of the Terán Expedition into Texas (1691–1692). There are several texts to be found with slight variations in different parts of the Archivo General y Público de México. The record followed by the translator is a transcript from the group, known as *Colección de Memorias de Nueva España*, which forms the nucleus of the division named Historia. The precise title of volumes 27 and 28, referring to Texas is as follows: *Documentos para la Historia Eclesiastica, y Civil de la Provincia de Texas.* Another text may be found in volume 182 of the division called Provincias Internas. Quite recently documents from the ancient Convento Grande de San Francisco have been made available at the Biblioteca Nacional in Mexico City, and reproductions by photostat of this relevant material have been provided by Professor Carlos E. Castañeda, Latin-American Librarian at the University of Texas. A comparative study of these documents has been carried on and differences observed and noted. These efforts have helped greatly in giving a more exact and faithful rendition of these original sources. Throughout the whole text used, the translator found many colloquialisms, pleonasms and inaccuracies. The editor and translator wish to acknowledge with thanks several careful readings of the manuscript by Professor Castañeda and the aid given by him in interpreting many passages that were peculiarly involved and difficult.

Paul J. Foik, C.S.C.
Chairman of the Commission and President of the Society

---

*Vol. 2, No. 1, appeared in January 1932

The Expedition of Don Domingo Terán de los Ríos Into Texas (1691–1692)

INTRODUCTION

The expedition of Don Domingo de Terán into Texas, in the years 1691–1692, the third official *entrada* into the region, marks the true beginning of missionary work among the Tejas Indians. It is therefore an important link in the story of the Spanish occupation of the country and of their attempt to place a barrier against the westward expansion of the French of Louisiana. The instructions for the guidance of the leaders, military, and ecclesiastical, the record which forms Part One of the series of documents, presuppose absolute unity of purpose between Terán and the missionaries, under the direction of Damián Massanet. Part Two, however, the account kept by Terán, and Part Three, the story recorded by the priests, graphically picture the differences which arose at the very beginning of the journey and which so handicapped the work as to render the trip without any appreciable results.

To understand the situation, a brief résumé of the two previous expeditions is necessary. Alonso de León had been named as commander of the first expedition in 1689, as well as the second in 1690. His purpose was to clear Texas of all French interlopers, who had entered the country with La Salle, and thus to thwart the French claims and plans for possession of the country. In the first of these expeditions, De León had found "the fort he was seeking dismantled, the building sacked, and the Frenchmen dead." To be sure that all immediate danger of French aggression was removed, he and Massanet had an interview with certain of the Indian tribes whom they met in the vicinity, and in answer to their plea for Spanish priests had promised to return the following year to live among them. This gave the Franciscan Fathers of the College of Querétaro, who for some years had been trying to extend their labors among this "peculiarly intelligent and friendly nation," an opportunity to carry out their cherished plans. Fear of the French also had now forced the civil authorities in Mexico to undertake the permanent occupation of the country.

During De León's second *entrada* "the feast of Corpus Christi was celebrated in East Texas among the Tejas Indians on the twenty-fifth of May, in the presence of the chief and all his nation. When Mass was over, the ceremony of raising the standard in the king's name was performed, possession was taken of the country, and the Mission of San Francisco de los Tejas was founded." It was located between the Trinity and the Neches rivers, four hundred miles from the nearest Spanish settlement. Three Franciscans, Miguel Fontcubierta, Francisco de Jesús María de Casañas, and Antonio Bordoy were left under the protection of three soldiers to carry on missionary work in a remote wilderness among a nation whose ears were ever open to the seductive words of any Frenchman who might appear on the scene. Undaunted by these difficulties, Father Casañas at once founded a second mission nearby; while Father Massanet set out for Mexico City to arrange for a more aggressive campaign against the demons who were entrenched among the savages. The third *entrada* under the leadership of Massanet and Domingo Terán followed immediately and the records they kept are of great value to the anthropologist and the historian, particularly to those interested in the missionary work in Texas.

I

INSTRUCTIONS GIVEN BY THE SUPERIOR GOVERNMENT TO BE OBSERVEDIN THE EXPEDITION TO THE PROVINCE OF TEXAS, JANUARY 23, 1691[1]

1. It is to be understood that the principal purposes of the said *entrada* are to establish eight missions in the aforesaid Province of Texas and in adjacent territory and mountain ranges for the priests of our Holy Father, Saint Francis; to explore and describe the country; and to ascertain whether the French or any other Europeans live there, either in large or small numbers. The procedure shall be as follows:

2. The preliminary preparations for the journey having been decided upon, the *entrada* shall be made, starting from Villa de Monclova. A description thereof shall be kept. Unless some grave obstacle prevents, the journey shall be made directly northward to the said province and the principal settlement

[1]"Documentos para la historia eclesiástica y civil de la provincia de Texas," Ramo Historia, Vol. 27, ff. 16–23, Archivo General y Público de la Nación de México, photostatic transcripts, Catholic Archives of Texas. The citations for Terán's diary: ibid., ff. 23–74; Massanet's diary: ibid., ff. 87–112. Bruno's diary, declaration of Alonso de Rivera, the *parecer* of Massanet and his companions, and Captain Francisco Martínez's diary of his journey to the Texas coast are here omitted.

The copy from the Archivo de San Francisco el Grande carries the fuller title: "Instrucción á que se hand de arreglar en la nueva entrada á la provincia de los texas o techas, así el gobernador de la gente y armas de ellas y mi teniente el capitán general de Domingo Terán de los Ríos, como los demas cabos, ministros eclesiasticos, y soldados, cada uno por lo que le toca según su empleo." Further variations of texts will not be noted unless they involve a difference in interpretation.

of the Texas Indians, where their captain and governor resides and where the three missionaries and the soldiers of the previous *entrada* of 1690 remained.

3. When within sixteen or twenty leagues from the said settlement, or any other distance that may be considered proper, camp shall be made and a report of the trip and other information shall be sent forward by messengers. One of the missionaries and one other person of intelligence shall be chosen for this task. In view of the reply that may be brought back, measures for hastening and making the *entrada* successful can be considered and decided upon without arousing the suspicions, misgivings, or fears of the Indians. Whatever they may decide upon as to the number of priests and soldiers that are to make up the party entering, shall be agreed to. Their suggestions as to the location of the camp and other appurtenances shall likewise be considered. The spot selected should be one at a convenient distance from the village, and the necessity and wisdom of maintaining an adequate guard should be kept in mind.

4. After the priests and the soldiers who are to go into the settlement and build their quarters have entered, and after the stock and the supplies designated for use in gaining the friendship of the Indians and winning their affections have been taken—or sooner if it be thought wise—the aforesaid Don Domingo de Terán, in company with the prelate and commissioner, Fray Damián Massanet, shall proceed to distribute in the name of the king and myself, the gifts and trinkets that are to be delivered to the governor and captain of the said settlement, as a reward for his friendship, his acceptance of the religion of the Catholic Church, and his allegiance to the king, as evidenced by his oath. Efforts shall be made to satisfy his doubts concerning the death of the Indian.[2] My regrets over his death, the steps taken for the punishment of the aggressor, and other details that may help to satisfy him shall be explained. After he has been appeased, a conference and council shall be held to determine the best means of establishing the missions and providing for their management, deciding upon spots for their location and the aid that is to be furnished in each case. The decisions should be made on the basis of progressive establishments proceeding by easy stages, without wasting effort by locating the most difficult, dangerous and troublesome one first.

---

[2]One of the Indians who had gone to Mexico with De León. See Lilia M. Casís, trans., "The 1690 Letter from Fray Massanet to Don Carlos de Sigüenza," *The Quarterly of the Texas State Historical Association* 2, 4 (April 1899): 307, and Herbert E. Bolton, *Spanish Explorations of the Southwest, 1542–1706*, Original Narratives of Early American History Vol. 18 (New York, 1925), 405–23.

5. If, as seems proper, a trip to the country of the Cadodachos[*] and the pueblos of these Indians,[3] or to those of other Indians should be decided upon and carried out for the purpose of establishing missions among them, the same policy followed in the case of the Texas Indians shall be observed in case the conditions are similar. It is to be understood that neither the above named nations nor any other dealt with, shall be reduced to royal obedience or brought under the dominion of the king, or of the Catholic religion, or of the missionaries by force or violence. They shall be controlled by persuasion, kindness, gentle and considerate treatment. Arms are not to be used except in case of self defense, or for the protection of friendly Indians, or those who have sworn allegiance to the crown. Neither are the Indians to be encouraged or induced to wage offensive war against other tribes.

6. It is our desire, first of all, that this undertaking shall have as its object the establishment of missions, and the spread of the Catholic Faith and the Holy Gospel. It is our desire, also, that all the money furnished in the king's name shall be applied to this end and to the development of the proposed evangelical work. To this end the governor and military commander, as well as his corporals and soldiers must avoid all carelessness in conduct and example. They must be anxious to prove their honesty, their religious faith, and their charity by their acts—especially before the Indians. They must not cause the Indians any trouble, either in persons or property. They shall not arouse their anger by interfering with their women. They must conduct themselves with that respect and reverence which is their duty to show the missionaries because of their office, especially with regard to the commissioner and prelate, Fray Damián Massanet, who is the director and leader of the undertaking and of the spiritual conquest. This the governor shall do and cause to be done without permitting any excesses among his subordinates.

7. The supplies, the horses, and cattle destined for the establishment and support of the missions and for the gratification of the Indians must be under the care of the said commissioner. They shall be given out and distributed at his discretion, without the intervention of the governor, who shall exercise jurisdiction only over his soldiers and subordinates. The governor shall watch over their conduct and see that they protect the supplies and stock. He shall endeavor to see that these reach their destination without loss or damage and that they are not wasted or misapplied under any pretext whatever.

---

[*]E.i. Kadohadachos, the Caddo confederacy occupying the northeastern corner of present-day Texas, and portions of Louisiana, Arkansas, and Oklahoma.

[3]See map of the Cadodacho settlement, Herbert E. Bolton, *Texas in the Middle Eighteenth Century: Studies in Spanish Colonial History and Administration*, The University of California Publications in History vol. 3 (Berkeley, 1915), frontispiece.

8. Concerning the orders and instructions of the preceding paragraph touching the military leader and commander of the troops, Don Domingo Terán, it must be understood that it is his duty to explore the said province of the Texas Indians and the surrounding territory and mountain ranges, and especially, to see if there are any habitations established by the French or other nations of Europe, be they large settlements, or scattered individuals, ecclesiastics or seculars. It shall be his duty to ascertain the occupation and employment of the latter, and, in case the settlers are seculars, to make them prisoners, to take their declarations, and to bring them to this court. However, their treatment shall not be very harsh. He is reminded, in this connection, that information has been received concerning four Frenchmen who, just before the arrival of the members of the previous *entrada*, sent a messenger to the principal settlement of the Texas Indians, believing it to be a more distant settlement which this nation has further to the northward, asking for the friendship of the aforesaid nation and trying to persuade them not to have friendly relations with the Spaniards. For this purpose, the messenger left a note at a settlement two leagues distant from the main settlement of the Texas Indians. Terán shall try to secure this paper. It is also understood that information was at the same time secured from the Province of the Cadodachos that a white nation was located to the northward of the river which divides them, where presents of knives, beads, and other things had been made to the Indians, and that the priests of our Holy Father Saint Francis had been seen traveling through the country with staffs and crosses, baptizing and teaching them the Christian doctrine. In case the aforesaid governor shall meet these two, he shall, without using any force—since they are Apostolic Catholic priests—secure information concerning their nationality and the reasons for their entry into the region, as well as concerning the commissions or patents under which they have entered and the dates of the said instruments. He shall at once try to secure their cooperation and bring them to an agreement with the missionaries of his own company. He shall not consider it improper to make an effort to have them labor together, but shall endeavor to do so by means of conferences between them and the prelate, Fray Damián Massanet.

9. Information shall also be secured in regard to the river above mentioned which separates the settlements of the Cadodachos as well as in regard to another very large river which flows two leagues distant from the principal habitations of the Texas Indians. In case it flows toward the Atlantic [Mar del Norte] and the coast thereof, it is important for the government that the said governor, Don Domingo Terán, explore its source, its crossings, and its point of entry into the sea. He shall investigate the truthfulness of these reports—as far as possible—but this shall not serve as an obstacle in the way of carrying out the other provisions of this expedition. With this in view, he shall try to

measure the depth of the rivers, especially in the last third of the course toward the ocean, and explore the country for several leagues around the bays and ports where they may enter—in case there be such—indicating the size and shape of these and giving the latitude of each.

10. To facilitate further the more perfect execution of all that has been enumerated, especially the exploration of the said rivers, he is to receive by sea at least forty persons trained in seamanship, boat-making, and other allied crafts. The vessel in which this voyage is to be made is to be in Bahía del Espíritu Santo toward the end of April of this year. The said governor shall arrange for his lieutenant, Captain Francisco Martínez, to be within sight of this bay at this time with twenty of the soldiers who are in his company and the munitions, horses, and necessary supplies, so that, in company with the people from the vessel under their own officer, he may proceed by land from the bay, following the governor and his party. From there the said governor shall make an examination of the rivers in the manner described. This done, the said officer shall perform the duties prescribed in the instructions. Don Domingo Terán shall perform the duties assigned him in the subsequent paragraphs of these instructions.

11. For the better and more accurate execution of all that has been ordered, after the necessary arrangements have been made, the supplies collected, and the people gathered together for the expedition, the said governor, in conference with the prelate and commissioner, Fray Damián Massanet, and with Captain Francisco Martínez—who is his lieutenant in all duties entrusted to him—shall divide the soldiers into groups and shall assign to each the task he is to perform. He shall give them the instructions they are to observe, and shall take pains to see that the orders given are the best suited to the ability of each soldier for the accomplishment of the purposes desired, thus uniting mental and physical effort in carrying out the main object of the expedition, the establishment of the missions.

12. The description of the trip to be undertaken must be kept in the form of a diary, written after consultation with the said commissioner and the accompanying priests, the said Captain Martínez, and the other members of the company who seem to be most intelligent and best fitted for deciding what is to be done. The recording of what happens and of what is discovered every day shall not be postponed until the subsequent day; but, as soon as the camp is made and the said conference held, the events and explorations of the day shall be carefully written down. This record is to be approved by the said governor, his lieutenant or, in his absence, some other official, and by the commissioner of the missions. The character of the country explored shall be noted, together with the numerous kinds of fruits, plants, and animals that abound, and a statement made of the climate, the altitude, the valleys, the

mountains, the principal rivers, the distance between them, the tribes found living in each section, their civilization, government, customs, religious rites, and other notable things that may be thought essential. As a result of the information secured and after the consultation provided for has been held, the place for the halt or encampment shall be decided upon. It is to be understood that a detailed examination of conditions shall not prevent the prompt execution of the plans as specified and the prosecution of the expedition for the purpose of founding the missions, since this detailed examination is to be undertaken only in case it is thought necessary for the execution of the main purpose and to guarantee the compliance of the orders listed in the previous paragraphs.

13. After the consultation provided for, the said governor shall give names to such important places, rivers, and woods as have no name or which were not given names during the *entrada* of Captain Alonso de León; and these shall be recorded on the day they were examined.

14. The said governor, Don Domingo Teráu, shall see that the soldiers he has under his command shall perform their duties with precision, keeping their arms, munitions, and horses in good condition and in such state that they will be able to use them in an emergency or in case of an unexpected development. He shall see that they post sentinels and that they are trained in the use of arms and in horsemanship while on the trip. Those who may not be sufficiently familiar with the use of either shall go through the necessary training with the proper application, zeal, and prudence.

15. If there be any differences or lack of agreement with any of the missionaries, the officers, or the intelligent persons selected for the conferences mentioned above regarding any operation whatever, the said governor, Don Domingo Terán, shall see that the matter is referred to a formal council of the said persons, who, after consultation, shall decide what is best for the royal service. In case the forces should be divided for the examination of any section of the country or for any purpose whatever, the governor shall form them into squads, following the same procedure with each. In each case, the officers shall consult with the missionaries that may be in the squad and the persons of the greatest experience and intelligence therein. The governor shall exercise great care in establishing the missions, giving careful consideration to their location, their supplies, and their garrison, and acting upon the advice of the principal missionary, the commissioner and prelate, Fray Damián Massanet, and abiding by the general opinion of all in deciding what is most conducive to the best and most efficient accomplishment of the end sought.

16. The said governor, Don Domingo Terán, shall also keep in mind the state of his supplies, the munitions, and the number of men, in order not to undertake any operation that presents insurmountable difficulties, or that may

serve to delay the establishment of the said missions, or occasion an excessive loss of the people under his care, thus making it impossible for him to retreat safely or to protect his men from lack of provisions or from any other cause.

17. When he has executed the principal duties prescribed in the preceding paragraphs, the said governor shall plan his return to this court to give me an account of what he has accomplished. In case he does not entirely retrace his course or any portion of it, he shall describe the new places and the country through which he passes in the manner and form above described. He shall not bring back with him, from among the nations he may visit and examine, more Indians than he may need as interpreters or guides, or for safety on the return trip to Villa de Santiago de Monclova, unless the said nations suggest the sending of certain Indians who in their name shall come to visit me in proof of their friendship, obedience, and gratitude. In order that each of the officers and the principal missionaries in the said expedition shall meet the conditions set down for each in the preceding paragraphs of these instructions, the said governor, Don Domingo Terán, shall make these duties known to the prelate and commissioner, Fray Damián Massanet, to his lieutenant, Francisco Martínez, and to such other of the priests and officials as may be considered essential, in order that each may make the necessary preparations for the trip and carry out his obligations in every particular. This I expect from his zeal and application to the service of God and of His Majesty, the King. Mexico, January 23, 1691.

II–A

ITINERARY AND DAILY ACCOUNT KEPT BY GENERAL DOMINGO DE TERÁN, BEGUN MAY 16, 1691, FINISHED APRIL 15, 1692[4]

MAY

On Wednesday, the sixteenth day of the said month and year, the march was started. Our troops moved forward in military formation and with proper

[4]The fuller title in the Archivo de San Francisco el Grande is as follows: "Description, Daily Demarcation of the Country, Exploration, Examination, and Sounding of the Bays in Search of a Port, and the Diary of the Journey Made by General Domingo de Terán de los Ríos, Military Governor of the Kingdom and Province of Texas, in Command Both by Land and Sea of the Aforesaid Country and of the Territory to the North and South, and Representative of His Excellency, the Viceroy, in Obedience to the Order and Express Command of His Excellency, Conde de Galve, Viceroy, Lieutenant Governor, and Captain General of these Kingdoms and Provinces of New Spain, in Response to Repeated Royal Cedulas Issued by the King, Our Lord, for the Purpose of Carrying Out Certain Measures Conceived by this Monarch, Noted for His Wisdom as well as for His Zeal and Application to the Service of Both Majesties, Certain Points, Cases, and Things for the Time Being Omitted. Dated, May 16, 1691."

precautions from the Presidio of Coahuila, en route for the Kingdom of the Texas Nation and the other provinces lying to the northward, the troops, the Fathers of the Holy Evangel—in the order of their rank—the supplies, munitions, horses under my charge, and all the retinue following. We traveled one league north and set up our standard.

On the 17th we continued our journey with our royal standard, going down the river toward the northeast, a quarter north. We marched seven leagues over a level country and camped at a good spot, which I called Nuestra Señora de Guadalupe.

On the 18th we pursued our trip in the same direction along the south bank of the river below Nadadores, between two mountain ranges which, in the previous expedition, had been called Baluartes. At this time I named them Los Dos Farallones. This night we camped on the river at a splendid location which had been agreed upon and described. Here we found a large cottonwood tree which towered above all the rest of the trees. We traveled seven leagues toward the above mentioned kingdom over a level country with good pasturage. I called this place Nuestra Señora de Guía.

On the 19th we proceeded toward the east, a quarter northeast, down the river to the junction of the streams called Coahuila Nadadores and Sabinas. I named them San Francisco and Sabinas, because in them and on the banks thereof there were a great number of *tarayes*.[5] We found a crossing above the junction. After we had gone six leagues we pitched camp and waited until the 24th for the troops and the people from Caldera.

On the 24th of the said month and year, we continued our march down the river over a hill. After fording the river in an easterly direction, we traversed seven leagues over open country, leaving behind us the crags and peaks of New Spain. We set up camp at a place called in the preceding journey, El Real de Pescados; but in this expedition under my direction I named it Ascención del Señor, because it was His day. On this day and the following I prepared a formal and detailed report of how the Fathers of the Holy Evangel, the cavalry under my charge, the troops, the supplies, the baggage, and all the people composing the expedition had assembled. This I sent to the viceroy by a soldier.

On the 26th, after moving toward the northeast, a quarter north, we established our camp between two ponds of rain water, having marched five leagues over a level country, in which there were thickets of brambles that are commonly called cats'-claws. I named the said ponds and the camp San Ementerio and San Celando.

---

[5]A tamarind, a tree indigenous to India, but used in Texas when speaking of small willows growing in swampy ground.

On the 27th we continued our march toward the northeast along the bank of an arroyo on which, in the preceding journey, the Indians found the Frenchman Juan.[6] After traveling four leagues we set up our royal standard according to military requirements and I called it San Francisco de Borja.

On the 28th we proceeded north, taking the direction of the Rio Grande, which was so named in the preceding expeditions. In this expedition I called it Río del Norte because it really was this river. I set up our royal standard on the bank thereof and remained at this place four days, because on the night of our arrival, there was a stampede, causing the loss of sixty horses from the herd, and I may add, nine mules besides. Eight soldiers went out in pursuit. During the search they were scattered in squads over a distance of fifteen or twenty leagues. Within this radius, but eighteen horses could be found. The Indians of the Odoesmades, Mescaleros [Mexcales]* and Momones nations, and others, who are their allies, inhabit this region. On the previous journey many had been found but on this trip none were encountered. The area supports a great number of buffaloes in regular herds, like those seen along the Río de la Plata and the surrounding country. The region is marked by canyons and peaks which dominate the territory. The soil is harder than the preceding section. Many medium sized willows were seen, while among smaller plants was one which is commonly called cats' claws. I named this river Santa Elvira and Río del Norte, its real name. We marched this day six leagues along its banks. We crossed to the other side with a loss of forty-nine saddle horses. While transferring the whole train composing my expedition, three head of stock were drowned. The current is exceedingly rapid, where it is narrowest from bank to bank. Here the river's width must be about a gunshot. I mention, too, that with great rejoicing and solemnity, I left three crosses set up and built arbors at the spot where our camp had been located, in order that our Holy Faith may be preserved and that the Indians of the region, who were known to be apostates, might resume their conversion and reduction into the bosom of the church. I encouraged the people to cross the said river on horseback carrying seventeen hundred head of small stock in their arms against the strong current. The water was rising so rapidly as to endanger the life of every person in my expedition. However, the great power of our Lady of Guadalupe, the North Star and Protector of this undertaking, carried our weak efforts in this task to a successful ending. There was a storm that night with lightning and thunder, wind and rain, with the gale whirling in from all directions. It blew down all the tents and exposed us to its fury. The

---

[6]Jean Gery, probably an early deserter from La Salle's colony. See "The 1690 Letter from Fray Massanet," 282.

*Not to be confused with the Mescalero Apaches.

tempest lasted from one o'clock at night until four in the morning. Most of the trees were washed up by the roots, and the general's tent and trunks were damaged by the waters of an arroyo which deluged them.

JUNE

Saturday, June 3rd of the same year, we proceeded toward the north, a quarter northeast. After traveling four leagues, we set up our royal standard at the spot called in the previous expedition El Charco del Cuervo. However, in my *entrada* I called it San Alexo.*

On the 4th of the same month, we continued our march toward the north, a quarter northeast, over a level country. After advancing five leagues, we halted on the banks of an arroyo called in the preceding trip Ramos. At this time I named it San Cayetano.†

On the 5th we directed our steps toward the north, a quarter northeast, over a level country, with mesquites in some of the sections. After traveling four leagues, camp was struck on the highest point on the bank of an arroyo, called Caramanchel in the previous expedition, but in this one, San Francisco Solano.‡

On the 6th we resumed our journey towards the north, a quarter northeast over a country partly broken and partly level. We crossed two ravines and stretches of timber and entered a region covered with mesquites. This lasted until we reached the banks of a river, which had been named Nueces in the preceding trips. On this expedition I named it San Diego. We traveled four leagues.

On the 7th we worked our way toward the east about two leagues through timber and big pecan trees, cutting a passage for the troops. After penetrating these woods in single file, we continued two leagues toward the north, inclining somewhat toward the east. The country was level and covered with mesquites and cat's-claws. The trip was a hard one, because the journey was into the timber lands and this delayed us. Camp was made after we moved forward six leagues. During the march we lost six head of cattle. It was not possible to locate them in the forest. It was necessary to stay in camp next day, because the packs had been damaged and some of the small stock had staid that night in the woods.

---

*Terán's proclivity for renaming geographic features already named by previous explorers (and even by himself) contradicted his orders and has produced some confusion for scholars. The problem is compounded by Fray's Massanet independent naming efforts. Needless to say, with one notable exception, the names applied during the Terán expedition did not survive.

†Comanche Creek.

‡The same stream.

On the 9th of the said month, the march continued toward the north, over hills and plains. After advancing six leagues, we camped on the bank of a river called in the previous expedition El Hondo, but in this one under my direction, San Pedro.* On the night of the day mentioned, there was a storm and a hurricane that caused a scattering of our horses. This forced us to stop on the 10th. We finally recovered them all.

On the 11th of the said month, our royal standard and camp moved forward toward the north a league and a half to an arroyo which had not been named in the previous expedition, as we were traveling in a different direction. It was considered a shorter and easier route from the Hondo River to the Kingdom of the Texas. Besides there was a different guide. I named the arroyo San Diego. From this point our journey was a quarter northeast. We marched six leagues to the bank of a larger arroyo. I named it San Simón.†

On the 12th, continuing our march toward the east, we discovered a new road and traveled over a level region like that along the Rio de la Plata with its herds, until our royal standard halted on the banks of another arroyo, which, at various points, on previous trips, had been called the Medina. There were great numbers of buffaloes here. On this expedition, I named it San Luis Beltrán. We traveled this day five leagues.

On the 13th our royal standard and camp moved forward in the aforesaid easterly direction. We marched five leagues over a fine country with broad plains, the most beautiful in New Spain. We camped on the banks of an arroyo adorned by a great number of trees, cedars, willows, cypresses, osiers, oaks, and many other kinds. This I called San Antonio de Pádua,‡ because we had reached it on his day. Here we found certain *rancherías* in which the Peyaye nation live. We observed their actions, and I discovered that they were docile and affectionate, were naturally friendly, and were decidedly agreeable toward us. I saw the possibility of using them to form reducciones[7]—the first on the Rio Grande, at the presidio, and another at this point. Different nations in between could be thereby influenced. We did not travel on the 14th because it was Corpus Christi day.

On the 15th we marched towards the east five leagues, across a country much like the preceding, with buffaloes and a great many oak trees. It is suited for all kinds of agriculture. We set up our camp that night upon the banks of

---

*Frio River.

†Hondo Creek, according to William C. Foster, *Spanish Expeditions into Texas, 1689–1768* (Austin: University of Texas Press, 1995), 72.

‡The one stream that Terán named which kept its name was the San Antonio River.

[7]*Reducción* has a special meaning, when applied to the Indians. Here it signifies the conversion of the infidel to the true religion. Evidently, the Peyaye tribe was here singled out as the possible forerunners in the great work of evangelization.—*Editor's note.*

a certain arroyo, where there is a considerable quantity of water. This I named San Ignacio de Loyola.* This night we had a terrible storm.

The 16th our royal standard and camp moved forward in the same direction four leagues across a country much like the preceding, to the banks of an arroyo with as much water, which I called Santo Domingo. This region had more trees.

On the 17th we continued our march towards the east, a quarter northeast, for four leagues and camped on the banks of another arroyo, which I named San Pedro de Alcántara.. The tract was good grazing ground, but in other respects like the preceding section. There were great numbers of buffaloes.

On the 18th our royal standard and camp proceeded in an easterly direction as before for four leagues until camp was made upon the bank of another arroyo. This I called Santa Rosa Peruana. The country was like the preceding and there were buffaloes.

On the 19th we advanced toward the east. After traveling four leagues, our standard was set up on the banks of an arroyo which I named San Agustín. The country was like the preceding. This stream had been named the Guadalupe by various expeditions which had followed different routes. Upon its banks, I found the Jumana, Cibula, Casqueza, Cantoma, and Mandones, having formal patents from the governors of Vizcaya and New Mexico. They came out to meet us about a league ahead with manifestations of peace. On this night, with four companions, I examined their *rancherías*, the number of the whole crowd being estimated at two thousand. The second night, seeing that they had left their own country far behind them, we decided that they had done so to make war against us as is their custom. During this day, therefore, we observed the precautions prescribed by military regulations. We gave them a feast in the afternoon. The next morning, the location not seeming to be a good one, we marched on, for I was uneasy because of the greed of the soldiers. I had a "talk" with the Indians through an interpreter and a private conversation with the governor and his lieutenants. They spoke Spanish and were fairly intelligent. They asked for new patents in place of the ones mentioned. I promised to present them upon my return trip. I watched their actions, movements, and expressions closely and I concluded that they were very brave, haughty and numerous.

On the 20th of the same month, the march was continued toward the east, a quarter northeast, from the banks of the said river to this one, which is supposed to be a branch of the one first named. After marching four leagues, camp was made. At night there was a disturbance among the one hundred and ten horses. Twenty-five soldiers were sent out in search of them to round

---

*Cibolo Creek, according to Foster, *Spanish Expeditions*, 72.

them up; but, after searching five days, they were not able to find them. At the end of this time, thirty-five were found. I started again, having lost seventy-five head. This delayed us until San Juan Bautista day. The country was rougher than that already traversed, because there were hills. The banks of this stream were covered with a great number of trees—pecans, cedars, willows, and other kinds found in the country.

On the 25th our royal standard was directed toward the east; having traveled four leagues, camp was set up on the banks of an arroyo. The country was more level than the region passed through and there were a great many buffaloes. This place I called Santo Tomás.

On the 26th our royal standard was moved toward the east, a quarter northeast. After going four leagues, camp was made on the bank of an arroyo, which contained a considerable amount of water. In preceding journeys it had been called the San Marcos and Colorado on various routes. At this time it was named San Pedro y San Pablo Apóstoles.* The land, as well as the timber which beautified it, were like those at San Juan Bautista. We stopped here on the 27th and 28th of the said mouth, due to the exhausted condition of our small stock.

On the 29th, the day of San Pedro y San Pablo Apóstoles, having been celebrated with unusual rejoicing in cooperation with the Fathers of the Holy Evangel, our royal standard moved forward and together we crossed the river twice, the passages being a league apart. For this reason I halted the march in order that the small stock might rest on the 30th.

JULY

On July 1st the general review of the year was held. Our standard and camp moved forward from the second crossing, traveling in a southerly direction. After marching six leagues over a rough and wooded country, our camp was set up at a third crossing of the river, the banks of which were made beautiful by the same kinds of trees as were at the other fords, especially pecans. We remained here until the 3rd, when, according to the orders of the viceroy and in fulfillment of his instructions, Captain Francisco Martínez departed with twenty soldiers from my troops, one hundred and fifty horses, forty mules, the necessary food, ammunition, and, I may add, the proper military equipment and peons to drive them, according to instructions. In obedience to the wishes of his Excellency, the march was suspended until the captain's return. The trip down to the old fort and back to this camp on the river consumed the time from our arrival on the 3rd until the 19th. I omit giving the reasons for this until I confer personally with the viceroy. This time includes the trip down, the stay

*Colorado River.

there, and the return. I may add that they brought back with them two boys of the French nation,* that the coast Indians obtained for them without any great difficulty, after a little firm yet kind insistence. During the six days' sojourn there, the said captain found that our vessels had not arrived in that bay, nor on the coast in that region. Today, the 21st, a council of the Holy Fathers of the Evangel and of the military authorities was called to consider sending the captain back to the old fort with the same number of horses as before to make fresh investigations. He was to remain for twenty days, and if the vessels failed to arrive, he was then to return to our camp on the river bank. After this attempt, I was willing to start the day after his arrival for the Texas country. But by common consent, the council finally decided to postpone the trip down to the old fort, and to continue the journey to the aforesaid kingdom on the following day. Upon arriving at that point, a force was to be sent down to the coast, and such other things as might be necessary were to be done. To the end, it was my opinion that the second departure down to the old fort should take place immediately, allowing twenty days, six more than the captain had taken for his previous journey. However, this did not coincide with the common opinion. Although my vote remained unchanged, they compelled me to continue the march on the 22nd.

On the said day, July 22nd of the same year, our royal standard moved forward toward the north, a quarter northeast. After traveling five leagues in the said direction, following a narrow trail with woods on either side, we camped upon an arroyo where there was water in holes only. The surrounding country was filled with buffaloes. Great numbers of them were in the nearby woods, covered with ticks, red bugs and other vermin. We called this place San Emeterio y San Caledón.

On the 23rd of the said mouth, our royal standard advanced six leagues in the same direction over a level country and we camped on another arroyo, the water being almost filled with buffaloes, because of the great number in the vicinity. I named it Santiago.

On the 25th our royal standard directed the course to the north, a quarter northeast. After marching four leagues we camped on the banks of a stream which the natives called Colorado. I called it San Gerónimo.† We remained upon the banks two days. During this time we built a bridge over which to cross the small stock because the stream was rising and the passage was hard enough for our horses. The small stock was so tired out, we could not go on.

---

*Eustache Bréman and Jean-Baptiste Talon.
†Brazos River.

We camped on the opposite side after traveling one league to a stream which I named San Bernardino.*

On the 28th our royal standard and camp moved toward the north, a quarter northeast. After proceeding six leagues over a level country, through a narrow passageway with many trees of various kinds on each side, we camped upon an arroyo which I called San Cipriano.† I remained in this place two days because of the exhausted condition of the small stock.

On the 31st our royal standard resumed its trip toward the north, a quarter northeast. After going four leagues through a wooded country, partly level and partly rough, we crossed an arroyo, and within about two leagues, we camped beside two water holes which I called San Isidro Labrador, Patrón de Madrid.

AUGUST

On August 1st our royal standard and camp were directed toward the north, a quarter northeast. After marching five leagues this day over mountainous and wooded country, we camped upon the banks of a river which, in the preceding journey and by different routes they called the Trinity. On the present trip I called it, La Encarnación del Verbo. We stopped one day because of the exhausted condition and fatigue of the small stock.

On the 2nd, about nine o'clock in the morning, the said Fathers of the Holy Evangel, without any cause or reason and even without notifying me, continued the march—an action so strange that it caused great consternation and worry in the whole camp, because the mode of our entry had not been decided upon. After a prolonged discussion of the motives that could have led to this, a decision was made to continue the journey on the following day.

On the 3rd our royal standard and camp continued the march toward the north, a quarter northeast from the aforesaid bank, penetrating through a dense wood and over a rough country. Our camp was set on a small arroyo that I called San Salvador. We marched this day five leagues.

On the 4th our general muster was held and our royal standard and camp moved forward in search of the Texas or Teija. The nation is called by the natives Asinay or Teixa,[8] which in their language means "friend." We made this day five leagues through the same kind of dense woods and through a rough country. The same day, about ten o'clock, after we had traveled about four leagues, one of the soldiers, whom my predecessor had left behind on the last trip, met us, bringing news about the reverend Fathers at the missions, and

---

*Probably the Little Brazos River, according to Foster, *Spanish Expeditions*, 73.

†Probably Cedar Creek, according to Foster, ibid.

[8]These variations are found in the transcript employed for this translation. Frederick W. Hodge in the *Handbook of American Indians North of Mexico*, Bureau of American Ethnology Bulletin 30, 2 pts. (Washington, D.C., 1907), lists the following: Tehas, Tejas, Teisa, Teixa, Texia, Teyans, Teyas, Teyens.

an order for us to stop a half league from the nearest one. Our royal camp was, therefore, set up in a small open space in a grove two hundred yards distant from a small arroyo. During the day we searched for and enquired after a better location, where we could quarter our troops, one better for the Indians as well as for the soldiers. But no suitable place was found within the radius of twelve leagues; for there is no open country nearby even as far as the Cadodachos nation, which is sixty leagues, more or less from this place in the same northerly direction with variations, as the road we traveled is to the San Marcos. The whole country is wooded to a distance of about twenty-five leagues from this spot. On the same day, about three o'clock in the afternoon, the governor came with all his people and all their followers to render their homage. They bore no arms. On the 6th I marched with all the cavalry, arms, munitions, and the necessary rear guard, all in military formation. At nine o'clock in the morning, after having given instructions to the governor and all his people and followers, he was expressly given to understand through three soldiers as interpreters, who had remained here at the time of the last expedition, as well as through Pedro Muni, that the king, our master, had sent us in his royal name to conduct and bring thither the Fathers of the Holy Evangel, the herds of small stock, the horses, the cattle, and all the other things according to promises made them. They were told that the king, our master, had sent them the stock, which was to be kept by the Fathers, and that the increase alone was to be used for the support of the natives and for the establishment of the missions that were to be founded. When the Indians heard this speech and this proposition, the said governor again and in the presence of the Fathers of the Holy Evangel, proceeded to repeat it to them. I told him that his Excellency, the viceroy, had directed me, as the representative of the king, and acting in his name, to deliver and place in the hands of the aforesaid governor the baton, and likewise to present him the gifts which his Excellency had sent, so that he might be able to keep his people in peace and lead them in war as occasion might demand. The said baton was offered and handed over to him, together with the trinkets sent along to gain his good will. This was done also in recognition of his obedience and his inclination toward the Christian religion and the Catholic Faith, and as a token of royal protection. I added that our coming had been for the purpose of aiding and safeguarding these natives, and I promised them our everlasting friendship. Concerning the Indian who died at Querétaro, I set his mind at rest, through the said interpreters, and I satisfied the family of the deceased by explaining my personal sorrow at his demise, the regret of his Excellency and the strenuous efforts he had made to secure the punishment of the aggressors. I used other arguments, calculated to convince them, and I cleared up the point to their entire satisfaction by explaining the measures taken. I was greatly aided by the Indian, Bernardino. They were contented and did not realize the seriousness of the case. The Indian's wife, Doña María, joined in with the rest of her people in being composed in a matter which we had considered difficult and dangerous. The powerful Virgin of Guadalupe, being our North Star and Guide, calmed and soothed all by her extraordinary assistance, and our uneasiness on this point vanished. On the day of the delivery of the baton to the governor a celebration was held, the cavalry under my command discharging six volleys. This, with the beating of the drums and blowing of the bugles, preceded our entry into the church in company with the governor and the Fathers. Mass was celebrated and thanks were given for the successful outcome of our journey. I named the region, Nuevo Reino de la Nueva Montaña de Santander y Santillana. I then held a general review.

II–B

DIARY OF THE RETURN TRIP[9]

AUGUST

On August 24, 1691, our royal standard and camp started for the old fort in search of our vessels and the people whom we were to have met at the end of April last. We had not found them, and if we did not find them this time, we were to continue the march to Monclova or to the court. The journey from Reino y Nueva Montaña de Santander y Santillana was on a route toward the southwest, a quarter south. This day we traveled five leagues over a rough wooded section and set up our royal standard on an arroyo which I called San Salvador on account of the feast day.

On the 25th I continued the march from the above mentioned place along a road to the southwest, marching five leagues, as on the previous day. We set up our royal standard on the bank of the river which, on previous occasions, had been called the Trinity, but on this present one was named La Encarnación del Verbo.

[9]The fuller title of the Convento Grande copy is as follows: "Diary and Daily Demarcation of the Return Journey from the New Kingdom of Nueva Montaña de Santander y Santillana, Kept by General Don Domingo de Terán de los Ríos, Military Governor, by Land and Sea, and Lieutenant Captain General of Montaña, after having Remained Twenty Days among the Asinay Indians Studying Them and Observing their Movements, the Said Trip Being Made for the Purpose of Locating Our Vessels at the Old Fort on Bahía del Espíritu Santo after Having Previously Gone to the Spot without Being Able to Find Them. It May Be Added that on the 13th of the Month, Three Captains of the Cadodacho Nation Arrived Offering to Be our Allies. They Were Accompanied by Two Captains of the Nasitos Nation who Lived Beyond the Cadodachos Who Are Located about Fifty Leagues to the North of Montaña and the Two Captains Still a Little Further On in the Same Direction. The Diary Is in Detail."

On the 26th our royal standard and camp moved forward five leagues, traversing level spaces and rough wooded hills. We camped on an arroyo which, in the preceding trip, I had called San Isidro Labrador, Patrón de Madrid.

On the 27th our royal standard and camp proceeded to the southwest, a quarter south, the land being rough in some places and wooded and level in others, though some areas had no woods. After marching four leagues, we camped at two ponds or reservoirs of rain water, which I called San Isidro Labrador on the trip over.

On the 28th our royal standard and camp again plodded along to the southwest, a quarter south, through broken country, part wooded and rough and the remainder level. We set up our royal standard on an arroyo, which I called in my preceding journey Santiago. We traveled this day six leagues.

On the 29th our royal standard and camp continued the return trip, traveling toward the southwest, over a country rough and wooded in places and level in others. After going five leagues, our royal standard was set up on the banks of the river called Colorado.* We halted because we found the water high. When I crossed it before, I called it San Carlos and Arroyo Salado, because the stream was so low, one could cross it on foot, without getting wet and it was more salty than the sea.

On the 30th our royal standard and camp still continued the march toward the south, southwest. After moving in this direction for three leagues, we turned slightly to the west, a quarter southwest and followed this course for about one league. We advanced this day five leagues over a country partly rough and partly level, having some woods, and camped upon another small arroyo, which, on the return trip, we found without water. Nearby in a pond, we obtained water enough for our horses and for camp use. On this same plain, as we traveled on in the same direction, we saw more than thirty herd of buffaloes. But our horses did not come up because they were so worn down and so poor. This misfortune forced us to go thereafter on mule back. I really believe that not a single horse will reach New Spain, due to the drought, for as we traveled on, they continued to fall behind a half dozen at a time. This was due to the hurry of the trip down to the old fort in search of our vessels, for this meeting was considered of paramount importance. It was believed that on this journey we had in the beginning about one thousand head under five years of age. Since we left Coahuila we have had only two showers and the country is without grass or water. If God does not favor us in this crisis, I foresee great disaster in our march back to New Spain and that our trip will have to be on foot, over a road infested with wild and hostile

*Brazos River.

Indians where we will be exposed to every danger. We now have only one hundred horses that were furnished by the king, and they are so poor that, in spite of the men walking and urging them on, they are unable each night to catch up with the main body. But we press on, because not even a winter's rest could save them. They rested twenty days at Nueva Montaña de Santander y Santillana and they were worse off than at the beginning.

On the 31st we continued our return trip toward the south, southwest; and, having marched eight leagues, we were forced by the lack of water to enter a region that was rough and wooded in spots and level in others. This was almost covered with buffaloes. We set up our royal standard on the banks of the river which, on previous occasions, had been called San Marcos and Colorado at different points where it was crossed. I called it San Pedro y San Pablo Apóstoles.* I remained there on the first of September because of the impossibility of moving the stock.

SEPTEMBER

On the 2nd of September of the said year, our royal standard and camp went onward in search of the old fort for the purpose of finding our vessels and our people, directing our steps away from the banks of the San Pedro y San Pablo towards the southwest. After traveling about two leagues, we veered a little, and then continued towards the south, southwest, for three leagues. We camped on the banks of a running stream which, in the preceding journeys had been called Las Tres Cruces. On this occasion I named it San Christóbal.† The country is in places, rough, in places level. There were likewise some small wooded spaces and good pastures.

On the 3rd our royal standard and camp continued the return trip, leaving the banks of the said arroyo and marching for the Guadalupe and the old fort. We traveled southwest for about a league, then another league to the south-southwest, then two to the south. We then set up our camp after having marched four leagues over a section that was partly wooded and partly rough and untimbered. There were here more than four thousand head of buffalo. We set up our royal standard on a little arroyo which was almost filled with buffaloes. I named it San Sebastián.

On the 4th our royal standard and camp continued the march traveling toward the south, southwest about a league. We then went about two leagues to the southwest and then two to the south, southwest. We camped on a level spot covered with trees. We had advanced this day about five leagues over a rough country, interspersed with level spots and heavy woods. I will not give

*Colorado River.

†Buckner's Creek.

all the deviations of the road, but I will only say that I covered nearly the whole circuit of the compass. The road followed in the previous expedition could only have been opened by a man in his sleep. The route was toward the Guadalupe, and although the trail as traveled was five leagues, it was not actually a league and a half straight through. I therefore believe that it would be well for New Spain, if the Indian guide, who led the previous expedition, were with us now.

On the 5th our royal standard and camp proceeded toward the south-southwest. After marching four leagues in this direction through thick overhanging woods, and rough country, where there was no water, we changed our course and traveled along a hill for two leagues to the northwest, setting up our royal standard on the south hank of a stream, which in the preceding journey, when traveling the same route, had been called the Guadalupe. I named it at various points crossed in my expedition, San Agustín and San Juan Bautista, because at its source it has two branches. On the 6th we suspended our journey, remaining on the said bank because it was necessary to go down from this location to the fort in search of our vessels and people. The better to execute the sovereign commands of the viceroy, I ordered volunteers enlisted for this journey and held a general muster. They were well equipped and supplied with ammunition according to military usage. On the 7th, at five o'clock in the morning, I started in person, marching light with the above mentioned number of cavalry. I left at this place in my stead, during the time until my return from the expedition from the said fort, the captain of the cuirassiers, Don Francisco Martínez, my lieutenant, with the remainder of the people, the provisions, and the supplies of the expedition. In case I do not find the vessels and the people there, I will find myself obliged to return to New Spain to give an account to his Excellency of everything that has been done, and of my failure to carry out the principal points of my orders and the sovereign commands of the viceroy through lack of definite instructions.

On the 7th of the said month our royal standard and camp continued the march in search of the old fort, the vessels, and the people belonging thereto. We traveled toward the north, a quarter north, about two leagues of this distance being through a wooded region. We then made three additional leagues toward the east. I may add that we went three leagues toward the southwest through a level country. Here there were more than a thousand head of buffaloes. We traveled two leagues, or a little more to the southeast and camped on the banks of an arroyo where there were great swarms of mosquitoes and the water was crowded with buffalo. We marched this day ten leagues.

On the 8th the journey was continued. We walked toward the southwest over a level country in search of our people. Before we arrived at the old fort, we saw two men at a distance of about a musket shot whom we thought were Indians from the coast, for we were looking for some of them in order to secure information. I ordered them overtaken. Shortly after being seen by our people, they fired a shot. Thereupon I hurried up with all my party. When we overtook them, we found that they were from the command of Captain Don Gregorio Varona, who had sent them as lookouts for us. We continued our march until we camped on the banks of the "Río de los Franceses." Here we found barracks constructed and the aforesaid Captain Don Gregorio Salinas Varona with the soldiers. They received us with the usages prescribed by military usage. They had sighted land, made ready, and put ashore on July 2nd of the present year. They had remained until this day, the 8th, with the determination of staying there until they heard of my arrival.

On July 3rd I had started Captain Martínez in search of them. On the 19th he returned to our camp on the river called San Pedro y San Pablo without bringing any information whatever. For instance, he had not learned of Salinas' whereabouts nor did he know the course he had taken. Besides, he had abandoned the place without any orders from me to this effect, and he had not made any report to me before doing so. Besides, he had seen the vessel on July 5th. Although I asked him why he had not remained at the old fort near the coast, after having dispatched a report to me, since he could have made an examination of the vessel, he answered that he had presented a request to be allowed to go back and make another attempt, but that the council of the Fathers of the Holy Evangel and the military authorities which I had called, had voted to postpone the trip to the fort and the bay and to continue the journey to the Texas country, although it was my opinion that the trip to the coast should be made at that time.[10] My opinion remained unchanged; but, by unanimous vote of the council I was forced to continue the journey. I sent an account of the incident from the aforementioned river bank by an Indian who was a native of Caldera. He carried the message in the form of a letter, which I addressed to the governor of Nuevo Reino de León, asking him to place it in the viceroy's own hands. On the 8th, the day of our arrival, Don Gregorio delivered to me three letters from the viceroy, two of them dated April 25th, the other dated June 5th last. I may add that he informed me of the new orders and instructions of his Excellency. I therefore, at once sent two of my aids, one as commander of arms, the other as the lieutenant representing the viceroy, with orders to Captain Martínez, whom I had left in command. I instructed him to set out with all the camp, ammunition, food, and troops for the designated fort, in order that from this point might be put

---

[10]Martínez's own story is contained in "Documentos para la Historia eclesiástica y civil de la provincia de Texas," ff. 112–116. See also Massanet's diary, ibid., ff. 87–112.

in execution the superior commands in regard to Nueva Montaña Santander y Santillana, from whence I had just come as is shown by the detailed diary of the trip.

II–C
NEW JOURNEY

I started from Real de Santa Margarita de Buenaventura[11] to Nueva Montaña de Santander y Santillana, on September 27, 1691, after having remained at that place eighteen days, waiting for the munitions, provisions, and people from the vessels which, his Excellency in his wisdom had been good enough to send out for the execution of his orders in regard to the exploration of the rivers and their openings into the sea. I am sending a report of everything from this place by the vessel *Don Joseph y las Animas*, Don Joseph Arambarú, captain. I transmitted these papers through *Alférez* Gaspar Tremiño. I am giving therein a full account of all I have noted among the natives as set down in my diary of the first lap of my journey, to which I refer.

On September 27th of the said year 1691 our second trip was begun after the proper preparations for the best possible outcome thereof had been made. We set out from Real de Margarita de Buenavista [Buenaventura] in quest of Nueva Montaña de Santander y Santillana, Reino de los Texas, and the other provinces lying to the north. Our royal standard, camp, and newly added people from the vessel, the troops, food, cavalry under my charge, and the people composing the entire expedition, according to the list, started toward the west-northwest and traveled in this direction until we crossed a creek where our cavalry watered. We then turned toward the northeast, a quarter north, from this stream until two in the afternoon, when we set up our camp on a water hole. We traveled five leagues in this direction and I called the place San Opio.[*]

On the 28th our royal standard continued toward the northeast over a level country, where we found the buffaloes which we have previously mentioned as being between the San Marcos River and the said Real de San Buenaventura. We traveled six and one-half leagues in this direction, varying therefrom for a distance of one and one-half leagues to the north, northeast. At three o'clock in the afternoon our royal standard was set up after we had passed a dry waterhole. In this second journey, I named the place San Exuperio.

---

[11]In the text used by the translator, Buenaventura and Buenavista are both found and employed indiscriminately.

[*]Lavaca River.

On the 29th we pursued our journey toward the north over a level country. We traveled six and one half leagues, after having gone one and one half leagues to the north, northwest. At two o'clock, our royal standard was set up after we had crossed a dry arroyo. In the second expedition, I named the spot San Miguel.*

On the 30th we advanced toward the north, northwest, over a region composed of mountain ranges interrupted by some ravines and finally sloping into foothills. I have already described this country and I refer to the entry in the first part of my diary. We traveled seven leagues in this direction until our royal standard was set up at a place which I called San Gerónimo de la Mota,† where there was a small pool formed by a stream coming from a hill.

OCTOBER

On October 1st we continued our march toward the northwest across a country of the same character, rough and barren. We traveled until two o'clock, when we could see the banks of the river which I called San Pedro y San Pablo. On this trip I named it Rosario, because it was that feast day. It has the trees on it that I have already described. Its water was so high that it prevented our crossing. We went in this direction five leagues.

On the 4th, after remaining here during the 2nd and 3rd because of our inability to ford the river, we crossed and continued our march, directing our steps a little more to the northeast for a league and a half, when I reached a place I had previously selected as a meeting place with the Reverend Fathers of the Holy Evangel. I named it Padre San Francisco.

On October 5th we resumed our journey on a route toward the northeast and traveled seven leagues over a country of the character already described in the first part of my diary. On this day the old captain of the Cantu nation was my guide, serving with three other natives who promised to accompany us as far as the Asinai‡ nation. We lacked water on this day, because we found only hills in the buffalo country. For this reason we traveled until about three o'clock, when we camped on an arroyo which I named Santa Catarina.

On the 6th our royal standard and camp moved forward on the road toward the north, in which direction we traveled for six leagues. We crossed two arroyos which contained a small quantity of water. We set up our camp near another, which had still less water. I sent a description of this place in the first part of my diary. I called it San Bruno.

---

*Navidad River.

†Also near the Navidad River.

‡Hasinai confederacy: affiliated Caddo tribes of the Nacogdoches-Natchitoches region.

On the 7th we continued our march toward the northeast over the same kind of a country I have described. There were some clumps of trees and wooded spaces which we had passed on the previous trip. By these we recognized the banks of the river which in the first part of my diary I called San Gerónimo. We forded this and found many indications that there had been a rise. The country and the timber were the same as I have described. After crossing to the other side with great difficulty because it was very boggy for a distance of a half league, our royal standard was set up on the banks of a stream which I think was a branch of the same. I called this place San Martín.

On the 8th our royal standard and camp pushed forward on the journey toward the north, a quarter northeast, over a country whose character has already been described, with some woods and clumps of trees. We traveled seven leagues in this direction until we set up camp in a good place which I called San Pedro de Sevilla.

On the 13th, after remaining in this place for four days to secure a little meat, the bad weather and rain causing delay, I started on this day and continued the trip following the route toward the northeast, a quarter east. After going three leagues we set our royal standard in a spot which I called San Fausto.

On the 22nd, having remained until this day on the banks of the preceding arroyo, at the spot named, without being able to cross because of the rise, and seeing the long delay caused by waiting for the stream to go down, I was obliged to build a bridge in a favorable location, because not all of them were suitable. We crossed over on this constructed passage, and then plodded our way along with much difficulty, on account of the muddy condition of the road. We pitched camp on the hill at noon, having made one league. I named the place San Melancio.

On the 23rd, our royal standard and camp moved forward toward the northeast across the same hilly country I have described in the first part of the diary. We traveled four and a half leagues and set up camp at a place where there was a small waterhole, which was serviceable to us. I named it San Germano [Fernando] y San Servando.

On the 24th we continued our march on the road and route toward the northeast, a quarter north. I have already sent a description of the country in the diary. We advanced seven leagues in this direction. In this distance we passed two small lakes of rain water and some level flooded sections with high grass that could be cut for the stock. We placed our camp on a small arroyo which I called San Frutos.

On the 25th our royal standard and camp moved forward on the march en route toward the northeast. At midday, we reached the banks of a river which

I named Encarnación.* We crossed this and continued our journey on the other side, following the same direction. We pitched our camp on an arroyo which I called San Frontón. Pines, oaks, and live oaks made the place beautiful. I omit a description as I gave one in the first part of my diary. We traveled six leagues.

On the 26th our royal standard and camp went on in search of Nueva Montaña de Santander y Santillana y Provincia de la Nación Asinai, taking a route toward the [north]-northeast, over a country with sparse woods and ranges of rough hills like that already described. We crossed various ravines on the way. After traveling ten leagues, we camped at the Mission of Santísimo Nombre de María, administered by the Reverend Father Fray Francisco Jesús de María. We located on the bank of a stream, making use of the water from the said arroyo, which I named El Arroyo de la Misión. In preceding trips I had called it Río de San Miguel.† The place where our camp was situated, I named San Valentino. Here we remained.

NOVEMBER

On November 1st continued at this same place, as I was delayed by bad weather—frost and rain. When the weather permitted, I decided to explore the arroyo in company with the two captains, Don Gregorio Salinas Varona and Don Francisco Martínez, and the royal *alférezes*, Don Pedro Fernández Cenrra and Don Alexandro Bruno, who were pilots. We traveled up and down the bank of the said arroyo about three leagues. After returning to camp, I called a council of the persons indicated. I secured their unanimous opinions that the arroyo was of no importance and not navigable. This is shown by the signed report of the said council. I was already aware of the relations existing between this Texas tribe and the Fathers of the Holy Evangel. I knew of the hostility of the Indians, of their dealings with the Indian Bernardino, their leader, of their importunities, of their rebellious attitude, and of the excesses to which they had been led by Bernardino. I was aware also of the danger to which the said Fathers believed themselves exposed as a result of the bad conduct of the natives. I knew, likewise, that, in perfect union and accord with another nation, called the Guatsas, these same Indians had and were still stealing the horses, cattle, and other livestock. And besides, I knew that the Asinai Indian [Bernardino] himself was in rebellion. On the next day, I received a note from the Reverend Father Superior, Fray Damián Massanet. In this he asked my help in apprehending some Indians of the Guatsas nation who had been injuring the stock. In answer to this request, I at once (ten o'clock at night)

---

*Bedias Creek.

†Neches River.

sent out ten men with a guide to search for them because I had information that the guilty parties were in the vicinity. These soldiers of mine brought five Indians, bound, who were said to be ones that were guilty of killing the stock. They were identified by the Reverend Father Fray Francisco de Jesús, as native Asinai Indians. The Indian governor and Bernardino were known to have been caught by some herdsmen with three of our mules in their possession. These the herdsmen recovered. Their guilt was also evidenced by the fact, that they had not been willing to come to the mission, although they were so near, being only about three leagues distant. I will add that this happened at a place called San Servando y Germano. The governor at that time claimed that he was hunting game, and that he was going straight back to his province to prepare a feast for us. In this same place he turned over to me two horses that were known to belong to the Reverend Fathers. He tried to make me believe that they had been brought to him by his Indians after they had been stolen. I really believe that he was the guilty one. I omit other points for personal communication to your Excellency. On November 3, when I was ready to start, I sent my commandant of arms, Juan García de Quintanilla, as a corporal in charge of ten soldiers and fifty fully equipped mules and the necessary servants to wait for the receipt of fresh orders from the viceroy. The said commandant started on his journey but I halted, for it began to rain during the day. This continued until the 6th of the month. I will also add the determination the Reverend Fathers had formed for withdrawing. This was shown by their desire to go on the trip with the assistant. They even saddled their animals for the journey. The reason they did not go was that they had to wait for my withdrawal and they held a council to consider this point.

II–D

JOURNEY, ROUTE, AND REPORT OF THE COUNTRY EXPLORED FROM NOVEMBER 6, 1691, DURING A NEW EXPEDITION TO THE CADODACHOS NATION FROM NUEVA MONTAÑA DE SANTANDER Y SANTILLANA IN EXECUTION OF THE ORDERS AND SOVEREIGN COMMANDS OF HIS EXCELLENCY, CONDE DE GALVE

On the said day, the Reverend Father Commissary arrived at my camp with two other priests of the Holy Evangel and a lay brother. They came for the purpose of carrying out the said orders as far as he was responsible. He joined the camp and the new expedition proceeded. I held a general muster according to military usage, observing the proper precautions.

On November 6, at noon, our march was started in search of the nation of the Cadodachos, on the road one league to the south, southeast, to the crossing of an arroyo, which I named Santísima Trinidad de María, but which, in preceding expeditions, as I have already stated, was called Río de San Miguel del Arcángel. From this point we continued our journey toward the northeast, passing through the level spots that were occupied by the natives. The country is very rough and is well timbered. There were no open spaces save clearings of about two hundred feet in circumference that were occupied by their quarters. In places there were ravines, and in other spots sand, all reduced to cultivation, as I reported to your Excellency from San Buenaventura. I may well add that beyond the arroyo there is a different jurisdiction with a different captain over the natives. The governor before mentioned has no power or authority here. Neither is the last mentioned captain acknowledged or obeyed by the first named. The one who rules in this jurisdiction has the same authority here as the other one has beyond the said arroyo. Each is really subject to the Indian called Ceñez.* In this same direction, including the distance to the crossing, we marched four leagues and then set up our royal standard on a hill near the stream. This I called San Severo.

On November 7th our royal standard and camp moved forward in the same direction to the northeast, a quarter north, over a country of the same character, there being no difference whatever in hills, woods, and open spaces. There were, likewise, many *rancherías* on this route. These were the last settlements of the Asinai nation, according to the statement of an Indian, a native of Nueva Montaña. I further add that there are also some pines in the woods which overshadow the other trees. After traveling four leagues in the said direction, our royal standard was set up on a hill covered with the varieties of trees named, because there was no other place more suitable. I named it San Amaranto.

On the 8th our march continued in the same direction in search of the Nazonis nation over a rough country of the same character as that described. It also had *rancherías* and cultivated patches. After passing some of these, our royal standard was set up on a hill nearby. I called it San Castor. Five leagues had been traveled.

On the 9th we followed a northeasterly route or road, for a distance of four leagues. Our royal standard was set up on a hill near a water hole which I called San Ermen[gil]do.

On the 10th our royal standard and camp moved forward in a northeasterly direction for five leagues over the same kind of a rough country as that we

---

*Xinesi: hereditary title for the leader of each Caddo confederacy. See W. W. Newcomb, *The Indians of Texas: From Prehistoric to Modern Times* (Austin, 1961), 303.

had passed. In this distance we came upon various small arroyos that were hard to cross. Our royal standard was set up on a hill, by a small water hole, which I named Santa Victoria.

We remained in this camp during the 12th waiting for some mules that were worn out with their loads and were unable to proceed, because of the lack of grass from which they suffered, for none had been found after we had passed the spot called San Frontón, before reaching the Asinai nation, and pasturage was not found there in sufficient quantities to feed them. The animals did not like even what was provided, because it was so coarse. They very much preferred the moss that grows on the trees in this section. It seemed apparent that if the pasturage continued to be of the character described, we would not only have to travel loaded like freight, as they commonly say, without a change of horses, but it would be necessary to make the whole trip on foot, without any doubt whatever. As a matter of fact, we were already practically afoot as was shown by an examination of the horses. At this time, not one of those I had set out with, is left, in spite of the fact that not one of them had been ridden. On this day, our royal standard moved forward on the road toward the northeast, a quarter east, over a country like the one previously described. Camp was pitched upon the bank of an arroyo containing considerable water. This forced me to remain on the same side. I named it San Diego de Alcalá. We traveled three leagues this day.

On the 14th, after remaining on the bank during the 13th waiting for the building of a bridge over which to transport the standard and camp to the other side, we started our march and crossed over. From the far bank we continued our journey north, a quarter northeast, over a country level in places and much like the preceding area. Our royal standard was erected, after we had traveled five leagues in that direction. I called the place San Prudencio.

On the 15th, continuing our march, we advanced toward the north-northeast, over the same kind of a country. Our camp and royal standard was set up near a lake, the size of which demanded the building of a bridge. This I ordered constructed immediately. The work was started and I named it Puente de San Eugenio and then added the name of Arzobispo de Toledo. Our troops proceeded in the same direction four leagues.

On the 18th, having remained at the lake during the intervening days because the weather was stormy, with rain and ice, I crossed over the bridge that had been built, carrying all my equipment. I followed a route toward the north, a quarter northeast, for three leagues until I reached the shore of a lake filled with low trees growing in the bed. Having crossed a ford that had been found, our royal standard was set up on the other bank. I named the place San Gregorio and called the lake Tamauturgo, for the saint.

On the 19th our march was continued toward the north, a quarter northeast, over the same kind of a country, with a great number of deer. We traveled five leagues in this direction, camp being made on the slope of a hill, due to the various delays encountered. Half way down the incline there was a spring which I named San Crispino Obispo.

On the 21st we remained at this spot waiting for nine mules that had been tired out by their heavy loads. They arrived this day and our royal standard and camp moved forward on the march toward the north over a rough country like the preceding. We could not travel more than two leagues because of the fatigue of the stock, the horses as well as the pack animals, for they were all together. Our royal standard was set up, and I named the place La Presentación de N[uestra] S[eñora].

On the 22nd we continued our march toward the north, a quarter northeast. We proceeded two leagues in this direction and reached the bank of an arroyo which, because of its size, I named El Grande. The rest of the day was spent in finding a good place for building a bridge. After locating it, we withdrew a gunshot from the bank. This place I called Santa Cecilia.

I lingered in this vicinity until the 27th. The first two days were spent in building the bridge which could not be completed sooner on account of the ice. We stayed the rest of the time because the sun was hidden by the heavy snow that fell on the 25th and 26th, the freezing weather continuing until the country was covered to a depth of two spans without any exaggeration whatever. Even the trees could not be distinguished because of the heavy snow which overspread them, not to mention the condition of the royal camp. But, as I had a part in this work, I will leave it for other chroniclers to recount and to tell how pitiful it was to see the animals come up to the protection of the fire, abandoning what poor sustenance the country furnished, for practically what little the country contained had been covered by the heavy snow of the preceding days. I may add that if the mules died from this exposure and lack of food, the suffering of the poor half-clad people, who had no roof but the sky, and like the mules, nothing but the bare ground to lie upon, must have been intense during this bitter weather. Due to these conditions, I finally determined to leave the camp on this day, taking with me thirty men with light equipment because I saw that it was impossible for all the men to proceed due to the bad weather and lack of food for the animals. I turned over the camp to Don Gregorio Salinas Varona, as the captain of the cuirassiers, Don Francisco, my lieutenant, was crippled and in bed. I started, carrying the thirty men with me, among them the royal *alféreζes* and pilots Don Fernando de Cenrra and Don Alexandro Bruno. Our supplies were loaded on the best and most dependable mules. As a precaution I had six mules loaded with arms, as well as forty-three additional animals. We came to the bridge but did not recognize it, because of the snow, until I had crossed it on foot, leading my mount with my right hand. All the people with me crossed in the same manner. After reaching the opposite side, and having recognized the direction of the route, we trudged on toward the north, a quarter northeast, over the worst road that it is possible for the human mind to conceive. After having gone about two leagues, we continued our journey, traveling still in the same direction and over somewhat the same kind of country. Night forced us to make camp on a small hill with an inadequate supply of muddy water. Here we stayed. I named the place San Fausto.

We took up our journey toward the northeast in search of the new province of the Cadodachos nation, traversing a country that was not quite so rough and had now and then some level spaces. The area was broken by certain plains, although they were covered with open woods of the kinds of trees I have already mentioned. There were various obstructions, due to the arroyos which overflowed the route for a quarter of a league in fearful torrents. Thickets of blackberries and other plants covered the fields and there was not a spot where one could put down his bare foot without imitating the meek and lowly St. Francis. On every side were barefooted men who were forced to travel on foot as the mules bogged down, because the snow had soaked the ground. This plight lasted for a distance of not less than two leagues. The snow deceived the men into the belief, that they could pass safely, because the blackberry bushes were covered with a white mantle and the troop could not see them. When a person would put down his foot to take a step, he would sink to his knees before he could change his position. In this way, they received "the blessed wounds" above mentioned. I could say a great deal more on this point, but I will not do so because, in truth considered calmly, it seems more the figment of the imagination, prone to create difficulties, than reality supported by facts. These descriptions I leave to others who accompany me. I may add that good fortune furnished small logs for crossing the small arroyos. A single piece of timber in each case served for the passage of both men and animals, and I may add, the equipment. Taking only the time demanded for the transfer, we traveled five and a half leagues in the same direction until at last we reached a level tract. It was less than a league straight through, in a northerly direction, or six leagues around the edge. The Indian guides informed me that at long intervals it was covered by the waters from the river in the territory occupied by the tribe. We crossed this level space, still going in the same direction, passed two lakes and came to a grove of trees. From this point we caught sight of one of the *rancherías* of the nation. It was located on a hill, which commanded the whole country. As soon as I arrived, I had the place examined as a precaution against an ambush, in case the French might be in the country and attempt to surprise us. After reconnoitering it, the Indian guide informed us through Brother Antonio, who served as an interpreter, that this was the temple in which the Indians worshiped and made offerings to their gods. We proceeded from this place and we made camp at the home of an Indian whom they called *Caddi,** located about half a league, more or less from the temple or *mezquita.* He was a young fellow about twelve or fourteen years of age, very good looking, and apparently quite friendly. According to the interpreter mentioned above, he offered us his *rancho* as a shelter for our people, due to the bad weather. I named the place Santa Galia. We traveled six leagues.

On the 29th, having taken a look at the river about nine o'clock in the morning, I asked the *alférezes* and the pilots their opinion regarding it. To this they answered that, according to appearances, it was navigable at that time, but that they could not be sure without having a longer time to verify the fact. The *alférez,* Don Alexandro Bruno, agreed with this opinion. He added that he would have to navigate it to be perfectly sure, and that there was not sufficient time in which to build a vessel and prepare the necessary provisions for a trial. He declared also that we lacked the requisite equipment. I agreed, realizing his willingness and his regret at the labor of the exploration, and the necessity for returning without carrying out the instructions of the viceroy in any particular. Besides the labor involved in the trip that had already been made, I had in mind the hardships yet to be endured on the return trip. While coming back to our camp from the river, we discovered a canoe in a slough. In this the aforesaid pilot, two of the men, and myself set out to explore the source of the stream and to find its mouth. We sounded and found it to contain about fifteen fathoms of fresh water. It had no current whatever. We could not find the source, nor could we even determine the direction in which it ran. We therefore decided that it did not open directly into the river. We consequently went back to camp, leaving the canoe. We located at the home of one of the Mandones Indians. We ordered the stock collected there, since it seemed to be the best place. From this point, I sent my aide, Marcos de los Reyes to Real de Santa Cecilia in search of the Reverend Father Commissary and his companions and Captain Don Gregorio Salinas, so that they might know what this province was like, and in order that they might bring me two head of stock, on foot or butchered, as food for the people, while they remained in this region. The aide left at once with the order and *Alférez* Don Alexandro [Bruno] came to me to suggest that we launch the canoe and make such soundings as we could. I agreed to this and suggested that the exploration of the lower stretches of the river ought to be continued for several days. Those to whom I mentioned the plan, objected on the ground that the canoe was not

---

*Caddi: hereditary title for the chief of a Caddo tribe. The caddices were subordinate to the Xinesi.

suited for this work, as it would require sails to make it possible to come back up the stream. They suggested alternatives, none of which were very helpful. On the 30th it was not possible to carry the canoe to the river, because the interpreter told me that the *caddi* was displeased because I had left his home. On this point I may state that lie has control and authority over the two captains of his tribe, whom I mentioned as being among the Asinai. Besides these two allies, he has five other captains who follow his lead, making seven in all. Each of these captains recognizes the position of the other captains and they all, in turn, recognize the authority of the *caddi.* I studied this *caddi* and found that he also had a considerable following of strong robust troops, all friendly among themselves. I noticed his resentment, and this forced me to return and set up camps at his *ranchería.* On December 1st, after the *caddi* had seen my willingness to meet his wishes, and my appreciation of his feelings, he summoned an older brother of his to approach and receive the baton, emblem of authority—it being the custom for the younger to thus bestow it—and ordered this brother to go to the aforesaid lagoon in company with certain Indians and aid us in carrying the canoe over to the river. This was done immediately, with the precaution suggested to me by *Alférez* Don Alexandro [Bruno], that of taking the mule ropes with which to haul the canoe. By means of these my people and twenty of the Indians succeeded in getting it to the bank. The *alférez* got into it immediately with two men. He carried a pole about twenty spans long, which he asked me to have cut for him. With this he sounded the river from the point at which the canoe was launched to the place we finally landed. On returning to camp I found that the Reverend Father Commissary and his companions had arrived, but that Captain Don Gregorio Salinas had not been willing to come, because the first order he had received had been in writing, while the second was verbal. There was not a scrap of paper on which to write. On the 2nd it was not possible to accomplish anything whatsoever, because of the sleet and rain which fell. On the next day, I again started for the river. There was in my company *Alférez* Don Alexandro Bruno and the pilots. Approaching the place where the *alférez* had fastened the canoe, he immediately got into it with his arms and instruments. Three seamen and myself accompanied him. We went down the river until he estimated that we had gone three leagues by the stream's windings. He declared that the soundings showed fifteen or twenty spans along the main channel and that, allowing for deeper and shallower spots, it must average a depth of nine or ten spans in its main course. He remarked to me that the river was at this time in its regular bed. However, the three seamen using their oars [and] the *alférez* [with his pole] could not make the return trip against the current, until it was decided to move close to the bank, that is in the still water. Two men towed the boat and the *alférez* and the other man kept it from running aground. In this way we continued the trip at a fairly good rate of speed, about a league an hour. It took us from about one o'clock in the day until dark to cover the distance to the starting point. From this place we then returned to camp. Brother Antonio reported to me that, under the instructions of the Father Comissary, he had asked the Indians in their own dialect if they desired to become obedient to the holy evangelical law, and they answered that they were willing to do so. I will state also that, in company with the *alférez*, the pilots, the *caddi,* and the companions of the Reverend Father Commissary, I went to the opposite bank of the river to examine the settled region. I found it the same as on this side. Through the *caddi,* as an interpreter, I learned from the native Indians that the settlements extended down stream along the river bank. During this visit I noticed the respect showed the *caddi* by the Indians. They offered him a seat as soon as they saw him, a deference they did not show in the case of the others who accompanied us. I noticed, too, that they had a captain, but that he is under the orders of the *caddi,* the latter being the arbiter and ruler of the entire nation. I came back from this visit to my camp for the purpose of continuing my return trip on the morrow to Bahía de San Bernardo and thence to the Kingdom of New Spain.

II–E

THE RETURN OF DON DOMINGO TERÁN TO BAHÍA AND LAGO DE SAN BERNARDO AND THENCE TO NEW SPAIN

DECEMBER

On the 5th our people started the return trip from the aforementioned new province of the said Asinai nation to pursue our journey to Bahía and Lago de San Bernardo. When I reached the first arroyo, in company with my people, I found the crossing difficult. Taking three men of my company I went on, leaving the rest to search for a better passage. I traveled in the same direction until I reached the arroyo named Santa Cecilia. I here set up my standard with the intention of building a raft so that we could float over in case the bridge was under water, as it was reported to be. The people had halted, planning to cover that distance on the following day.

On the 8th we remained in camp at Santa Cecilia waiting for the people and for the rounding up of the stock that had been scattered as well as for the mules that were coming on behind. Because of the bad weather about twenty of them had died during the time I remained with the Cadodachos nation, when it was impossible for me to take my departure. The conditions I then faced, I have already indicated. We traveled on and reached a spot which I named La Presentación de Nuestra Señora. Here the road became much worse and most of the people were on foot. Even I was of this number, because I had no animal I could ride. I dismiss this with the remarks I made on the day I went in search of the Cadodachos nation. I merely state that the difficulty was so great that I could not find words to describe it, even though I should attempt to do so. The distance has already been indicated.

On the 11th we remained in camp waiting for the stock that could not catch up until this day. We proceeded on the return journey and reached the place called San Crispino. Here camp was again made.

On the 12th I made ready to continue the trip. I called for those who had the courage to undertake the march on foot as the mules were worn out. This was done to give the cavalry a chance to continue the transportation of the supplies which the viceroy, in his wisdom, had sent along for equipping the vessels that were to have been built on these rivers for the purpose of exploring them to their mouths, as well as other streams in the region. Even this was not sufficient to keep a drove of mules from breaking down on the expedition and they were able to make only a league and a half a day.

We remained at this spot, waiting for the mules that had been left behind. We then took up our journey in the opposite direction from that we had made on coming to the country. We set up our standard on a lake called San Gregorio Taumaturgo because we were unable to cross.

On the 15th, after the people had built a pontoon bridge with two ropes, our royal standard proceeded south, a quarter southwest, after the supplies and equipment under my charge had been carried over. We traveled one league and set up our camp on the shores of a small lake, which I called San Cándido.

On the 16th, after we had transferred the supplies, we advanced again in the same direction. We traveled two leagues and then halted. I called the place San Eugenio. The bridge we built I called Toledo, for the saint. We pitched our camp at another lake which I named Santa Fructuosa.

On the 17th, the herd having caught up with us, I ordered the march continued. The day being rainy and freezing. I hated to have the people travel on foot, as they had since the day I called for volunteers at the camp called San Crispino. The weather permitted me only to reach San Lázaro.

On the 18th the Reverend Fathers of the Holy Evangel did not catch up with us. For personal reasons they had not wished to continue the journey on the previous day. We continued, however, traveling still south-southwest, until we had gone three and a half leagues, and there we set up our standard at a place I called San Prudencio.

On the 19th the royal standard proceeded in the same direction. After marching four and a half leagues, camp was made on the other side of an arroyo which I named San Diego Alcalá. Finding the bridge which the seamen had constructed inundated by a fresh rise, we used as a transport a little raft made by the Indians which we found at that point. We did not have time to gather up the stock and put the herds under an escort, as provided by military usage, for all of this would have delayed us much longer. The small amount of provisions I had would not permit of this, especially as it was necessary to travel a long distance with poor equipment over a country infested with savages and where no supplies save the buffaloes that could be secured after we crossed the Trinity River. I omit a description of the difficulties of my return trip, hungry and afoot, with the weather already giving us warning of worse to come.

On the 21st, after remaining in camp waiting for the herd, and the people carrying the supplies on their shoulders to and from the rafts—the one we had found, the other we had hastily built—our royal camp moved forward one league. We stopped at a place which I called Santo Tomás.

On the 22nd we continued our march south, a quarter southwest. We traveled two and one half leagues and set up our camp at a spot which I named San Haviano.

On the 23rd the day was cloudy and snow was falling. Our royal standard and camp moved south-southwest three and one half leagues. We made camp at a location I named Santa Victoria. None of the herd reached the point.

On the 26th the herd, for which we had been waiting for two days, came up, as well as two men who had been sent in pursuit of a negro trumpeter who had run away a second time. He had been severely punished for the first offense, and it was not proper to omit it in the second case. The men assured me that they had obeyed orders implicitly in the search, but that in the nine days they had spent in the effort, they had not been able even to catch sight of him, nor had any of the Indians they met on the road obtained any information regarding him. Our royal standard, therefore, continued the return in the same direction. We examined the *rancherías* of the Nazoni nation, who live in this region. We advanced two and a half leagues and camped at a place which I named San Esteban.

On the 27th our royal standard continued the return trip, traveling to the southwest. We traveled in this direction for three leagues. We camped at a spot I called San Juan Evangelista.

On the 28th we again took up our journey toward the *ranchería* of the Asinai Indians, who live on the north bank of the arroyo. Our royal standard moved in search of them, southwest, a quarter west for about four leagues where we found some of them. We camped in a very poor location because neither at this place nor within a radius of a league could even the poor pasturage which the country affords be seen, due to the flooded condition of the meadows. I called this place Los Inocentes.

On the 29th our royal standard and camp retreated toward the southwest, a quarter south in search of the Real de San Severo. To reach it we traveled three leagues. Here I decided to wait for the herds, which had not caught up since we left Real de Santa Victoria. Two Indians from the mission came to this place and informed us that the corporal I had left in charge of [a] detachment in these frontiers, had run away. I may add that they reported that he had abandoned his post once before but had returned.

On the 30th our royal standard was again en route for the province and nation of the Asinai and the Mission of Santísimo Nombre de María, marching from the said camp toward the southwest, a quarter south in search of the passage at the arroyo called Río de San Miguel. We forded it, though it was slightly up, directed our steps toward the said mission, where our royal standard was set up. Here most of our herd came along, also five men who had lost their way soon after they left Real de San Esteban, in trying to get ahead and travel faster than the herd. Since those who accompanied me were afoot, I was unable to send anyone in search of them. They were finally guided to our camp by an Indian of the Nazoni nation.

JANUARY, 1692

On January 4, 1692, after remaining at the said mission waiting for the herds, during which days there were heavy rains and ice, I continued the march from this mission until I reached Mission San Francisco, where I set up our royal standard and camp. We had traveled a league and a half toward the southwest. I stayed here until the 9th, the weather being bitterly cold. During the journey, the people were exhausted by the trip, and at San Cipriano they demanded the mounts which I had promised them. I recalled their implicit obedience, and that there were at this mission a number of horses that had been delivered to the priests under orders of the viceroy. Therefore, in order not to leave our supplies on the route, where there would be no possible chance of recovering them, I promised these horses to the people so as to avoid greater difficulties. On that account, they could not refuse to let me have the horses they were riding to use as pack horses for the supplies. They immediately agreed to my proposition and delivered them on the spot, offering to walk to the mission. In view of their attitude, my own promise, and the fact that the stock in question was of little or no use at the mission, I asked the commissary to furnish me with such horses as he could spare, so that I might be able to report to the people that we would be able to continue our journey. However, the Father Superior refused, declaring that the animals were not good for anything and that, moreover, he could not round them up, either all or even a part of them. As a matter of fact, he was killing time. Neither did he issue orders in an attempt to assemble them nor did he permit me to do anything.

In this state of affairs, and convinced that none of the mules were able to travel, much less to carry loads—not being able to stand even the harness—I determined to call a council on the 7th to consider the advisability of leaving at the mission such loads and supplies as were of no use to us on the return trip, so as to show my good will in the welfare of the mission. The mules, relieved of the loads, could then be turned over to the troops, in case the pasturage failed and an immediate continuance of the journey was necessary. It was unanimously decided by the council that all the munitions should be left. The Reverend Father Superior requesting that the catapults be left and that the four seamen who had volunteered to remain be allowed to stay. Agreeable to this request and the decision of the council, these things were turned over to the corporal of the troops and were left there, as evidenced by the receipt given by Captain Don Gregorio Salinas Varona. The troops were satisfied with the proceedings. During the remaining time before my departure, I again asked the Reverend Father Superior for the horses, but my request went unheeded. Neither was the request I presented for thirty cows to supply my party with food until we reached the buffalo country answered. On the 8th I decided to send three of the most able soldiers in search of the horses. They hunted for them that day, found them, and returned to camp to give me a report. It is to be understood that I decided upon this measure on the 8th, as mentioned, because it was then that I ran out of military supplies. This was the reason why I could not start without these animals. It was demanding too abject an obedience to expect us to risk such a long journey in the middle of winter, naked and without food. I believe time will prove that there was no hope, especially since experience had shown how very difficult the roads were even in summer, when there was a supply of food on hand, as was the case during the first part of our trip. These are the existing conditions. Would that they did not exist and that there was no reason to add to the confusion in this vast sea of trouble!

On this day, the 9th of January, my royal standard and camp started again on the return march from the said nation in the direction of the Bahía and Lago de San Bernardo in search of El Real de Santa Margarita de Buenavista [Buenaventura]. On the said day six of the missionaries of the Holy Evangel of the said mission joined my royal standard for the purpose of retiring to our kingdoms and provinces. I beg to withhold their reason for so doing, as well as my own, until I speak in person with your Excellency. They were admitted into our camp and we continued the march toward the southwest for one and a half leagues when the royal standard was set up. The members of the expedition made the journey to this point on the mules which I had relieved of the munitions as well as of most of the loads. With my own hands I adjusted the packs they were to carry. I named the camp Los Mártires de Zaragosa.

On the 10th, a very bad day with heavy fog, our royal standard and camp trod heavily along in the prescribed direction. We pushed on, our cavalry horses already tired out, and most of the people on foot due to the roads, which were boggy and under water, even the pastures in the highlands being more than two spans under water. The areas did not furnish the scant herbs usually found, and furthermore each meadow land looked like an ocean. To be sure, one might say that we were here faced with the dark waters of a vast expanse that turned each of the pastures that had hitherto been valleys, arroyos, and plains into a new Red Sea, whose confines seemed infinite and without chance for drainage. We traveled on under these difficulties for three leagues, when we struck camp. I named it San Pablo.

On the 12th, after the mules and the people who had fallen behind caught up with us and joined our royal standard, we proceeded further. All the people were now on foot, because on the previous day they had found that all their efforts to push their animals on was harder work than to travel on foot. The mules were used to lessen the loads of the other pack animals and we continued our march northeast [*sic*] until our royal standard was set up on a small arroyo, whose swollen and raging torrents prevented our crossing. We traveled three leagues along its bank to a place I named San Victoriano.

The 13th we occupied ourselves in building a raft and in getting the equipment over to the other side of the arroyo. We traveled on about a gunshot and set up our royal standard on the banks of La Santísima Trinidad, which greeted us with a great flood, which seemed unbelievable to those who had crossed it when low, as my people had done on three occasions. And here we were on its banks!

My royal standard remained on the river bank, engaged in hunting up and down stream for a better crossing. The weather was bitterly cold. To forget our hunger, we busied ourselves in building a raft, which was finished on the 14th. There being no other way, it was decided that, since the sea forces were our best swimmers, they should man the raft rather than the land forces. None of them would get aboard and none would dare to carry over to the far side a towline as a guide rope for the transport. Of the three men, who were brave enough to try to swim the stream, two reached the far side, but were benumbed by the cold and lost the line without knowing it. They emerged naked and half frozen, and preferred to remain on the far bank rather than to risk death by trying to cross the stream again. The third man, not wishing to join the others in the bitter cold, turned back from the middle of the stream. The two on the far side had fire, for one of the men had suggested to the other to provide for it. On the 15th it was still cold but another man decided to try to carry the line across. He reached the far bank, half dead, after taking advantage of the upper part of a tree, which the waters almost covered. A part of it was above the water and he tied the rope to this. However, the current was so strong that it was hard for two men to pull the line. Finally, when this attempt failed, I ordered four oars made to see if it would be possible to cross on the raft, not for the purpose of carrying a corporal across, but to bring back the men who had crossed over so that they might not die from hunger and cold. This was not successful. On the 17th the difficulty still remained and we were just about to use up all the meat we had brought with us. I therefore ordered four scouts to see if meat could not be obtained without returning to the Asinai nation, for our need was urgent. The next day was very stormy. On the 19th, Don Gregorio Salinas Varona reported to me that the royal *alférez*, Don Alexandro Bruno, had told him that it was quite impossible to cross the river, that it was rising every day. This we knew by experience. He added that the said *alférez* had learned from the people who had reached the other side, that they had seen a hollow log that might be of use. He said that the carpenters ought to go and look at it and make a canoe. This they said would be a three days' job. The carpenters at once set to work to cut out the canoe. On the 22nd the people whom I had sent back came in with cows. We waited until the 23rd for the launching of the canoe. I immediately ordered the transportation of the camp to the other side. This went on with all possible haste until eight o'clock at night. We did more than seemed humanly possible during this time. On the following day the crossing was completed after nightfall. We set up our royal standard and waited for a day so that we might continue our journey. I should mention also how hard we worked in the canoe. The royal *alférezes* and pilots, Don Pedro Fernandes Cenrra and Don Alexandro Bruno took turns, each trying by sheer force of will to row across with animals tied by their heads to the said canoe. Thus a considerable loss in number was avoided. Because of the heavy rain, it was not possible to continue the march and we remained at this point.

On the 26th the royal standard and camp advanced the march toward the southwest following the route and direction of the previous journey. We crossed a half league of water where there were boggy spots. We could have gone five leagues in the time taken to cover this distance. We reached a ravine that had never been noticed before. It had not even enough water for little sparrows. On this occasion the passage delayed us. We hastily built a raft, for it was difficult to cross even in the carts, and the weather did not permit any setbacks whatever. Necessity forced us to labor on. I named the place El Desconocido.

We remained on the above mentioned small arroyo or ravine until the 28th, transporting the rest of the people and the Reverend Fathers of the Holy

Evangel. The people whom I had sent forward to explore the route to see if it was not impassable returned about two o'clock in the afternoon. They reported that the level space of ground where the camp I had named San Frutos had been, as well as the territory surrounding it, were all inundated and looked like an immense sea; that they had not dared to go farther because they did not know what to expect, and that they had attempted to find out its confines to the westward in the direction of certain hills they could see. They declared that they were disappointed, however, and had to return to report to me. After this account, I immediately left the banks of the said arroyo, because it was so high then, after twenty-four hours of observation, that we realized if we stayed, the torrent would cover the tops of the trees, thus flooding more than twenty *varas* of country. On this day, after being forced to move our camp, we marched through water. After trudging three leagues, we set up our royal standard on a small lake full of snags. I expected to come out of this day's experience scarred like the Indians themselves, and even worse, for a stick hit me in the ear and tore it until the blood ran. The wound was so bad that I did not know whether I still possessed this member on my head. I named the place San Julián.

FEBRUARY

On February 1st, after staying at the camp hunting for suitable pasturage so that we might start on the trip, I marched toward the hills mentioned above in hope that though it was a long journey, according to the information we had, we would at least be able to travel along that route above water. The days were cloudy, and there was ice, snow, and wind, the last resembling a tempest in its fury. In view of this the people began searching for the shortest and quickest route to our main road. After considering the report made by each of the explorers, I selected the Tlascaltecan Indian Pablo as guide. He tried various routes in his attempts to avoid the difficulty of marshes, but, after all, even the hills were boggy. Traveling in various directions we covered a distance of three leagues before we reached the road. Here we pitched our camp. Neither the cattle nor any of the animals were able to reach it. I will not describe the character of the country, for no rational person has ever seen a worse one. Even some of the unloaded animals mired down so deep that, to end my description, I will say that it took six men to pull some of them out. Delayed in this work, some of the men themselves would have been left behind, stuck in the mud like the mules, had we not come to their assistance. The name of this spot is San Celio.

On the 3rd the herd arrived (and I may add that we were without any supply of meat while in San Celio, because neither the stock nor the mules had been able to catch up). They approached about midday and our royal standard continued the march, traveling in the opposite direction from the former journey. We traveled half a league and came to a ravine which I called El No Pensado. This gave us the same trouble as the one I named El Desconocido. In our first journey it was of the same character as the one just described. Four of the seamen went ahead of us from this place in search of another ravine which was larger in order that if it were up like this one, they might make arrangements to avoid a day's delay.

On the 4th we traversed a low section extending beyond the camp, and I omit mentioning the difficulties encountered in making the animals cross it. We finally reached an arroyo which I named Carrizal. Here we found a bridge built. The mules went over it with the supplies. Two fell off and damaged the packs they were carrying. We proceeded beyond this point for about a league and a half and camp was made at a rather favorable location with sufficient water and pasturage. This I named San Andres Corzino.

On the 5th we advanced along our previous route and in the same direction to the southwest. Our party traveled five leagues to the spot named San Melancio on the banks of an arroyo called El Detenido. The water could be seen from the hill where the camp was located. The stream was out of its banks and extended for more than three quarters of a league. This prevented the passage on this day, for upon examination we found the flood to be as mentioned above. It proved to be one of the boggiest places on the whole trip.

On the 7th my lieutenant, Don Francisco Martínez, captain of the cuirassiers, after viewing the arroyo from the camp, went in person to examine it accompanied by six seamen. He built a raft to carry over the equipment; and on the day named, after arriving at the said arroyo and traveling a distance of more than a half league in water three spans deep, I tried to cross on the raft but capsized. I struggled against the current for quite awhile. The cook and men servants followed my example. We all came out wringing wet and shed enough water to fill a good sized keg. About fifteen men went aboard the raft and had the same experience. Then came the trunks and papers, which underwent a similar fate. The royal standard crossed from San Fausto all the way in water, the whole country being inundated up to this point. We were forced to go up on the highest hill, and even then we were not certain of our safety. Needless to say we were all obliged to sleep in our wet clothes, there being no alternative. We did not even have a fire, for the weather did not permit, the constant rain putting the fire out.

On the 11th the day dawned with a rain and wind storm. Our royal standard, nevertheless, resumed the journey toward the Colorado or Espíritu Santo River, as it is likewise called, while I went forward to reconnoiter. It was so high that none of the experienced soldiers who accompanied me could tell what to do, for it was so much like a sea. Finally, after firing three shots, I was answered from the other side. A discovery that comforted me as well as all the people and made us forget, to a certain extent, all the work and toil endured in our march to this place, giving us courage for the still greater task of returning to the spot, where the rest of the people had set up camp at a location called San Martín. We returned by the route the animals had worn. One could not leave the path because the timber would not permit it. The new camp was at Real de Consuelo—a matter of thought for all.

On the 13th the aide, Juan García de Quintanilla, came to this camp with papers and letter from His Excellency. These new orders and sovereign commands were to be implicitly obeyed. In view of this I called into council the two captains, Don Gregorio de Salinas and Don Francisco Martínez, the two *alférezes,* Don Alexandro Bruno and Don Pedro Fernández Cenrra, who voted unanimously. The record appears in the report signed by the council. I may add that on this day Captain Francisco Benavides gave me an account of the supply of horses which His Excellency, in his great wisdom, had sent under his charge. He also gave me an account of the epidemic that had raged as a result of the cold winter. The total number of those left amounted to one hundred and thirty. He did not know how many had died during the month he had waited on the banks of this river; but he stated that the remainder of those with which he started from the Kingdom [of León] were not of much account. On the 14th I sent the drivers ahead to mark the route as best they could, and to open a way wherever it might seem best to them for us to cross. On the next day the aide mentioned above brought thirty mules under his charge and some horses, as I had instructed him to do. I started out with such as could carry loads. I still recall with vexation the trouble experienced in making our way through the woods, leaving the packs stuck up on poles. The amount carried by each mule did not exceed four arrobas [one hundred pounds]. The epidemic that has afflicted us along the way continued, and became more serious at this place, where we stayed for such a long time, where we were afoot amid frequent rains that gave our poor people many a soaking. It was a rare thing for them to save even the ragged clothing that protected them so scantily. The intervening days until the 22nd were spent by some in hunting a supply of meat, by others in bringing up the provisions for our journey as well as my trunks, all of which were sent on ahead. I was without all conveniences, for I did not even have paper or a change of clothing for more than three days while the rain lasted. I was waiting for the train of mules I was to take with me. They were supposed to have started at the same time as the ones belonging to the aide, but the latter had had the advantage of fairly good pasturage afforded by the place. Mine could not travel with even the moderate load of four arrobas.

On this day, the 22nd, with clouds and some rain, the royal standard continued the march in a south-southwesterly direction. We traveled thus six leagues until I made camp at a place which I named Catedral de San Pedro. This day such beasts as were available were used.

On the 23rd we pursued our way toward the south-southwest. Our camp went forward seven leagues in this direction until we set up camp at a good place with pasturage and water. This I named Santa María. The whole country was filled with buffaloes. On the 24th our royal standard directed its course in quest of the banks of the San Marcos River or the San Pedro y San Pablo as I called it in the first part of my journey. Continuing the march to the south-southwest, we traveled five leagues and reached the banks of the said river. Here, at the spot I named San Francisco del Valle on this trip, I caught up with the rest of the people under the command of Don Juan García and those under the orders of Captain Francisco Benavides, all of whom were together. I had them sound the river immediately, as we saw that it was rising so fast that it would prevent our crossing.

On the 26th, after sounding the river on the previous day, and not having found a good ford, I ordered a float built to carry over the provisions and other supplies. This took all day. On sounding it again today we found it possible to cross, though with difficulty. After passing to the other side, we carried the royal standard to a place which on this second trip, I named El Rosario.

We remained here the 27th waiting for the people whom I sent in search of meat, and for the Cantuna Indian, who was to deliver to me certain horses of mine that I had left in his care on my second trip to the Asinai province and nation. He brought them in, but in very poor condition. On this day we continued our march to the southwest, a quarter west. We traveled six leagues to the place called Las Cruces, which on this return trip, I called La Cruz de San Román.

On the 29th we went toward the southwest, a quarter south, until our royal standard was set up at a distance of six leagues. At this time I named it San Miguel. On this day Captain Francisco de Benavides received news that one of his soldiers and five seamen had drowned in Bahía de San Bernardo.

MARCH

On March 1st our royal standard and camp again set out on the return march from the above mentioned place. We traveled in various directions, unable to follow any straight road. We had to do this to avoid the heavy woods lying along the direct route. In these variations we roamed over sections which we had not traversed either in the first part of our journey or in our countermarch to the Asinai nation. It was a rich land with few or no water holes in the summer season and a great number of buffaloes. There were more than three thousand in the distance we covered to the point where we set up our royal standard. This place I called El Angel de la Guardia.

On the 2nd I received information that three men were missing from those under my charge. I sent a party to search for them and our royal standard continued its journey in a south-southwesterly direction going six leagues. Here we made camp, joining the party and horses under the command of the said captain [Benavides]. I called the place Las Bocas de San Pablo. At midnight two of those who were missing out of my camp came in and a little later followed those whom I had sent in search of them. They told me they had no news of the other man save that certain Indians told them that they had found a man hurt, but that they did not know where he had gone.

On the 4th, after remaining in the said camp waiting for the man who was missing, and having again sent a party in search of him, the captain, Francisco Benavides, held a general review. Of the one hundred and twenty horses provided at the expense of His Majesty, not a single one was found to be of any account at all. Our royal standard continued the return march along the route and road to the south. The people composing my camp covered a distance of a league and a half on horseback. In this short distance each of the horses had to be changed once at least, fresh ones being secured from the extra drove. Seeing the impossibility of continuing thus, our royal standard was set up. I called the place San Casimiro.

On the 5th, with a cold wind from the north and some rain, our royal standard and camp resumed the journey, in spite of the weather, in search of Real de Santa Margarita de Buenavista [Buenaventura] and of the vessels, and the reserve party intending to return in the said vessels. I also intended to turn over to His Excellency the fifty men whom he, in his great generosity, had been good enough to add to my troops to help carry out the orders given me. We traveled toward the south, a quarter southwest, from the said place over a very rough country with bad roads. We continued thus for three leagues until our company joined the party from the vessels under the command of Juan Enríquez Barroto, captain of artillery, whom we found waiting for us at the said place. He reported that they had kept a constant lookout for us at this location for more than two months, and that a vessel had been stationed there also. At the time we arrived we found two *fellucas* and a launch. One can imagine what a comfort the meeting was to the people of my camp as well as to the others mentioned. It seemed that they had kept going forward urged by the very hardships endured—and these are the only reward these humble vassals of the king have received for their long journey, during which they were unable to accomplish a single one of the many orders entrusted to them by His Excellency. This was not due to the lack of courage or of noble souls

who were willing to obey the orders of His Excellency implicitly, but it seems that it must have been so ordered by Divine Providence. Finally, it must be said, that the descriptions here given of various occurrences cannot be anything save inadequate sketches which my humble faculties have been able to produce. I have recorded them in plain fashion in fulfillment of the orders of his Excellency. I remained at this place from the day above mentioned until the 22nd engaged in preparing a report and in writing other documents which I will lay at your Excellency's feet as evidence of the truthfulness of my account. I occupied the time also in holding a council to determine what to do with the horses which were unanimously voted by all present to be worthless. On the said day Captain Francisco Martínez, my lieutenant, took charge of the camp and I embarked on the frigate. I remained on board the vessel which lay at the mouth of the bay, at a point called San Francisco, until the 24th awaiting for a favorable chance to sail along the coast to the east to make explorations in obedience to the orders of his Excellency.
Dated at Lago de San Bernardo de San Francisco, May 24, 1692.

III
DIARY KEPT BY THE MISSIONARIES[12]
BEGUN ON MAY 16 AND FINISHED AUGUST 2, 1691

On May 16, 1691, I [Damián Massanet][13] set out from the Mission San Salvador del Valle de Santiago, in the jurisdiction of Coahuila, with the following missionaries and ministers: Fray Francisco Hidalgo, Fray Nicolás Revo [Recio], Fray Miguel Estela [Estelles], Fray Pedro Fortuni, Fray Pedro

---

[12]The variations here indicated are the result of a comparative study of the different texts with the original documents contained in Provincias Internas, Vol. 182, Archivo General y Público de la Nación de México. This investigation was carried on by Herbert E. Bolton. The variations are placed in square brackets.

[13]Father Massanet was a member of the Franciscan College at Querétaro. He had begun his services on the Coahuila frontier as early as 1687; and having become interested in the Indians across the Rio Grande through the story of the miraculous conversions by Mother Agreda, had eagerly embraced the opportunity of going with Alonso de León to Matagorda Bay and to East Texas. He had supervised the founding of the first Texas mission and had been instrumental in inducing the viceroy to inaugurate a comprehensive program on the northeastern frontier. He continued his efforts for the Christianization of the Indians of this section until 1693, when the work was temporarily abandoned through the orders of the viceroy. Contrary to the expectations of Father Massanet, the Texas Indians had proved unmanageable, even threatening to kill the missionaries, if they did not leave the country. His writings constitute our most important sources for the beginnings of missionary work in Texas and it is unfortunate that it is impossible from the records to trace his history after he retired from the Texas frontier, a disappointed man. Some of his most striking characteristics can be gathered from his letter to Don Carlos de Sigüenza y Góngora and from the diaries of the *entradas* of Don Alonso de León, already cited.

García, Fray Ildefonzo Monge, Fray Joseph Saldaña, Fray Antonio Miranda, and Fray Juan de Garicochea [Garaiicochea], three brothers and a boy whom I brought from Querétaro, all chosen for the undertaking and the spiritual conquest of the souls of the barbarous Texas Indians and the other nations allied with them, and all holding patents from our most Reverend Father, the Commissary General of New Spain, Fray Juan de Capistrano, and under orders of His Excellency, Conde de Galve, Viceroy and Captain General of this New Spain.

On this day, after having celebrated Mass, I turned over the mission of San Salvador to the Licentiate Presbyter, Juan Bautista de Zepeda, who by order of the most illustrious Bishop of Guadalajara, was awaiting our departure for the purpose of residing in the said mission as curate, and of serving the said Indians who remained there, as is shown by the declaration which the said licentiate gave me.

After leaving the said Mission San Salvador, we traveled toward the northeast over a level country containing small wooded sections of mesquites which were not very large, always within view of the river upon which the mission is located. This day we traveled five leagues and halted on the banks of the river, where there is a high hill without trees, a spot which the Spaniards call Real de Chocolate. I gave it the name of San Hubaldo, because it was his day.

Thursday, 17. We left Hubaldo and traveled toward the northeast, across a level country without timber. At a distance of three leagues there were some lakes of brackish water, which in rainy weather flow toward the east. In these lakes there are a great many fish—*bagres,* and great numbers of perch. We crossed these lakes and then came to a mesquite wood and immediately saw at a distance some high bare hills, which extend from west to east, along the bank of the Sabinas River. We traveled to the point where these hills are low. We arrived at the crossing of the said river and halted. We advanced this day five leagues. I named this spot and the river San Pascual Bailón because it was his day. In the language of the Indians it is called Guansan, which means Little River.

Friday, 18. We did not travel on this day because we spent the time transferring the stock and the mares. The ford is rocky and is passable for mules even when loaded, but it is difficult. This crossing is, however, the best on the river. There are many cedars, cottonwoods, and ashes at this point. The stock was able to wade over very well, thanks to God.

Saturday, 19. We set out from San Pascual Bailón and Sabinas River. We traveled toward the north over level country with small clumps of mesquites and *nopal* A league and a half away there is a large salt lake, which, when the water dries up, furnishes very fine salt in places. We passed close to and above it. We continued to move in the same direction over very level country. At the foot of a range of hills, there is a very large lake of water, but in times of drought, the water usually fails. We went six leagues on this day. We bestowed upon this place the name of San Félix, because we were there on his day. In the language of the Indians it is called Chacalep while the Spaniards call it Charco del Pescado.

Sunday, 20. We did not travel because we were expecting the governor, Don Domingo Terán, who was coming down from Coahuila with the soldiers.

Monday, 21. The military governor, Don Domingo Terán arrived at the place with the soldiers. Upon reaching the Sabinas River, Captain Don Francisco Martínez had sent two soldiers down the river to meet the governor and guide him to the spot where we were waiting for him. The reason for our waiting in this place was that we had started with our stock and mares from Nuevo León and hence the trip to Coahuila would have needlessly made us go more than forty leagues over bad roads. The stock would have found this impossible and would have been eventually lost. The night after we joined forces there was a great blowing of trumpets and beating of drums. Declaring that the horses would be frightened and run away, the governor, Don Domingo Terán, had ordered the men not to play. That night there was a stampede of the horses and the next morning one hundred and fifty were gone. In catching them, those that were left were almost killed, for the soldiers rode them very hard to round up the horses that had been frightened and had run away.

Tuesday, 22. We did not travel because the governor, Don Domingo Terán, declared that he had to write and send letters to His Excellency.

Saturday, 26. We set out from San Félix and went northeast over a level country. After traveling three leagues, we came upon a deposit of saltpeter which extends toward the south. Next there are ranges of low hills. This day, we made five leagues and halted at some lakes to which we gave the name of San Felipe Neri, because it was his day. In other expeditions they were called Agua Verde. In the Indian tongue they are called Asanquan, which means heart.

Sunday, 27. We left San Felipe Neri and proceeded northeast, following certain hills and. halted on an arroyo of brackish water. This day we traveled five leagues. During the day the Indians of the Mescaleros, Yoricas, Chome, Parchacas, Alachome [Machome], and Pamais [Paman], tribes accompanied us. All these tribes live between the Río del Norte and the Sabinas. They are not located in any definite place but always roam about hunting buffaloes and searching for whatever the country affords. They do not plant crops nor do they like anything that resembles work. This place was named San Juanico. The Indians call it Guagual.

Monday, 28. We left San Juanico and traversed northeast over a level country, though somewhat broken, but still good for travel. After we had gone about three leagues, we saw the river, from the high hills, not the water but the banks along its borders. We directed our way north through mesquite woods over level country. About a league before the river is reached there is an arroyo which flows into the river. At the crossing of the river there are some tall reeds. This day we went five leagues and halted on the banks of the Río del Norte, which some call Rio Grande and others Río Turbio because the waters are always muddy. We called this place San Fernando because we were there and celebrated Mass on his day. In the Indian language it is called Pulapaexain [Pulapexam], which means the place where chickens are raised. The Indians also call it Ganapetuan [Guanapetnan], that is to say, Rio Grande.

Tuesday, 29. The soldiers set out to look for the horses which during the previous night had stampeded. There were forty horses missing.

Wednesday, 30. A squad of soldiers continued searching for the horses which were still missing. They did not find them and the said forty horses were an absolute loss. Another squad went out to kill buffaloes, of which there was an abundance.

Thursday, 31. We crossed the large stock in safety, thanks to God.

JUNE

Friday, June 1. All the soldiers and the herders began to look after the sheep and goats, all of which had to be transferred on horseback, because the ford of the river is about a musket shot across and the current is strong. The small stock could not be moved on foot and there was no wood for building rafts. During the day most of the stock was carried over. That night about eleven o'clock a terrible hurricane came up, one so constant in violence that the big mesquites that are found at this spot were pulled up by the roots and the tents were blown down and carried away as if they were straw. It lasted about three hours. It rained during the whole time and the water seemed to fall in bucketfuls. We weathered this storm with no protection save that of repeating frequently the litany of the Most Holy Virgin and the prayers to the saints who had been selected as patrons of our voyage and our success. Each morning before leaving the camp, all the priests, on bended knees, said the aforesaid prayers and the litany to the Most Holy Virgin, the Most Holy Cross, Saint Michael, Saint Joseph, Our Father Saint Francis, Saint Anthony of Padua, Saint Rose of Viterbo, and to the souls in Purgatory.

Saturday, 2. We started taking the small stock across at about noon and finished this task successfully by five o'clock in the afternoon. The river by that time was rising so high that it would have been impossible any longer to get to the other side.

Sunday, 3. Espíritu Santo Day, after Mass, we left San Fernando and Río del Norte because the place was lacking in pasturage for the cattle and horses. We continued toward the north, over broken country, with arroyos, hills, and mesquite woods. It was like this for about three leagues. After that the country is good and level. We stopped at some water holes that are in a woods of tall trees called hackberries. In past expeditions it had been called Charco de los Cuervos. I named it San Bernardo. In the language of the Indians it is called Guampachet [Guanpache], which means Muddy Water. During all the previous days, we had seen many buffaloes. Today there were more.

Monday, 4. After Mass, we left San Bernardo and proceeded northeast over a level country with but little timber. After we had gone about a league we saw the woods along an arroyo which runs from the northeast toward the south. This arroyo has no water further south. We continued on our direction, turning from the northeast to a quarter east through certain ranges of hills covered with mesquites. We reached the banks of the arroyo which has considerable water. At the distance of a gunshot there were four tall oaks close together with heavy foliage. Here we camped. In previous journeys this place was called Arroyo del Pullón because a soldier caught a *bagre de pullón* as they call them. I named it San Matías. In the language of the Indians it is called Samenpajo.

Tuesday, 5. After Mass we left San Matías. We advanced toward the northeast, over level country where in places there were open mesquite woods. We made four leagues and reached an arroyo containing considerable water. During droughts this usually fails. In the other expedition this arroyo was called Arroyo de Caramanchel. I named it San Lucas. In the language of the Indians it is called Guanapacti, which means Arroyo de Dos Aguas. At this spot, and the one just passed, there came out many Indians of the Quems, Pachules, Ocanas, Chaguan, Pastaluc, and Paac nations. The *ranchería* was on the banks of the said arroyo, about three leagues from the spot named. This day we went four leagues.

Wednesday, 6. We set out from San Lucas and traveled toward the northeast, over level country, without trees. After having gone about two leagues there was a dry arroyo running to the south. It was heavily wooded. In rainy weather it has water in holes. Before reaching it there is a mesquite woods. Across this arroyo the country is level without woods until El Monte Grande is reached, which is on this side of the river. It is a dense thicket of large mesquite trees. After reaching this woods one turns to the east until one can see a high hill covered with trees that lies to the northeast. After crossing this one emerges from the woods and enters a country (which lies in the river bed itself) where there are no trees. Here we set up our camp for there was no other place. This was once called the Nueces River on account of the many pecans there. I named it San Norberto because it was his day. The Indians call it Chotilapacquen. This day we traveled about six leagues and stopped on the banks of the river. There were great quantities of buffaloes. In the river were many fish—*bagre*, and perch.

Thursday, 7. We left San Norberto, or the Nueces, by its other name. We crossed the river and immediately entered a valley filled with very large pecan trees. We turned towards the north, a quarter northeast. As one comes out of the said valley there are many large mesquites and oaks. Then one turns northeast, a quarter east. A high hill covered with trees can be seen in the distance toward the northeast. We pushed east, a quarter southeast, until we reached a little hill which can be seen to the south. From a distance it looks white because it has no woods. As we approached it, we left it to the southward and tended toward the east over a chain of low hills covered with many mesquites. After traveling about a league, we turned northeast, a quarter east, until we reached a dry arroyo where there was no water but which was heavily timbered. The river is about a league distant and there is a very large pecan tree at the crossing. This day we went six leagues and halted after we had forded the Río Frio. I named it San Feliciano* because I left it on his day. In the language of the Indians it is called Guarapacavas [Guanapacaus] which means Cold Water.

Friday, 8. We did not advance because the previous day the stock was unable to reach the place [where we camped] because of the dense woods. During these days we had abundant buffalo and fish, of the latter there are a great number in the river of the kind they call *bagre de pullón.*

Saturday, 9. We left San Feliciano and Río Frio and traveled toward the northeast, a quarter east, about two leagues and a half over a range of hills covered with mesquite woods, though not very large ones. We at once entered a level untimbered region. Towards the northeast some tall trees could be seen. These were oaks. Toward the east could be distinguished a small, pointed hill and somewhat further on in the same direction, and towards the same large oaks, lay the Hondo River. This day we made five leagues and halted upon the bank of the said river. I gave it the name of San Bartolomé.† In the language of the Indians it is called Guanapajac [Guanapajao]. This day we traveled five leagues.

Sunday, 10. Feast of the Most Holy Trinity. We did not march, because on the preceding night there was a stampede among the horses, and they carried away with them cows, mares, and goats. On the next day, thanks to God, all were found. To this spot came the Indians of the following nations:

---

*Leona River.
†Frio River.

Sanpanal, Patchal, Papanaca, Parchiquis, Pacuachiam, Aguapalam, Samampac, Vanca, Payavan [Payauan], and Patavo [Patauo]. I distributed tobacco, rosaries, knives, and beads to all of them. Afterwards, in the evening, others came, the Pitanay [Piutaay], Apaysi [Apayu], and Patsau.

Monday, 11. We set out from San Bartolomé and Rio Rondo. On this day and from this place, we started for the Texas [Techas], a route pursuing a direction different from the one followed by the two previous expeditions. After crossing the river we proceeded toward the north, a quarter northeast, over level country without trees. We reached a mesquite woods and observed some cedars. We traveled towards them and found them to be on the banks of an arroyo with a running stream, where there are great quantities of fish. To cross it one turns eastward. After passing through it we went north over a level country with heavy mesquite and oak woods. To the east were some low hills. After we had gone about a league we saw a high, black, round hill, which has some tall oaks on the north side. We skirted it leaving it to the north of our route. After passing this hill, about a league beyond, we climbed other ranges of low hills covered with mesquites and oaks. To the northeast could be seen a level, untimbered country except for some very large oaks that were located at a considerable distance from each other. After entering this level stretch, we traveled toward the northeast and reached another mesquite woods. We entered it through a glen and could then see the woods along a large arroyo. They were cottonwoods, tall oaks, and mulberries among which vines were thickly scattered. In this arroyo were many fish, and on this day there were a great number of buffaloes. We halted on the banks of the arroyo. We had advanced six leagues this day. To this place we gave the name of San Bernabé because it was his day. In the Indian language it is called Potopatana which means a well.

Tuesday, 12. We left Arroyo de San Bernabé and proceeded northeast through a mesquite and oak woods. The country was easy for travel. At a distance of about a quarter of a league we emerged from the woods at the foot of a high hill. We immediately entered a level region without trees, the whole forming a beautiful prairie, where there were great numbers of buffaloes and deer. From this prairie could be seen a tall round hill in a northeasterly direction. We turned east and in line with the said hill we could see another one farther east. We passed this which is covered with tall mesquite woods. half a league beyond is the arroyo. It is crossed below its junction with a dry one. We went this day five leagues and camped on the far side. We gave it the name of San Basilio.* In the Indian language it is called Panapay.

*Medina River.

Wednesday, 13. We left San Basilio after having said mass. We continued northeast, a quarter east, until we passed through some low hills covered with oaks and mesquites. The country is very beautiful. We entered a stretch which was easy for travel and advanced on our easterly course. Before reaching the river there are other small hills with large oaks. The river is bordered with many trees, cottonwoods, oaks, cedars, mulberries, and many vines. There are a great many fish and upon the highlands a great number of wild chickens.

On this day, there were so many buffaloes that the horses stampeded and forty head ran away. These were collected with the rest of the horses by hard work on the part of the soldiers. We found at this place the *ranchería* of the Indians of the Payaya nation. This is a very large nation and the country where they live is very fine. I called this place San Antonio de Pádua, because it was his day. In the language of the Indians it is called Yanaguana. We traveled five leagues.

Thursday, 14 and Corpus Christi Day. We did not continue our journey because of the presence of the said Indians. I ordered a large cross set up, and in front of it built an arbor of cottonwood trees, where the altar was placed. All the priests said mass. High Mass was attended by Governor Don Domingo Terán de los Ríos, Captain Don Francisco Martínez, and the rest of the soldiers, all of whom fired a great many salutes. When the host was elevated a salute was fired by all the guns. The Indians were present during these ceremonies. After Mass the Indians were given to understand through the captain of the Pacpul nation, that the Mass and the salutes fired by the Spaniards were all for the honor, worship, and adoration we owed to God, our Lord, in acknowledgment of the benefits and great blessings that His Divine Majesty bestows upon us; that it was to Him that we had just offered sacrifice [of His Body and Blood] in the form of the bread and wine which had just been elevated in the Mass.

Then I distributed among them rosaries, pocket knives, cutlery, beads, and tobacco. I gave a horse to the captain. In the midst of their *ranchería,* that is, their pueblo, they had a tall wooden cross. They said that they knew the Christians put up crosses in their houses and settlements and had great reverence for them, because it was a thing that was very pleasing to Him Who was God and Lord of all. On the day we left, the said Payaya captain, as an expression of thanks and appreciation, declared that he wished to go with us and guide us as far as the *rancherías* of the Chomanes. He also ordered four Indians of his tribe to help the Spaniards round up the stock and do whatever else might be needed.

Wednesday, 15. We left San Antonio de Padua and traveled east, a quarter northeast, over level lands without woods. Along the road were many ranges of low hills covered with oaks. We continued the whole day in the same direction. After going five leagues, we halted upon an intermittent arroyo. There were a great many buffaloes, and in the lagoons there were alligators and fish in abundance. I named this spot Santa Crecencia because it was her day. In the Indian language it is called Ymatiniguiapacomicen [Smatiniguiapacomisem] which means river where there are colors for painting shields.

Saturday, 16. We left Santa Crecencia and traveled northeast, a quarter east, over level country without trees. To the north there are some low ranges of hills with but little timber. A still higher hill could be seen in the distance. This had tall timber on it. As we progressed on our journey it was left to the north. Near this hill there is a heavy mesquite woods which rapidly descends to a dry arroyo . There are very large mulberry trees, pecans, vines, oaks, and hackberries. By ascending this hill from the northeast, a quarter east, and taking the same direction as before, some big hills running from the north toward the east may be seen. After ascending again we arrived at a low stretch of mesquite next to an arroyo with water, which is hot and salty, and in it also there is a rock with an opening from which fine cold water runs. We went four leagues. I named the spot San Félix because it was his day and because it had been a good day for buffaloes, prairie chickens, fish, and good water. In the language of the Indians it is called Papulcasa.

Sunday, 17. We departed after Mass at San Félix and proceeded northeast, a quarter east, over a level country without timber. There could be seen in the distance toward the north some tall hills untimbered. These run from northeast toward the east. There is a mesquite woods at these hills. The country is good for travel and has no rocks. When the last hills are reached there is an oak woods. From this point can be seen the woods on the banks of an arroyo, whose banks are red. First there is a dry one running east, a mesquite woods, and at a short distance there is another arroyo with water. These two unite lower down. There are many mulberries, oaks, and cottonwoods. There are many buffaloes and fish. We made four leagues. I named the place San Marcelino because we were there on his day. In the language of the Indians it is called Xoloton [Xaloton], which means black nuts. I noticed that from the mission founded in Valle de Santiago, under the name of San Salvador, which I turned over to the ordinary of Guadalajara, up to this place there is only one language spoken.

From this place to the Tejas country different languages are spoken. One encounters the following nations in the order named: Catqueza, Cantona, Emet, Cavas, Sana, Tojo, Toaa, and others. Here is the border region of various Indian nations. They speak several tongues (but they understand each other) because they are all friends and have no wars. The aforementioned place, called Xalaton is called Bataconiquiyoque by the other nations in the country of the Texas. These tribes are all located on the road to the Tejas [Techas].

Monday, 18. We left the place called San Marcelino [Marcelliano] going through a mesquite woods and traveling north, a quarter northeast, until we reached some high hills where the timber ceased. At this place we came upon an Indian who on horseback was coming to meet us. He told us how the captains of the Choma, Cibola, Cantona, Chalome [Choloma], Catqueza, and Chaynaya were coming out to receive us in peace. We marched on with the said Indian and after we had traveled about a half league we met the said captains with other Indians who were accompanying them, all on horseback. When they met us they all alighted from their horses and with great courtesy saluted us. They brought two letters they had received from the missionaries who had remained among the Tejas Indians [Techas] the year before. The missionaries had sent these to us by an Indian who had come from the Tejas [Techas]. I opened the said letters and found that the missionaries had written me to say that the Tejas Indians had been visited by a great deal of sickness and that many of the Indians had died; and that God had been pleased to take unto Himself the soul of the Reverend Father Fray Miguel Fontcubierta on the fifth day of February of the present year. *Requiescat in pace.* I had left this priest as president and prelate of the missionaries when I departed from the missions. He died from a fever which lasted eight days. He spent the entire time in deeds of kindness and in praying to God, our Lord, for grace for himself and for those poor unfortunate Indians who were still unredeemed. The said captains then told us that their *ranchería* was on the river at one of the springs which form the Guadalupe. We all traveled on together under the guidance of the said captains. We marched toward the northeast over a level country without woods where there were low ranges of hills. The *ranchería* was in a woods. We went five leagues on this day, and I named the place San Gervacio, because we set out on his day. In the language of the Indians it is called Conaqueyadita [Conaquedista] which means where the river rises.

Note.—When we met the said captains, they all were mounted on very small saddles which resembled riding saddles with stirrups. When we asked them where they got these little saddles, they told us they had taken them from the Apaches in war.

On the afternoon of our arrival, all the captains, each with his own people, held a parade. The first in the parade was Don Juan Safiata [Sabeata] with his tribe and some Chomas. Next came the captain of the Cantona tribe who led his people and some Chomas. This captain marched in front of his men carrying a cross of wood which he said he had guarded with great care and veneration for many years. Next came the captain of the Cibola tribe with his own people and those of the Chalome and Guanaya tribe. This captain likewise marched in front of his people carrying an image of our Lady of Guadalupe, one of those that had been distributed among the captains the previous year. They had been sent for this purpose by His Excellency, Conde de Galve, Viceroy and Captain General. After these came the captain of the Catqueza tribe. He was an Indian named Nicolás, well versed in the Mexican dialects and in the Spanish language, understanding everything that was said to him. This Indian was reared in Parras [Saltillo and Parral].* He went to New Mexico and later returned to his own people to live in a wild state with no restrictions whatever. Besides this, he enjoyed great prestige, for according to the faulty judgment of this people and their barbarous nature, a man who is wicked and expert in cruelties and in war is considered as the greatest among them and he has also a large following among them. Since he knows the Spaniards and knows how to talk to them he makes the other Indians believe whatever he wants, and in particular that the Spaniards are his friends and that they have promised to help him in his wars and whenever he needs them. Among these barbarous nations any Indian who is clever in languages is looked upon with admiration, for these wild creatures are not reasonable beings. Because of the reasons cited the said Captain Nicolás of the Catqueza was also very highly regarded. He came on this day with his people and bore an image of our Lady of Guadalupe, like the other one referred to. He did the same as the others, that is, marched in the procession with his people divided in two columns and kissed my habit and my hand.

After all were gathered together, large and small, I called the captains and gave each of them presents for his people: for the men tobacco, pocket knives, and other cutlery; for the women, rosaries, earrings, glass beads, and red ribbons. They were all very much pleased and their contentment reached its limit when two loads of flour were sent to their *ranchería* with instructions for their captains to distribute a *tercio* to each of them.

The above mentioned nations, the Choma, Cibola, and Canaya, are Indians who live in and about the country along the banks of Río del Norte. They border on the Salineros Indians who live on the banks of the Salado, a river that runs into the Río del Norte. They also border upon the Apaches, with whom they are often at war. The Apaches live in a mountain range which runs from east to west. They are at war with all the other nations, except the Salineros, with whom they are at peace. They have always been at war with the Spaniards of New Mexico, for although they have sometimes made peace, it has never lasted but a short time. In the end they dominate all the other Indians. The other nations say that the Apaches are not brave because they

---

*Parras is located about seventy miles due west of Saltillo, in southern Coahuila. Parral is a major mining center in southern Chihuahua, near the border with Durango.

fight on horseback, armed with offensive and defensive arms. These Indians are very quick and warlike. May God, our Lord, bring them to the true knowledge of our Holy Catholic Faith. The Chomas are the same Indians who in Parral and New Mexico are called Jumanes [Jumares]. Every year they come to the headwaters of the Guadalupe River and sometimes as far as the Tejas [Techas] country. They come to kill buffaloes and carry away the skins because in their country, there are no buffaloes. When it gets cold they return to their own country.

Don Juan Sabiata [Sabeata], captain of the said Chomanes, (whom they call Jumanes) showed us a commission as governor of the Indians of his nation and others that may join him. Another Indian of the same nation exhibited a commission as lieutenant to the said Don Juan Sabiata. The governor of Nueva Vizcaya, Don Isidro Pardiñas, gave them both these commissions.

The next day, Don Juan Sabiata, captain of the said Chomanes, and another Indian who speaks Spanish, came and told me that I must stay with them, that among their people there were many Christians who had been baptized in Parral and Paso del Nuevo México. I asked him in what region we would find the pueblo, and he answered me that we had to return to his country, that he could not stay away any longer, that he had come for buffaloes and for skins, which he had to carry back. To remain friends and not displease him, I told him I knew full well how far away his country was, and that it was not possible to go at the time because our missionaries who had stayed alone the year before among the Tejas were in great need, but we would come next year. All these arguments that I used with him were for no other purpose than to distract his attention, because if they really wanted missionaries in their country, they doubtless could have had them before this, as they go to Parral and Paso de Nuevo México every year. We remained friends and at peace, thanks to God.

In this same place Captain Tomás[14] of the Catqueza nation told the soldiers they ought not to leave that place, because they were laboring under a misconception, that the country of the Tejas [Techas] was a very poor and unhealthy country, that the Tejas Indians had tried to kill the missionaries and that they had stolen all the cows, horses, clothing, and the things from the church. All this was for the purpose of seeing whether it were possible to keep us in that place, which was his territory, and in order to see whether he could keep, as well, all we were carrying to found missions among the Tejas [Techas]. These reasons found a ready echo in the apprehension of some and more especially in the case of the governor. The said Captain Tomás hid from

[14]Captain Nicolás is the name recorded elsewhere in this account.

me when I went into the *ranchería* with Captain Don Francisco Martínez to look for him. Captain Martínez never gives credence to these things or pays any attention to such Indian stories.

Tuesday, 19. We left San Gervacio and traveled two leagues to the east in order to separate ourselves from the *rancherías* and put an end to the familiar intercourse that had developed between the soldiers and the Indians. The Indians, large and small, must have amounted to about three thousand souls. The country is level and without trees. At a distance of two leagues, the woods, which are very extensive, begin. We stopped at the edge of the timber because there were some ponds there and the next water was very far away. We halted to allow the stock to catch up as it had started late. The forest consists of mesquites and oaks and extends toward the east. That night the captains came to our camp and brought five boys as captives. These they gave to the governor, Don Domingo Terán, and to the soldiers in exchange for horses. The captives were children of the Muruam nation who live in the vicinity of the Guadalupe River.* These Indians are at peace with those of the coast of Bahía del Espíritu Santo. We traveled on this day two leagues.

Wednesday, 20. We set out from San Silvestre and went north, a quarter northeast through hills where there were scattered mesquites and many rocks. We advanced five leagues and reached the other branch of the Guadalupe River to which I gave the name of San Juan.† In the Indian language it is called Canocanoyestatetlo [Canocannayesttetao] which means hot water. This water is very hot when it first comes out of the ground but it cools after running. There were many buffaloes and fish. We traveled five leagues.

Thursday, 21. We did not move on, because on the previous day the horses stampeded and the following day one hundred and sixty were missing. In the morning Captain Francisco Sánchez and nine soldiers set out. They returned with sixty horses at noon. The afternoon was spent in search for the rest, of which forty were found. Sixty were lost altogether.

Friday, 22. We did not advance, but continued the search for the horses that were still missing. We did not find a single one, not even a trace. That same afternoon two Indians arrived from the Cantona nation saying that they had heard in their *ranchería* that our horses were missing. They said the captains and other Indians were coming to help the Spaniards search for them.

Saturday, 23. Before sunrise the said captains came to the camp with their Indians. As soon as it was announced that the Indians had arrived, the governor, Don Domingo Terán ordered the Frenchman Pedro Muni to tell the Indians not to come into the midst of the camp with their arms. What

---

*San Marcos River.

†Blanco River.

might have been the consequences, I dare not say, since that is not my business. There were sixty Indians in all. Flour was immediately given them so that they might eat and later tobacco was distributed. Twelve soldiers set out with the said Indians to look for the horses that were missing. Some of the Indians who went out unaccompanied by the soldiers said that they had seen and found the horses but the animals escaped because the searchers were on foot and were therefore unable to corral them. They declared that the horses went into the woods which are very thick and extensive.

Sunday, 24. After Mass twelve soldiers went out with some of the Indians, who had seen the lost horses on the previous day. The Choma Indian governor, Juan, went with them. They did not find anything, not even the tracks of the herd, because of the great number of buffaloes that roamed over the country and the woods. They returned without the horses. We lost fifty in all. Juan, the governor of the Choma Indians, was given the task of looking for them with his people. He was told to take them to the San Marcos River where Governor Don Domingo Terán said he would wait for him until the tenth to bring all the horses to that river, that is to the last spring, one of the arms that forms the Guadalupe. I gave it the name of San Juan Bautista.

Monday, 25. We left San Juan Bautista and crossed the river. We went about a league to the east and reached some small hills. We traveled northeast, a quarter east, over a rough country without timber where there were many arroyos and little hills, all of which we were able to cross. We advanced six leagues and came to an arroyo of running water. There were a great many trees, tall mulberries, ashes, hackberries and grape vines. There were many buffaloes. I named the place San Juan y San Pablo. In the language of the Indians it is called Techaconaesa which means place where there are prickly pears and mesquites.

Tuesday, 26. We left San Juan y San Pablo and proceeded northeast over low ranges of rocky, unwooded hills, for three leagues and came to a heavily wooded arroyo. We traveled all day in sight of a mountain which law [sic] to the eastward. After crossing the arroyo we ascended some small hills and could see the woods along the river. After ascending the hills we went east. Between the river and the mountain there is a valley filled with small mesquites. We stopped on the banks of the San Marcos, which the French called the Colorado River* because the soil was red and even the water seemed to be. The river has on its banks a great many trees, oaks, cedars, brazil woods and grape vines. There were many buffaloes. This day we traveled five leagues.

Wednesday, 27. We left the camp on the San Marcos, and crossed the river, we then proceeded east over a level country, leaving the mountain to our

---

*Present Colorado River.

north, while the San Marcos River was to the south of us. After traveling about two leagues we crossed the San Marcos River again, where we looked for a place to set up our camp and found a good one. We traveled this day about three scant leagues.

In setting out today we had to follow the river with much difficulty, in order to find a place where the stock could swim over. This situation could not be avoided, because to the south there is an impassable mountain which reaches as far as the Guadalupe River, while to the north there is another like it. To find a place suitable for those who had to go down to Bahía del Espíritu Santo, it was necessary to descend the river and look for a less difficult route for the cattle, horses, and other stock. This river is called Carcayantico in the language of the Indians.

Thursday, 28. We did not travel, because the preceding night the horses stampeded and in the morning fifty two were missing. That same morning Captain Francisco Sánchez brought in twenty seven. The other twenty five were lost. I named this place San Pedro because I said Mass on his day.

Friday, 29. After Mass we left San Pedro and went about two leagues south, a quarter southwest, over level country without woods until we came to a running arroyo. We advanced east over rough country with arroyos, hills and many trees—pecans, oaks, pines, and grape vines. This day we made more than six leagues, and stopped again on the banks of the said river, the San Marcos. This morning, when we set out, Captain Sánchez went ahead with five soldiers to see if they could find the horses we had lost, but they were not found and not even a trace of them was seen.

Saturday, 30. We did not travel because the stock had not arrived at the camping place with us on the previous day. We stopped on the banks of the San Marcos River. I named the place San Pablo because we arrived on his day. On the trunk of a tree where we stopped, a hackberry (for this is what it is called in this country) I carved a large cross and the numerals of the year we were there, that is, 1691.

Sunday, July 1. After Mass we left the place called San Pablo and traveled east about a half a league through a forest, among tall trees, cottonwoods and oaks. After penetrating the woods about two gun shots distance there is a tall, sharp-pointed hill with a steep ascent. On top there is a level spot with oak trees, but not very thick. From this point there could be seen a level space covered with oak trees, and about a league away there was a lagoon running from north to south. The Indians call this in their language Nenocodadda. The lagoon contains many fish and alligators. From this point the woods on the San Marcos River which was near could be seen. To reach the river from the said lagoon one proceeds northeast. This day we did not cross the river because we were hunting a better ford for the herds. We went three leagues. This lagoon, Nenocodadda, I named San Nicolás.

Tuesday, 3. After Mass, Captain Don Francisco Martínez set out for Bahía del Espíritu Santo. He took twenty soldiers and eight herdsmen, one hundred and fifty horses, and fifty pack mules, some loaded and some unloaded to transport whatever cargo was secured from the vessels. All of them were to be used to bring back the soldiers that His Excellency, Conde de Galve, Viceroy and Captain General of this New Spain, had sent by sea in the vessels which were secured by his orders in Vera Cruz. We remained on the other side of the San Marcos River waiting for Captain Don Francisco Martínez to return with the soldiers he had taken and those who were to land from the vessels. We did not go on because the soldiers who remained were not sufficient to drive the stock and herds that were left.

On the next day some Indians of the Cantona nation and one of the Texas nation arrived and reported to Bernardino that the missionaries in his country were well, that they had planted a great quantity of corn, and that nothing at all had happened.

Monday, 2. We crossed the San Marcos River in safety, thanks to God, and stopped on the other side of the river in a level spot where there was good pasture for the cattle and horses. Near the river were many springs of cold water, but that of the river itself was very hot and muddy.

On the following day I sent two Indians of the Cantona nation with a letter for the missionaries who were among the Texas [Texhas] Indians, advising them that we were on the San Marcos River waiting for the soldiers from Bahía del Espíritu Santo and that, if there were any news, they should notify me immediately.

The Texas [Techas] Indian, who came with those of the Cantona nation, told Bernardino that there were four Indians of the Cadodachos nation in his country and that they said that in the Cadodachos country there were ten white men, former companions of those who had lived at Bahía del Espíritu Santo, that they had given them many glass beads, jingles and other things not previously known to the Indians. These white men had declared that they had come from the direction in which the sun rose and that they lived there on the banks of the river.

Wednesday, 18. Captain Don Francisco Martínez arrived from Bahía del Espíritu Santo with the soldiers and the mules and horses. He brought back two small French boys who were captives among the Indians of the Concosi [Coancosi] [Karankawa] nation. This nation live on the shores of Bahía del Espíritu Santo, and were the same Indians who killed the Frenchmen who had landed on the gulf coast and at Bahía del Espíritu Santo. The vessels were not found and the Indians of that region declared that there had been no

Spaniards along the whole coast. They reported that five moons previously a vessel loaded with corn had been shipwrecked, but that the people had gone away in another smaller vessel they had with them, taking part of the things that were on the one that was wrecked. The said Captain Francisco Martínez left a letter with the Captain of the Concosi [Coancosi] nation so that if any Spaniards came, he could give it to them and could send us word to the Texas country by an Indian.

Thursday, 19. The Indians of the Choma nation brought fourteen horses of those that were lost on the Guadalupe River. That same night they planned to kill all of us. Two Indians of the Mission of San Salvador in the Valley of Santiago, whom I had always carried with me on my journeys and who were of the jurisdiction of Coahuila, warned me. One of them was the captain of the Paquiles [Pacpules] nation and the other of the Quems nation. All the soldiers kept a strict watch. That night they did not dare to make an attack. God be praised. The great number of deaths that might have followed were avoided.

Friday, 20. Early in the morning before the sun rose the Indians realized fully that we had been on the alert the previous night, aware of their intentions and warned by their actions. Don Domingo Terán could not rest until he distributed blankets, knives and tobacco to the Indians. On the previous day he had given Juan, the captain of the said Indians, a gun, and on this morning, he gave him powder and balls. From this the Indians inferred that the Spaniards were afraid of them. After receiving all these things the Indians departed, while we remained at the same place.

Saturday, 21. We left San Buenaventura and the San Marcos River. We traveled north over level country where there were many oak woods. About five leagues away we could see a tall hill with heavy woods, toward the northeast. After marching for a league directly towards this hill we entered an unwooded section and stopped at the summit of a mount which lies to the northward. Here there is a dry arroyo that has some water holes. I named the place Santa Praxedis. In the language of the Texas Indians it is called Conaeted [Catdetda]. This day we went seven leagues.

Sunday, 22. After Mass we left Santa Praxedis and proceeded north over level country covered with woods—oaks and walnuts. At a distance of two leagues, the route continued northeast and we reached another large woods where there is a partly dry arroyo with many holes full of water. We left the woods and camped in an open level space near some of the water holes in the said arroyo. This day we traveled three leagues. I named the place Santa María Magdalena. In the language of the Indians it is called Sicoconotdeta.

On Monday the 23rd we left Santa María Magdalena and traveled continuously toward the northeast over a level unwooded section. At last we came in sight of a mountain toward the east. A league to the west after we had left the place, we met three Indians who were coming from the Texas country. The missionaries had sent them with the reply to the letter which I had written them from the San Marcos River. We went five leagues and stopped on a running stream. I named the place San Apolinario because it was his day. In the language of the Indians it is called Nateasba [Natteasba]. Another arroyo was crossed about a league and a half back which I called Nacosit [Nacasit] which means the place where there is red soil like *almagres*.*

Tuesday, 24. We left San Apolinario and traveled northeast over level country without woods and reached the edge of a thick woods through which we tracked in the same northeasterly direction, a quarter east. We went down to the river, which in the previous journey we named Bahía del Espíritu Santo. This day we advanced four leagues. This river is called Beatsi. I gave it the name of San Francisco Solano.

Wednesday, 25. We set out from San Francisco Solano and crossed the river at the widest place, where the water has no current; it is more like a lagoon at this point. The small stock was driven over a bridge made of wood. After the river was crossed, we found a large woods, very thick with willows, cottonwoods, and elms. We traveled through these woods north, a quarter northeast, and came to a dry arroyo which is at the entrance to the woods. After proceeding a quarter of a league we went down the arroyo about a gunshot and then turned northeast until we reached the woods. Then there was a level unwooded space and an arroyo with holes of water at intervals but with no stream. The water was salty and there were a great many alligators. There were also many buffaloes. We went two leagues. I named the place Santiago. In the language of the Indians it is called Baconatdesta [Baconetta].

Thursday, 26. We left Santiago and directed our steps north a quarter east over a level unwooded country, but we kept in view a very large mountain to the east and another toward the west. We found many dry arroyos because of the great number of buffalo. We advanced six leagues this day and camped on an arroyo of running water. It is at the edge of an immense woods that lies in the same direction, a quarter northeast, north. It is a very fine place for water and pasturage. There were a great number of buffaloes. I named this place Santa Margarita. In the language of the Indians it is called Canobatodeano.

Friday, 27. We did not travel because the small stock could not reach camp on account of the intense heat. Only the stronger ones succeeded in getting there.

Saturday, 28. We left Santa Margarita and proceeded northeast, a quarter east, over a level country. We crossed the arroyo and came to dense woods

---

*Red ochre.

which continued until the river is reached. This river is much wider at the crossing of this road than at the lower one which we followed last year. The Indians call it Babototo [Nabatsoto]. We forded the river. After emerging from the woods nearby, there is a lagoon with very good water and a great many fish and alligators. About a gunshot distance away the country is level and there is an open area. Here we halted. We traveled this day four leagues. I named the place Nuestra Señora de la Merced.

Sunday, 29. After Mass we left Nuestra Señora de la Merced and marched east, a quarter northeast, over a level country. We encountered a very tall woods of oaks and walnuts, but the course is very good. After leaving the grove there is an arroyo which has holes of water. Further on there is another one like it. Then there is a level open space and to the northeast, a quarter east, there is another large tract with timber like the one we passed. After leaving these there are some more water holes where we stopped. We advanced this day five leagues. I named the place Santa María [Marta]. In the language of the Indians it is called Asconascatavas [Asconaseattavas], which means where there is a very good fruit which they call *as*.

Monday, 30. We left Santa María [Marta] and traveled northeast over a level open country, keeping in view of the mountains both to the east and to the west. After we crossed the strip of woodland that lies between, there is a level spot; not the first woods, which is very extensive, but the last one named, and also an arroyo of running water which in the language of the Indians is called Soadds. After this stream is crossed there is another level stretch without trees. A little hill is next ascended and then one enters another grove and reaches a second arroyo of running water where we camped. This place is called Nuxnadte. It gave it the name of San Ygnacio. We made this day five leagues.

Tuesday, 31. We left San Ygnacio and traveled northeast. We crossed an arroyo. Wooded hills follow each other and then there are arroyos with many tall pines. We advanced this day six leagues and reached the Trinity River which, in the language of the Indians is called Conayentevantetsos.

AUGUST

Wednesday, August 1. I pushed ahead with the missionaries because we were so near our goal and because Don Domingo Terán moved so slowly. We went northeast. At a short distance there is an arroyo of very cool running water which the Indians call Naats. Immediately there follows a heavily wooded section, containing oaks, walnuts, and pines. They are all very tall and do not impede our course. At a distance of about two leagues we came to another arroyo of very cold water, which in the language of the Indians is called Nequebatse. This day we marched five leagues and camped on an arroyo of cold running water, where there are very beautiful tall pines. In the language of the Indians it is called Conandotdetra [Conenditetta]. I named this place San Esteban. Through all these four places we passed and on to the pueblo of the Tejas Indians. The road is a good one.

Thursday, 2. We left San Esteban and traveled north, northeast, over wooded country and many arroyos with water in them. We crossed six during the day, all with very good and cool water. After going two leagues, we turned east to reach the place where the governor lives, and where Mission San Francisco de los Texas is located. This day we made six leagues, thanks to God. Three leagues before arriving, we met the missionaries, Fray Francisco de Jesús María and Fray Antonio Bordoy, who came with the governor of the Texas Indians and many others of the tribe to greet us. As soon as they saw us, they alighted, came up, and embraced us, and then began to weep because of the death of Father Fray Miguel Fontcubierta and for the great number of the people who had died of the epidemic. We traveled on together and in this manner reached the church of the mission. We entered for the purpose of singing a *Te Deum Laudamus* in thanks and to say the prayers that we had repeated every day while on the road, prayers to the patrons we had chosen for the successful outcome of the Expedition—the Holy Cross, the Virgin, Saint Michael, Saint Joseph, our Father Saint Francis, Saint Anthony, Saint Rose and the Souls in Purgatory.

Sir: This is the diary and itinerary which, according to my limited capacity, I kept during the whole route. I have no doubt it contains many imperfections. May Your Excellency accept the good will that prompted me to give this pleasure. I could add many other things from what I have heard from the Indians, but I do not set them down because, since I am staying here, I will wait until I have investigated further and have explored the country, as I hope to do during the coming year.

May God keep Your Excellency many years, is my wish. Written at your Mission San Francisco de los Texas, August 20, 1691.

Your Excellency's servant and chaplain, who kisses your hand.

FRAY DAMIÁN MASSANET

THE VENERABLE PADRE FRAY ANTONIO MARGIL DE JESÚS

Peter P. Forrestal, C.S.C.*

FOREWORD

It is most opportune that the following work, a summary review of the life and labors of the Venerable Padre Fray Antonio Margil de Jesús, has been written from the most authentic and available source materials by Reverend Dr. Peter P. Forrestal, C.S.C. At a time when the cause of the holy servant of God is being resumed with the expectation of his beatification and canonization, it is well that the heroic deeds and virtues which he exercised, the services which he rendered for the evangelization of America and the miracles which he performed should be made known to Catholics for their spiritual edification and consolation. To the people of Texas this brochure has a particular significance, since it tells the story of the saintly Margil's zealous labors in the missions during the time when the conversions of the various Indian tribes here were seriously attempted, and when the permanent settlement of the country actually took place. This soldier of the Cross and his faithful companions, the sons of St. Francis, founded several missions and by their religious activities sowed the first fruitful seeds of Christian civilization in Texas.

The gratitude of the Historical Commission and of the Texas Catholic Historical Society is expressed to the staff of the University of Texas Library, and especially to Professor Carlos E. Castañeda, the Director of the Garcia Latin-American Library, in supplying the documents and other printed materials that have made this work possible. We also wish to thank the Reverend Dr. Gilbert J. Garraghan, S. J., for permission to reprint this contribution as one of the Studies of the Texas Catholic Historical Society.

Paul J. Foik, C.S.C.
Chairman of the Commission and President of the Society

---

*Vol. 2, No. 2, appeared in April 1932 as a reprint from *Mid-America* 3, 4 (April 1932).

The Venerable Padre
Fray Antonio Margil de Jesús

How beautiful upon the mountains are the feet of him that preacheth the gospel of peace. Isaias 7, 7.

Very few missionaries in the history of the Catholic Church have labored with such indefatigable zeal in winning souls for God as did Fray Antonio Margil de Jesús, one of the pioneers in New Spain. Although during his life his name was held in reverence and benediction by the inhabitants of practically every town from Panama to Louisiana, and although at the time of his death his obsequies were celebrated in many cities both in the Old and in the New World, today, strange to say, only an occasional scholar north of the Rio Grande is acquainted with the missionary activities of this humble but valiant soldier of Christ.

In presenting the following brief sketch of the life and labors of this great servant of God we shall aim at historical accuracy primarily. With this end in view we have made a very careful study of the letters of this venerable priest, the numerous sermons preached, both in America and in Europe, at the time of his death, the *Peregrino septentrional atlante* and *Nuevas empresas,* published by Espinosa in 1737 and 1747 respectively, the *Vida del V. P. Fr. Antonio Margil de Jesús,* published by Vilaplana in 1763, the *Vida* compiled by Arricivita in 1792, and published in the second part of the *Crónica del apostólico colegio de Querétaro,* the various documents presented to the Roman curia during the process of beatification and canonization in the last half of the eighteenth century, and works of several modern historians to which reference is made in the footnotes.

In the present article we do not propose to give a comprehensive treatment of our subject; we shall do little more than introduce it to our readers, and this with the hope that before long another and a more fluent pen may in a befitting manner describe the activities of this great missionary of New Spain.

BIRTH AND CHILDHOOD

Antonio Margil, son of Juan Margil Salumaro and Esperanza Ros, was born in Valencia, Spain, on August 18, 1657, and two days later was baptized in the beautiful church of San Juan del Mercado, which afterwards came to be known as los Santos Juanes Bautista y Evangelista. When still only a mere boy he showed promise of rare talent and virtue, and because of this his truly Christian parents procured for him teachers capable of developing in him studious and virtuous habits. When not at school, where he made rapid progress in his studies, he spent most of his time in building miniature altars at home or in serving Mass and making visits to the Blessed Sacrament in one of the many churches of Valencia. According to several witnesses whose declarations were recorded by the public and apostolic notary in the city of Valencia shortly after his death, his one desire during time of vacation was to visit the churches in which the Blessed Sacrament was exposed. There he would become so rapt in prayer and meditation that oftentimes he did not return home till after nightfall. When his mother, realizing that he had been fasting the entire day, used to reprove him for this, Antonio would answer respectfully that in the presence of the Blessed Sacrament all this time seemed but an instant and that he would not have left even then had he not been obliged to do so by the sacristan who wished to lock the church.[1]

ENTERS THE FRANCISCAN ORDER AND IS ORDAINED

Wishing to consecrate himself entirely to God, at the age of fifteen and with his parents' consent he called at the Convent of La Corona de Cristo[2] in Valencia and asked to join the ranks of the Friars Minor. The official records containing the names of those admitted into that monastery state that "after Compline, between 5 and 6 o'clock in the afternoon of April 22, 1673, Brother Antonio Margil, a native of Valencia, who had completed the fifteenth year of his age, asked to be admitted as a choir religious into the Convent of La Corona de Cristo; and, in the presence of the community that had assembled

---

[1]Hermenegildo Vilaplana, *Vida portentosa del americano septentrional apóstol, el v. p. fr. Antonio Margil de Jesús, fundador, y ex-guardián de los colegios de la Santa Cruz de Querétaro, de Christo Crucifado de Guatemala, y de Nuestra Señora de Guadalupe de Zacatecas* (Madrid, 1775), 8.

[2]So-called because in that convent was preserved half of one of the thorns from the crown of Our Savior.

for this purpose, received the habit from Fray José Salellas, actual guardian of said convent."[3]

In the novitiate Antonio was an exemplar of virtue. He took delight in performing the most menial services, and imposed upon himself such severe penances that the Master of Novices took away from him the hair-shirt and forbade him to use the discipline and other instruments of torture with which he was wont to lacerate his flesh. On April 25, 1674, before completing his seventeenth year, he made his religious profession in this same convent of La Corona de Cristo. As a professed religious Antonio made even greater efforts to advance in perfection and to detach himself entirely from the world with its allurements. One day, not knowing that he was being observed, he slipped off quietly to the church, and walking over to one of the tombs, raised the slab concealing a body that had been buried there for some time and that was already in a state of decomposition. He remained there beside that tomb until the Master of Novices, who had followed him down to the church, drew near and asked what he was doing. The young novice replied: "Reminding this brute of a body of what it now is and of what it will one day be."[4]

When he was eighteen years of age the superiors, convinced that he had a vocation to the priesthood, sent him to the Convent of San Antonio in Denia, where, according to the sworn declaration of Fray Vicente Andani, who had been a seminarian with him in the aforesaid convent and who testified in Guatemala on March 6, 1727, young Margil made constant progress in virtue and was greatly respected and admired by all because of his deep humility, his jovial disposition and winning ways. After he had completed a three years' course in philosophy at Denia he was sent back to La Corona Convent for his theology. Here during the time not devoted to study he followed the regular exercises of the novitiate, and every night after Matins went down quietly to the garden, where, laden with a heavy cross, he followed in the footsteps of the Crucified Christ, pausing to meditate before each of the fourteen Stations erected within the convent walls. When twenty-four years of age he was ordained to the priesthood, and after his first holy Mass, for which he had prepared by prayer, penance, and a humble confession of even the slightest faults, received from the Provincial Chapter an obedience as confessor and preacher in the town of Onda. Here his labors bore such abundant fruit that a short time after his arrival to this town his superiors decided to change him to Denia, a Mediterranean port much frequented by profligates from various parts of Europe and greatly in need of the ministrations of a zealous priest.

---

[3]*Summarium beatificationis et canonizationis Ven. Servi Dei Antonii Margil a Jesu,* no. 5, p. 50. sec. 48.
[4]Vilaplana, *Vida portentosa,* 12.

JOINS THE AMERICAN MISSIONS

He had not been here long before he learned that Fray Antonio Linaz, who belonged to the Majorca Province and who had recently been preaching with remarkable success in many cities of the peninsula, had obtained permission to take with him twenty-five volunteers for the missions in America. Burning with zeal for the glory of God and the salvation of souls, and realizing that in the far-off Indies the harvest was ready but the laborers were few, young Margil decided to enlist in this little band of missionaries. He took leave of his companions at the Convent of San Antonio, after having asked them to pray for the success of his undertaking, and set out for Valencia in order to pay a visit to the religious at La Corona de Cristo and to bid good-bye to his aged mother, who was now a widow.

His departure was felt keenly by all those religious, who had come to love him from the very day he first called at the novitiate, and it was felt still more keenly by that pious mother who had watched over and guided him during his childhood and who had hoped that he would be present to comfort and console her in her declining years. Informed that Fray Antonio was determined to leave for the Indies, she was deeply affected, and when he came to bid her good-bye the poor old lady said to him: "Son, how is it that you decide to go off and to leave me now when I was expecting from you some comfort and consolation, when I was hoping that at the time of my death you would assist me, that you would be at my bedside in that hour of trial?"[5]

Antonio, stifling the sentiments of filial love and affection that were welling up in his breast, answered:

> Mother, when I entered the monastery I left you, and I took the Blessed Virgin as Mother and Jesus as Father, for at that time I renounced all earthly ties. I am going to labor in the vineyard of the Master, to see if I can please my beloved Jesus. You will find consolation in the Lord, for His Divine Majesty will take care of you and, if He so permit, I shall not fail to assist you at the hour of your death. Do not be afflicted, mother, by these natural sentiments; we must leave all in the hands of Providence. Take this habit, which with my superior's permission I leave you in order that you may be buried in it. The fact that my brother-in-law and my sister remain here is for me a source of

---

[5]Isidro Félix Espinosa, *El peregrino septentrional atlante: delineado en la exemplarissima vida del venerable padre F. Antonio Margil de Jesús* (Mexico, 1737), 37.

consolation.[6] With all my heart I commend you to their care and, in case you be deprived of their assistance, my Father Jesus will take care of my mother Esperanza.[7]

Antonio cast himself at his mother's feet, and having received her last blessing turned his back upon his childhood's home and took the road leading to Cádiz. Shortly afterwards he and the other missionaries sailed from the aforesaid port, and after a three months' voyage, during which their lives were frequently in peril, they landed at Veracruz on June 6, 1683. At this port a most sad spectacle met their gaze. Shortly before their arrival the pirate Lorencillo[8] had sacked the city, desecrating the churches, and murdering or crippling great numbers of the inhabitants. Margil, deeply pained, hastened to the assistance of that wretched people, and spared no sacrifice in ministering to the dying, in burying the dead, and in consoling the afflicted.

REACHES QUERÉTARO

A few days later, accompanied by one of his companions and provided with nothing but a staff, a breviary, and a crucifix, he set out for Santa Cruz Convent in the City of Querétaro. On August 13th, after having given missions at all the towns and ranches along the way, he walked into the Convent of Santa Cruz, which, now erected into a college and seminary, was soon to send forth missionaries to all parts of the New World.[9] On the first Sunday of the following month he opened a mission in Querétaro, and the inhabitants, observing that he spoke to them with all the unction and sincerity of the anointed of God, and learning that he was accustomed to spend the entire day and most of the night in works of penance and in acts of charity, of humility, and of love of God, flocked to the churches, confessed their sins and made a firm purpose of amendment. This mission finished, he set out for

---

[6]Vilaplana uses the plural. Antonio had two sisters, one that was married and another that later on entered La Puridad Convent.

[7]Espinosa, *El peregrino septentrional*, 38.

[8]Fray Rogerio Conde Martínez, O.F.M., in his brochure on Margil states that the pirate was English and that his real name was Lawrence Jacome. At the celebration held in the Spanish capital in 1928, on the occasion of the VII centennial of the death of Saint Francis this work (Madrid, 1929) was awarded the prize for the best treatise on Margil, offered by His Excellency Dr. Francisco Orozco y Jiménez, beloved Archbishop of Guadalajara, noted benefactor of an afflicted people and humble but fearless apostle of Christ.

[9]At Santa Cruz College, with which Margil was now connected and which, as other apostolic colleges, was under the supervision of a commissary general for the Indies, the friars received special training for the work on the missions.

Mexico City, the emporium of the Western Hemisphere, where, with the assistance of several other religious, he succeeded in eradicating vice and in implanting such beautiful virtues as might have incited to emulation the most Catholic communities in Christendom.

Leaving the capital, he retraced his steps to Santa Cruz College, where he was most punctual in his attendance at the religious exercises, and where each night after Matins he made the Stations with a heavy cross over his shoulder and a crown of thorns upon his head, thereby unconsciously impressing upon his saintly companions the necessity of exemplifying in their own lives the doctrines of Christianity and of trampling under foot the world with its seductions before hoping to bring the pagan nations of America under the yoke of Christ.

GOES TO YUCATAN

Fray Antonio had been here about three months when he and three other religious received the obedience to labor for the spread of the faith among the barbarous tribes of Campeche or Yucatan.[10] Responsive to that call the four zealous missionaries left immediately for Veracruz, and while waiting for the boat to weigh anchor gave a mission at the Castle of San Juan de Ulúa.[11]

Accompanied by their commissary general, Fray Juan Luzuriaga, who was making his visitation of the American missions and who was soon to preside at the Chapter in Mérida, they crossed Campeche Bay, arriving at their new field of labor on Holy Saturday, April 1st of the same year, 1684.[12] Losing no time, they gave a mission at the port and at each of the towns, villages and haciendas along the road to Mérida, capital of the province.

At the Chapter now being held in this city the commissary general proposed that the Recollection-Institute, which for so many years had flourished there, be reestablished and that one of the four missionaries who had accompanied him from Veracruz be appointed as guardian. But, finding that not one of these cared to accept the office and that all were burning with the desire to carry the light of the gospel to nations that for centuries had sat in the darkness of paganism and superstition, he allowed them to leave for the Kingdom of Guatemala.

---

[10]Campeche and Yucatan are now separate states.

[11]This fortress overlooks and defends the port of Veracruz.

[12]Vilaplana (*Vida portentosa*, 25) states that they landed here in March, 1686. Here there is an evident discrepancy, for on page 31, Vilaplana himself tells us that after leaving Campeche they went to Guatemala and arrived there on September 21, 1685.

Happy in the thought that they were soon to bring to innumerable pagan tribes a knowledge of Christianity, they set out on their journey, but on reaching the mouth of the Tabasco River three pirate vessels gave them chase, and only by a miracle of God were they able to escape with their lives and to return, after eight days of mental and physical anguish, to the Port of Campeche. They presented themselves before the commissary general, who was stopping at this port and who, apprized of their ill fortune, addressed them in these words: "To me this seems a chastisement from God for not having remained here to establish the institute. I now command you to offer up special prayers in order that God may enlighten you as to the course you are to follow."[13]

Without the slightest manifestation of reluctance, they repaired to the choir, and after they had prayed there for a long time the superior called them, and in their presence had a little child draw lots in order to determine the will of God with regard to their future activities. On slips of paper drawn by the hand of that innocent child it was indicated that Fray Antonio Margil and Fray Melchor López were to go to the missions and that the other two religious were to remain in Mérida.

Imbued with the spirit of Paul and Barnabas, these two apostles of Christ, destined to be inseparable companions for fourteen years in the work of planting the good seed in the fallow lands of Guatemala, went forth once more on their sacred mission and arrived happily in the Province of Tabasco. For one whole year their days were spent in announcing the truths of Christianity in the towns and hamlets of this province and the greater part of the nights in keeping vigil before a beautiful crucifix which had been given to them at the aforesaid port and which they were to carry with them on all their travels.

Famished with hunger, drenched with rain, broken in health, but undaunted in spirit, these barefooted sons of Saint Francis, leaving behind them the Province of Tabasco, trudged along southward as far as Tuxtla in the present state of Chiapas. Here they became gravely ill, and Fray Antonio was given the last sacraments; but miraculously cured, they continued on as far as Ciudad Real, where their deep humility and their burning zeal for souls made such an impression on the inhabitants that many of both sexes dressed in sackcloth and joined the Third Order of Saint Francis. After converting the people of Ciudad Real they entered Soconusco on the shores of the Pacific, and as they passed through this province, announcing the glad tidings of salvation, thousands of people, with green branches in their hands and with holy joy in their hearts, came forth to receive those angels of peace, the fame

---

[13]Espinosa, *El peregrino septentrional*, 45.

of whose sanctity had already reached the utmost confines of Spanish America.[14]

LABORS IN CENTRAL AMERICA

Traveling by a circuitous route for a distance of more than one hundred leagues and preaching the word of God in all the towns through which they passed, Fray Antonio and Fray Melchor reached the capital of Guatemala, and entered the Convent of San Francisco a little after 1 o'clock on the morning of September 21, 1685.[15] But, shortly after their arrival these messengers of peace were summoned to Itzquintipeque to put an end to dissension and discord that had arisen between two companies of Spanish soldiers stationed on that coast, and as a result not until the beginning of the new year were they able to open the mission in the capital of Guatemala. For more than six months they preached in the cathedral, convents and other churches, and long after the mission had closed all the priests of the city were still busy hearing the confessions of the multitudes that, actuated by the fear and love of God, hastened to wash away their sins in the sacrament of penance.

From the capital they continued their journey southward, and, in 1688, entered Nicaragua, Nicoya, and Costa Rica, proclaiming the kingdom of God and exercising such a salutary influence that the natives of their own accord destroyed their idols and cut down the trees from which they had been gathering the fruit for their *chicha* and for their other intoxicating beverages. Whenever possible, they reached a pueblo about sundown, and, with crucifix in hand, walked through the streets announcing the mission and warning the inhabitants to hearken to the voice of God and to confess their sins. In each of those towns they erected the Way of the Cross, taught the people to recite the rosary and to sing the *Alabado*.[16]

Learning that there still remained vast regions in which the light of faith had not as yet penetrated, the discalced sons of the poor little man of Assisi turned east, and suffering untold hardships in crossing bleak mountains and

---

[14]Fray Juan López Aguado, *Voces que hicieron eco* (Mexico, 1726), 20. "Láurea Funeral Americana," in Genaro García Collection, Benson Latin American Library, University of Texas at Austin.

[15]Conde ([Margil brochure], 60) tells us that on September 21, 1685, Margil was back in Querétaro. This is obviously an oversight, for on page 46 of the same work he states that on this date he arrived in Guatemala. Strange to say, he falls into exactly the same error with regard to December 2, 1691.

[16]During our recent sojourn in Spain it was for several months our happy privilege to celebrate Mass at the Patronato de los Enfermos in Madrid and to hear this beautiful hymn of praise to the Blessed Sacrament sung on Sundays and feast days by the poor children and working classes of the capital, whose spiritual and corporal needs are ministered to by faithful and devout chaplains and by the self-sacrificing Damas Apostólicas founded by Doña Luz Casanova.

barren deserts, with scarcely enough food to keep them from starvation and with no guide other than the position of the sun and the stars, made their way into the interior of Talamanca.[17] With the assistance of some of the natives, who from contact with the Christians of Costa Rica had come to appreciate the blessings of our holy faith and through the good offices of several caciques, who realized that men who at such sacrifice had entered the territory of an unfriendly people with no weapon but the cross could be none others than messengers of the true God, they succeeded in establishing eleven *pueblos* and in making thousands of converts.

Success seemed to attend their labors in this new vineyard of the Lord, until certain tribes, incited to rebellion by their pagan priests, burned the church of San Miguel and threatened to take the lives of the missionaries. Saved from certain death only by a miracle, those two living exemplars of Christian fortitude, following the example of their illustrious prototypes at Antioch,[18] gathered up from the ground handfuls of dust and, casting it into the air as a sign of their unworthiness of eternal life, left them and went off to preach to the Terrabas.[19]

After they had instructed the friendly Borucas on the boundary of Costa Rica, they came to the land of the Terrabas. These, struck with holy awe at the sight of the saintly missionaries, cast at their feet the weapons with which they had gone forth to receive them, and learning that they could not be saved until they had abandoned their ancient rites and practices, they burnt their idols, razed to the ground their places of pagan worship, and built two temples to the God of the Christians. Fray Melchor remained here, while Fray Antonio journeyed back to convert the incendiaries of San Miguel; but, on August 25, 1691, when both were about to leave for Panama, they received from their commissary general an order to report to Santa Cruz College in Querétaro. Though regretting to leave those missions, the barefooted friars began immediately that long journey of more than six hundred leagues, and that they did so in the spirit of perfect obedience is evident from a letter which they sent to the guardian of said college from one of the towns of Costa Rica.[20]

As soon as they walked into the capital of Guatemala, on December 2nd, the President of the *Audiencia* of that city notified them that their commissary general, informed of their great apostolic labors and of the work yet to be done, had sent a counter order instructing them to remain in Central America. They did not advance another step, but, at the request of Bishop Andrés de

---

[17]A long strip of territory on the Atlantic seaboard of Costa Rica.

[18]Acts of the Apostles, chap. 13.

[19]Terrabas and Borucas: tribes inhabiting the southern portion of Costa Rica.

[20]Espinosa, *El peregrino septentrional*, 83.

las Navas, set out for Vera Paz to pacify certain pueblos that had revolted, and about five months later were called back to the capital to establish a hospice for missionaries. While awaiting the royal *cédula* authorizing this foundation, they suffered great hardships and imperiled their lives in leading back to the fold the apostate Choles of El Manché, and in endeavoring to convert the ferocious savages of the mountains of Lacandón, that long before had martyred two Dominican priests, Fray Andrés López and Fray Domingo de Vico.

Undertaking the last journey he was to make with that zealous apostle who for fourteen years had been his inseparable companion on the missions and who was soon to be appointed President of the new hospice, Margil made his way into the territory of the Lacandones; but, after enduring extreme hunger and thirst for several months and after braving death itself in the hope of evangelizing that indomitable people, he realized that the hour for their conversion had not as yet arrived, and decided to return to the City of Guatemala.[21]

One year later, January 17, 1695, that zealous missionary, accompanied by the President of the *Audiencia* and six hundred soldiers, again walked barefooted up the craggy heights of Lacandón, and after a sojourn of two years, during which he always spent from midnight till daybreak on his knees in communion with God, succeeded in exterminating idolatry and In establishing the Christian faith in all that country.

ELECTED GUARDIAN OF SANTA CRUZ

Here he labored with marked success until March, 1697, when, to the deep sorrow of his spiritual children who had come to love him as a father and who were now to be deprived of his ministrations, he was recalled to Querétaro as guardian of Santa Cruz. Without hesitation he answered the call of obedience, and after preaching in all the towns along his route, that great apostle of America, so fittingly titled *Atlante Peregrino* by his illustrious co-laborer and biographer,[22] reached Querétaro on the afternoon of April 22nd of this same year.[23] That day the entire community and all others who had gone forth to welcome him at the entrance to the city beheld, indeed, a novel spectacle as

---

[21]Fray Francisco de S. Esteban y Andrade, *Título glorioso del crucificado con Cristo y segunda azucena de la religión seráfica* (Mexico, 1729), 15. See also "Láurea Funeral Americana."

[22]Fray Isidro Félix Espinosa and Fray Antonio Margil worked together on the missions in Texas, Espinosa as superior of the missionaries from Santa Cruz and Margil as superior of those from Nuestra Señora de Guadalupe.

[23]Conde states that Margil arrived here on April 2nd. This is probably a typographical error.

the far-famed missionary came along that dusty road in the patched habit which he had worn in Guatemala, with an old hat thrown over his back and a skull hanging from his girdle.

As superior of Santa Cruz College, he evinced those admirable virtues of charity and humility that had characterized his work on the missions. He looked after the corporal as well as the spiritual needs of his subjects, built an infirmary for the sick religious, and considered himself merely as a weak instrument of the divine will, each night offering the keys of the cloister and of the hearts of his subjects to Jesus and Mary, the true guardians of that convent.[24] During the period of his guardianship at this college his days and nights, save three hours given to repose, were spent in penance and prayer, and in gaining souls for Christ, not only by his work in the confessional, but by the simple yet heart-stirring sermons which he preached on the streets of Querétaro. On several occasions his insatiable zeal led him out of this city to distant places, and numberless souls resolved to abandon sin and turn to God as he thundered forth the warning to repentance in the churches and on the plazas of Valladolid, Mexico City, and Celaya.

FOUNDS COLLEGE IN GUATEMALA

In 1700, he finished his term as guardian, and in April of the following year was called to Guatemala to establish peace between the people and the Royal *Audiencia.* Without taking leave of the citizens of Querétaro, once more he set out on that long journey of almost four hundred leagues, and toward the end of May or the beginning of June, after having preached and heard confessions along the way, that messenger of peace reached the capital of Guatemala, where he settled the disputed questions to the satisfaction of both parties.

On June 13th he founded in this city a seminary *de Propaganda Fide,* the nucleus of which was to be composed of the religious until then living at the Calvario Hospice, and, prompted by those same motives which at the age of seven had led him to place himself in the arms of Christ Crucified, named it El Colegio de Cristo Crucificado.[25] In the Provincial Chapter held soon afterwards he was elected guardian of this college by those saintly religious, who, acquainted with his missionary activities of fourteen years in Central America, realized that no other could direct so successfully the destinies of the new institute. Those virtuous men had cast their votes according to the dictates of conscience and they were not to be disappointed in their choice. Fray

---

[24]Espinosa, *El peregrino septentrional,* 125.

[25]Vilaplana, *Vida portentosa,* 7.

Antonio, by his faithful adherence to the rules of Saint Francis, inspired them to exemplify in their own lives the beautiful virtues of charity and humility, and by his continuous and arduous labors in the confessional and pulpit, aroused in them that spirit of self-sacrificing zeal so necessary for the work of the missions. Like the Apostle of the Gentiles, he preached Christ in season and out of season, and on Christmas night spoke for several hours on the plaza of the capital city endeavoring to prevent the scandalous abuses so common on this most sacred of festivals.

On a certain occasion, when preaching in the Cathedral of Guatemala, he took as his text the brevity of life and the uncertainty of death. In the course of the sermon he remarked, to the astonishment of his audience, that all those then present would not hear him on the following day, because before that time one of them would have been called to render a strict account before the Supreme Judge. Scarcely had he uttered the last words of the sermon when, according to the testimony of Father Jerónimo Varona of the Society of Jesus, who was present at the time, a woman fell dead between the Main Altar and Socorro Chapel, not having had even enough time to make her confession.[26]

Satisfied that the rules of the Order were being faithfully observed by all the subjects of that holy institute and that the doctrines of Christianity were being practiced by the inhabitants of Guatemala, he set out for Nicaragua, and after a journey of some two hundred leagues reached the City of León about the end of May, 1703. He left this capital and in a torrential rain made his way through swamps and over swollen creeks to the towns of Telica, Sevaco, and Granada, denouncing witchcraft, demon worship, and superstitution, and awakening in the lukewarm Christians of those parts a sincere detestation of idolatry and a deep sense of their obligations as followers of the Crucified Christ.[27]

In about three months he was back in the City of Guatemala, but he had been here only a short time when summoned to the Pacific coast to correct certain flagrant abuses that had crept into the provinces of San Antonio Suchitepéquez[28] and Zapotitlán, whose inhabitants, Christians only in name, still clung to the ancient rites and ceremonies of their ancestors.[29] That his mission was entirely successful is evident from the report which the *corregidor* of Zapotitlán made to the Royal *Audiencia* of Guatemala on October 12, 1704. This report states that with the visit of Fray Antonio the province became a

---

[26]Espinosa, *El peregrino sententrional*, 174.

[27]Later on the capital was changed to Managua, which, as León, is situated on the Pacific.

[28]On the Pacific in the southwestern part of Guatemala.

[29]Even at the present day much the same may be said of several of the Indian pueblos of New Mexico. It is to be hoped that before long the work of the zealous Franciscan Fathers of this state will be crowned with the success that in Central America attended the labors of their illustrious coreligious.

veritable paradise of God, for at all hours the people, that until then had been steeped in the most shameful vices, could be seen, both in the homes and on the streets, chanting the *Alabado,* or reciting the rosary and other prayers in honor of their Eucharistic Lord and of His Most Blessed Mother.[30]

FOUNDS COLLEGE IN ZACATECAS

As soon as his term of office had expired this giant pilgrim of America, accompanied by another religious, started out once more for Costa Rica with the hope of advancing farther southward and of bringing into the faith the numerous tribes of Panama and Peru; but, on July 25, 1706, as he was about to climb the Talamanca Mountains he received from the commissary general an order to return to Mexico for the purpose of establishing a new college on the outskirts of Zacatecas. Though he yearned for the conversion of those pagan nations and though his companion urged him to continue on his way, that slave of holy obedience, retracing his steps, began the long wearisome journey to the scene of his future labors.[31] Upon reaching the City of Guatemala he called at the College of Cristo Crucificado to visit the religious, of whom he had been a kind superior and whom he was never more to see,[32] and after addressing to them words of counsel and comfort bade them good-bye and continued his journey northward.

Faithful to his custom of preaching the word of God in all the towns and ranches through which he passed, the tireless apostle continued on until he came to Mexico City, where he spent a few days consulting the commissary general on certain points relative to the new foundation. During the months of November and December he was at Santa Cruz in Querétaro, and from this college took with him to Zacatecas five religious, who, with those already living at the Hospice of Nuestra Señora de Guadalupe, were to form the little community at the Apostolic Institute about to be established.

January 12, 1707, should always be a memorable day in the history of the Church in Mexico, for it was on this day that her greatest of apostles entered the College of Nuestra Señora de Guadalupe at the foothills of the Zacatecas Mountains and, casting himself on his knees before the image of Our Blessed Mother, thanked her for having watched over him during that long journey of

---

[30]Espinosa, *El peregrino septentrional,* 207, 208.

[31]S. Esteban y Andrade, *Título glorioso,* 20.

[32]In 1708, upon the death of Fray Tomás de Arrivillaga, guardian of the College of Cristo Crucificado, the Royal *Audiencia* of Guatemala begged Margil to accept this office. He wrote back that his heart was in Guatemala and that if possible he would fly to that kingdom, but that this was impossible, since the commissary general held him bound by the well-riveted chains of obedience.

more than six hundred leagues from the wilds of Costa Rica and commended to her care the destinies of an institute that was soon to play an important part in the work of evangelization in North America.[33]

From the very outset the new foundation began to grow both in a spiritual and a material way, and within a decade able and zealous missionaries from Zacatecas were spreading the doctrines of Christ in Northern Mexico, Texas, and Louisiana. In August of this same year, 1707, Margil, at the request of the Bishop of Guadalajara, left his college for three months to give missions in the capital and in several towns of Jalisco, and he spent the spring and summer of the following year laboring throughout the diocese of Durango.

Toward the close of the year 1708, he went to Querétaro to confer with the commissary general on certain matters of importance, and while there was asked to preside at the Chapter of the Zacatecas Province. Prior to the Chapter, which was convoked in San Luis Potosí on February 23, 1709, and which proved to be most successful in every way, Margil preached missions in this capital and in many of the neighboring towns. At the close of the Provincial Chapter he left for Zacatecas and preached and heard confessions at each of the towns and ranches at which he happened to pass the night. He reached Guadalupe College about the middle of Lent, and as religious from several of the provinces had entered the new institute a short time previously, he decided to spend the following year at the college in order to train for the work of the missions the young men committed to his care. During this year his voice was frequently heard in the churches and on the plaza of Zacatecas, and on one occasion he miraculously escaped death at the hands of certain comedians, whose performances he denounced publicly and whom he finally induced to abandon that life of sin and turn to God.

During March of 1711, in obedience to a *cédula* of Philip V, Margil undertook the conversion of certain barbarous tribes in the mountains of Nayarit. Accompanied by another religious from Guadalupe College and by four Indians, he set out for those mountains, and on May 9th sent from the town of Santa María de Guazamota a letter informing the barbarians of his coming and assuring them that no motive other than the desire to save them from hell induced him to enter their province. After five days two Indians whom he had dispatched with this message returned with the information that those barbarians, in answer to Fray Antonio's letter, had stated that they would at all costs cling to their pagan practices, that they were not afraid of the

---

[33]The royal *cédula* authorizing the erection of the Hospice into an Apostolic College was granted by Philip V in 1704, but did not reach America till 1706. See José Francisco Sotomayor, *Historia del Apostólico Colegio de Nuestra Señora de Guadalupe de Zacatecas: desde su fundación hasta nuestros dias*, 2nd ed., 2 vols., (Zacatecas, 1889), 1:32.

Spanish soldiers, and that under no condition would they embrace Christianity. Nothing daunted, both missionaries entered those mountains, but though ready for every sacrifice, even that of life itself, in the effort to convert that obstinate people, they came to realize that the hour of their conversion, according to the inscrutable designs of God, had not as yet arrived, and decided to return to their college.

For two years Margil endeavored to prevail upon the Viceroy in Mexico City and upon the Royal *Audiencia* of Guadalajara to assist him in the work of converting the pagans of Nayarit, but seeing that the proposed expedition to that province was being postponed indefinitely, he decided after being relieved of his duties as guardian in November 1713 to carry his spiritual conquests into the New Kingdom of León and across the Rio Grande.[34]

With the permission of the commissary general and of the new guardian,[35] and accompanied by another friar, once more he left the College of Guadalupe and during the early part of 1714 gave missions in Mazapíl, Saltillo, and Monterrey and in several other towns of Zacatecas, Coahuila, and Nuevo León. In the month of May he reached the Sabinas River and on its banks established and dedicated to Our Lady of Guadalupe the first mission founded among the pagan Indians by the Zacatecas Institute. He had been here but a short time when the Tobosos swooped down upon the neighboring pueblo of San Miguel, tore to pieces the sacred vestments, and stripped and threatened to take the life of the missionary. Through the assistance of certain members of this tribe who had once been Christians, the padre, almost naked, succeeded in making his escape to the Mission of Nuestra Señora de Guadalupe. He reached the thatched hut constructed by Fray Antonio, who learning of his happy escape and considering this a signal victory for the cause of Christianity, led him in triumph into the church, ordered that the bells be rung, and intoned the *Te Deum* in thanksgiving.

As the Tobosos still continued their depredations, the Indians who had been congregated at Guadalupe fled back to the mountains, and the three missionaries, seeing that under the circumstances any effort to reestablish the pueblos was useless, left for the Dolores Mission at Punta de Lampazos.[36] Though all hope of erecting a mission near the Sabinas had vanished, Fray Antonio was not discouraged. Awaiting the opportunity to labor among the Texas across the Rio Grande, he spent the remainder of that year and the

---

[34]Only a few years later missionaries of the Society of Jesus, to their great glory be it said, succeeded in spreading the Gospel throughout most of this territory.

[35]Fray José Guerra.

[36]The Dolores Mission was seven leagues north of that erected by Margil and was founded, in 1698, by Fray Francisco Hidalgo and Fray Diego de Salazar. It should not be confused with the Dolores Mission founded ten years previously at Boca de Leones, or modern Villa Aldama.

beginning of 1715 in preaching and hearing confessions among the Christians in Nuevo León. Toward the close of 1715 or in the early part of 1716 he set out with a military escort for the Mission of San Juan Bautista, located on the Río Grande del Norte near the present town of Piedras Negras. Though suffering from double hernia he walked all the way from Lampazos to the Sabinas River, where in spite of all protestations the corporal of the guard insisted that he make the rest of the journey on horseback. Having reached the Rio Grande he preached to the soldiers at the presidio and introduced the Third Order at the Mission of San Juan, but finding that he could not establish here a mission for the pagan Indians, he decided to return to the scene of his recent labors in Coahuila and in the New Kingdom of León."[37]

FOUNDS TEXAS MISSIONS

In the fall of 1715, steps had been taken to reestablish the long neglected missions on the Neches and thus to prevent further encroachment of the French upon Spanish territory. To accomplish this an escort of twenty-five soldiers, under Captain Domingo Ramón, was to accompany into the country of the Hasinai, or Texas, Indians a mission band from the College of Santa Cruz in Querétaro and another from the College of Nuestra Señora de Guadalupe in Zacatecas. The former, composed of five priests, was to have as superior Fray Isidro Félix de Espinosa, and the latter, made up of three priests, two lay brothers and one *donado*, was to be under the direction of Fray Antonio Margil de Jesús. The superior of the Zacatecas band was still busy visiting the towns and ranches of Nuevo León when, in the spring of 1716, word reached him that the expedition was already on the Rio Grande and was about to leave for Texas. Without delay he set out to join his companions, but along the way he became gravely ill and had to be taken to the Mission of San Juan Bautista, where his condition became so critical that he was given the last sacraments. Urged by Margil himself not to postpone the *entrada,* on April 25th the missionaries of both colleges bade farewell to their beloved friend and co-laborer, and the expedition, having crossed the Rio Grande, moved northeastward to the country of the Hasinai, which had originally comprised

---

[37]Because of the scarcity of priests at the San Xavier missions and in order to take care of the new missions among the Apaches, Santa Cruz College, in 1751, was obliged to turn over to the secular clergy that of San Juan Bautista, founded about fifty years previously. See Bolton, *Texas in the Middle Eighteenth Century: Studies in Spanish Colonial History and Administration,* University of California Publications in History Vol. 3 (Berkeley, 1915), 239.

nothing more than the strip of territory between the Trinity and Red rivers and part of what is now the State of Louisiana.[38]

The founder of Guadalupe College and superior of its little band of Texas missionaries had for many years yearned for the conversion of the Hasinai; he had redoubled his fasts, watched late into the night, and sacrificed everything life holds dear that one day he might be able to bring to this and to kindred tribes a knowledge of the true faith. His heartfelt prayer for the conversion of this people was born of the ardent zeal which had led him into Talamanca, Lacandón and Nayarit, and, at least in part, that prayer was not to remain unanswered. Margil, completely recovered, soon left the San Juan Mission and, following the route taken by the Ramón expedition, advanced toward the territory of the Texas Indians. When he overtook his companions he learned, to his great joy, that they had been well received by the natives and had been meeting with remarkable success in explaining to them the truths of Christianity and in inducing them to abandon their wild, nomadic life.[39]

The expedition reached the country of the Hasinai, in the eastern section of the present State of Texas, in the summer of 1716 and, setting to work immediately, the missionaries from both colleges made every effort to instruct the natives and to induce them to establish pueblos. The Friars from Zacatecas, in whom we are especially interested, began their labors with the Nacogdoches, and among them, near the banks of the Angelina, established their first mission, dedicated to Our Lady of Guadalupe.[40] At this mission Fray Antonio and his companions spent the remainder of this year, using a thatched hut as a dwelling, enduring every kind of hardship, mingling with the

---

[38]*Informe que se dio al Excmo. Sr. Presidente de la República Mejicana sobre límites de la Provincia de Tejas* (Zacatecas, 1828), 6. Bolton (*Texas in the Middle Eighteenth Century*, 2) tells us that the Hasinai "comprised some ten or more tribes, of which the best known were the Hainai; Nacogdoche, Nabedache, Nasoni and Nadaco." He states also, p. 1, that "early in the eighteenth century the boundaries [of Texas] were extended westward to include the settlements on the San Antonio River and Matagorda Bay." See also Hubert Howe Bancroft, *History of the North Mexican States and Texas*, 2 vols. (San Francisco, 1886), 1:604, n. 2.

[39]The date of Margil's arrival to East Texas is not at all clear; the fact that he is not mentioned in either the Espinosa or the Ramón diaries after the expedition had crossed the Rio Grande would seem to indicate that he did not rejoin the expedition until after it had reached the territory of the Hasinai. On the other hand, the *Informe* cited in n. 38 above, states that the expedition, accompanied by Margil, entered the Province of Texas on June 28th. Espinosa tells us that Margil did not leave San Juan Bautista till the feast of Saint Anthony of Padua, which falls on June 13th. There is, however, in the Zacatecas Archives a letter written by Margil to Fray Antonio Andrade, and dated May 29, 1716, "*desde el camino hacia los Texas.*" From several of his letters, which are preserved in the said archives and which state that "we entered Texas with only twenty-five men," it would seem clear that he overtook the expedition somewhere along the route.

[40]In the center of the present town of Nacogdoches Bolton has located the site of the old Mission of Guadalupe: "The Native Tribes about the East Texas Missions," *The Quarterly of the Texas State Historical Association* 11, 4 (April 1908), 258–59. At this same time the Santa Cruz missionaries founded San Francisco de los Tejas, La Purísima Concepción, and San José de los Nazones, somewhat north of the Zacatecas missions.

rude and illiterate natives, and endeavoring to impress upon their rude mentalities the grandeur and sublimity of the Christian religion with the hope of gaining souls for heaven.

Informed by the Nacogdoches that certain neighboring and friendly tribes might willingly receive the light of faith, in January of the following year Margil journeyed eastward to the territory of the Ais, and among them, at what is at present the town of San Augustine, established the Mission of Nuestra Señora de los Dolores. During March he crossed the Sabine, and at the site now occupied by the Town of Robeline, Louisiana, fifty leagues due east from Dolores and not far south of Shamrock and Spanish Lake,[41] founded San Miguel de los Adaes and left at this mission Fray Agustín Patrón, one of the friars who had accompanied him from Mexico.[42] From Dolores, for which he had a special affection and at which he spent the greater part of the year, he made regular visits to the other missions, and on several occasions, carrying with him the sacred vestments, walked from San Miguel to the French presidio at Natchitoches, a distance of about ten leagues, and there said Mass, preached, and heard the confessions of the soldiers.

Those were, indeed, years of trial for the religious in East Texas. Since their arrival they had received no letters from their brethren in either Spain or Mexico, and when, in August of 1718, Margil learned that almost two years previously he had again been elected guardian of Guadalupe College he wrote to his superior requesting that, as the term was then drawing to a close and as he was hundreds of leagues distant from Zacatecas, his resignation be accepted and that he be permitted to remain at the missions. Here Margil and the other missionaries suffered untold hardships and at times had scarcely enough food to keep body and soul together. 1717 and 1718 were years of veritable famine in East Texas; the corn and bean crops were a failure, the scant supply of provisions the missionaries had brought with them from Mexico had become exhausted a few months after their arrival, and for a time all they could secure to stave off starvation was the flesh of crows.[43] In 1717, the Querétaro and Zacatecas colleges, with authorization of the viceroy, sent

---

[41]For further data on the location of these missions consult Bolton, ibid.; also his letter to Father Engelhardt, published in the *Franciscan Herald*, August 1915.

[42]With regard to the friars that accompanied this expedition there seems to be some divergence of opinion. Consult the Espinosa diary, for April 25th, ["Ramón Expedition: Espinosa's Diary of 1716," *Preparing the Way: Preliminary Studies of the Texas Catholic Historical Society I*, Studies in Southwestern Catholic History No. 1 (Austin, 1997), 69]; Isidro Félix Espinosa, *Chrónica apostólica, y seráphica de todos los colegios de Propaganda fide de esta Nueva-España*, (Mexico, 1746), 417, and the Ramón diary for April 21st, ["Captain Don Domingo Ramón's Diary of His Expedition into Texas in 1716," below pp. 134–35.]

[43]*Mexicana Beatificationis et canonizationis Ven. Servi Dei Antonii Margil a Jesu: De Temperantia*, XXX, 32, (n.p.:Typographia Rev. Camerae Apostolicae, n.d.). Consult also *Información de Sucedidos a N. V. P.*, article 186. (*Proceso de Guadalajara*) [*sic*].

a supply of provisions to the padres. The expedition, comprised of a few missionaries with an escort of fifteen soldiers, reached the Trinity before Christmas of the same year, but as this river was overflowing its banks for a distance of about two leagues and as there was little hope of its waters subsiding, the supplies were buried in a woods west of the river, and by means of some Texas Indians who happened to be in those parts a letter was sent to the missionaries with information as to the location of the hidden supplies. The expedition returned to the Rio Grande, but due to impassable roads the letter did not reach its destination until July 22nd of the following year.

In these pages we cannot dwell at length upon this glorious chapter in the history of the Church in Texas, but those of our readers acquainted with the Castilian tongue can find in the first part of the *Crónica Apostólica y Seráfica*, written by Fray Isidro Félix de Espinosa, superior of the religious from Querétaro, a simple, yet beautiful and detailed, account of the sufferings and hardships endured by those zealous pioneers during their first two years of missionary activities among the Hasinai.

In 1719 war broke out between Spain and France, and in June of this year the commandant of the French fort at Natchitoches, without orders from superior officers, made an unexpected attack upon San Miguel, captured a lay brother and an unarmed soldier, the only persons present at the time, and seized the sacred vestments and whatever else was to be found at the mission. On the way back to the fort the commandant was pitched from his mount, and in the confusion that resulted the lay brother, putting spurs to his horse, dashed into a nearby woods, eluded his pursuers, and making his escape to one of the neighboring missions warned Fray Antonio and the other padres of the impending danger. The religious from both colleges and the few soldiers stationed at those missions recognized at once the utter impossibility of coping with an enemy so well equipped and retired to a place of relative safety, but seeing that in spite of repeated and insistent appeals the royal officials in Mexico were taking no active measures to restore those missions, on October 3rd all withdrew to the Mission of San Antonio, located more than two hundred leagues to the southwest of Natchitoches. In the meantime another and a more pressing appeal for assistance was sent to the viceroy, and while awaiting results Fray Antonio ministered to the spiritual wants of the soldiers at the presidio, and on the banks of the San Antonio River established the mission of San José, which was soon to become one of the most famous of the Zacatecas Province.[44]

---

[44]Juan Domingo Arricivita, *Crónica seráfica y apostólica del Colegio de Propaganda Fide de la Santa Cruz de Querétaro en la Nueva España* (Mexico, 1792) 101; Espinosa, *Chrónica Apostólica*, 467. Consult also the Solís diary of 1767. This diary, translated for the first time by the author of the present article, was published in

Finally, on April 4, 1721, the long expected expedition, made up of five hundred men under the Marqués of San Miguel de Aguayo, governor of Coahuila, reached the presidio of San Antonio.[45] Here it was joined by Father Margil and by the other Texas missionaries from Santa Cruz and from Guadalupe. On May 13th the entire expedition left San Antonio, and during the march each morning several Masses were celebrated, and at night a catechetical instruction was given, followed by the singing of the *Alabado.*[46] Traveling in a northeasterly direction, the expedition passed close to the sites at present occupied by the towns of New Braunfels, San Marcos, Austin,[47] Rockdale, and Waco, and having crossed the Trinity toward the end of July entered the territory of the Hasinai. Both missionaries and soldiers received a warm welcome from the natives, and the cacique of the Adaes, whom all Texas tribes recognized as their leader, assured them that all had been impatiently awaiting the return of the Spaniards and that had they delayed any longer he himself would gladly have gone to San Antonio to seek them.[48]

Shortly after the arrival of Aguayo, the French commandant reluctantly, but without offering any resistance, agreed to evacuate all Spanish territory and to withdraw to his fort at Natchitoches. A presidio garrisoned with a hundred men was built among the Adaes, and the abandoned missions, of which scarcely a vestige had remained, were restored and supplied with ministers. Fray Antonio took charge of San Miguel, and in the hope of reaping a rich harvest in that land that had lain fallow during his long period of absence, he became, so to say, one of the natives, helped them in their daily tasks and shared their joys and their sorrows. Faithful always to his religious exercises, early each morning he said the Divine Office and Holy Mass with scrupulous attention and devotion and spent several hours daily in mental prayer, spiritual reading, and visits to the Blessed Sacrament. His bed was a black sheet spread

---

the *Preliminary Studies* of the Texas Catholic Historical Society in March, 1931. [It is reprinted as "The Solís Diary of 1767," in *Preparing the Way: Preliminary Studies of the Texas Catholic Historical Society I*, Studies in Southwestern Catholic History No. 1 (Austin, 1997), 101–48.] Another translation, by Margaret Kenney Kress, of the Department of Spanish of Texas University, appeared as "Diary of a Visit of Inspection of the Texas Missions Made by Fray Gaspar José de Solís in the Year 1767–68," *Southwestern Historical Quarterly* 35, 1 (July 1931): 28–76.

[45]Juan Antonio de la Peña, "Derrotero de la expedición en la Provincia de los Texas" (Museo Nacional de México; Departamento de la Biblioteca Nacional, legajo 94, no. 20). This diary has not as yet been translated, but numerous references to it can be found in the scholarly article by Eleanor Claire Buckley, "The Aguayo Expedition into Texas and Louisiana," *The Quarterly of the Texas State Historical Association* 15, 1 (July 1911): 1–65. [The Peña diary appeared as "Peña's Dairy of the Aguayo Expedition," *Preliminary Studies of the Texas Catholic Historical Society* 2, 7 (January 1935), and is reprinted below, pp. 161–214.]

[46]Arricivita, *Crónica seráfica*, 2:101.

[47]Buckley ("The Aguayo Expedition," 38) states that toward the end of May "the expedition camped on what is now Onion Creek, and crossed it later, apparently at the site of the present McKinney Falls."

[48]Peña, "Derrotero de la expedición."

over the ground and his pillow the trunk of a tree, but frequently he denied himself even the three hours set apart for repose, for as one of the religious who had labored with him on those missions testified years afterwards, on many occasions Fray Antonio passed the entire night on his knees in communion with God. On Good Friday of 1722 he spent several hours in retirement, meditating upon the mystery of the Redemption. At 5 o'clock in the afternoon he left his cell, gathered the natives into the church, and there, after speaking for one hour on the sufferings and death of Christ, made the Stations, explaining in the most touching terms the excruciating pains endured by the God-Man along the Sorrowful Way to Calvary.

About this time the Royal *Audiencia* of Guatemala informed the commissary general for the Indies that much dissension and discord had broken out in that kingdom and requested that Margil be sent there as mediator; but, after consultation with the guardian and Council of Zacatecas College, the General concluded that for the present his services could not be spared at the new foundations, and decided to leave him in Texas. Appointed prefect of the missions *de Propaganda Fide* upon the death of Fray Francisco Estévez, one of Margil's first acts was to establish with the assistance of Fray Agustín Patrón, and near the site now occupied by the Town of Victoria, the Mission of Espíritu Santo de Zúñiga for the savage Karankawas.[49]

RECALLED TO ZACATECAS

Margil continued his efforts to congregate the Indians of East Texas. He continued, by word and example, his efforts to bring back into the fold the sheep that for two years had been left without a shepherd, that had wandered off to the woods and to the mountains during his forced absence at San Antonio; but, in the summer of 1722, when most busily occupied in these truly pastoral duties, he received the obedience to report to Zacatecas as guardian of the College of Guadalupe. Having appointed a successor as superior of the Texas missions, he set out on his journey and in June arrived in Zacatecas, where after that long absence of eight years he was given an enthusiastic and hearty welcome by the inhabitants and also by his fellow-religious at Guadalupe.

At the beginning of the new year he visited Mexico City, accompanied by Fray Isidro Félix de Espinosa, who was now guardian of the college in Querétaro, and during his stay of three months, awaiting certain concessions

---

[49]Bolton, *Texas in the Middle Eighteenth Century*, 284. Consult also Engelhardt's article in the April 1916 number of the Franciscan *Herald*.

in behalf of the Texas missions, addressed large audiences in the Convento Grande de San Francisco and in other churches of the capital. With the viceroy's assurance that the interests of those missions would not be neglected, he set out again for Zacatecas, but upon reaching Querétaro he stopped to visit the religious, and at their request preached several sermons in that city. A few days after his return to Zacatecas he was taken ill with ulcers of the liver, and his condition became so alarming that the doctors gave up all hope of his recovery and advised that he be given the last sacraments. In answer to the fervent prayers offered by the friars at Guadalupe and Santa Cruz and by all with whom he had come in contact and who had learned of his illness, however, God saw fit to restore him to health in order that he might continue his work in the monastery and on the missions.

There is no need of recounting here his many acts of virtue and penance in the cloister or his apostolic labors in the pulpit and confessional during his term as guardian. Suffice it to say that in the former he practiced to an eminent degree those virtues of prudence, charity, and self-denial that had always won for him the love and esteem of his fellow-religious, and in the latter that spirit of self-sacrificing zeal that had always characterized his work on the missions.

In keeping with the rules of the Order, at the Chapter convoked on February 17, 1725, new officers were named for the College of Guadalupe. As Fray Ignacio Hence, the newly elected guardian, was then in Texas, however, the community requested that Margil remain in office until his successor reached Zacatecas.[50] When Father Hence arrived six months later Margil, to prepare for further work on the missions, took leave of his companions and with the approval of his superiors retired to a place of solitude about five leagues from the college. Here he spent several weeks in prayer and penance and left this retreat only on feast days in order to devote himself to the work of the ministry.

Upon his return to the college he learned that the people of Guadalajara had solicited his mediation in the adjustment of serious differences existing between certain factions in their city. On the advice of his superior and that of one of the Fathers of the Society of Jesus, he decided to act as arbiter and to pay a visit to that capital. On the afternoon of October 18th he bade good-bye to his fellow religious, begged them to pardon any faults or offenses of which he might have been guilty, and left that holy institute. The following

[50]Vilaplana, who has taken most of his data and much of his phraseology from Espinosa, states that this Chapter was held on February 22nd. Espinosa states that the election took place on this date. Sotomayor, in his list of the Chapters of the Zacatecas Province, tells us (*Historia del Colegio*, 2:367) that the fifth was convened on February 17, 1725.

day, upon reaching the summit of a hill that dominated the surrounding country, he stopped for a few moments and looked back upon the College of Guadalupe, which loomed up in the distance and which he was never again to see. Imparting to it his last blessing, and having no doubt a foreknowledge of the glorious work still to be accomplished by its members and of the cruel persecution to which they were one day to be subjected, he turned his back upon the City of Zacatecas, and with a heavy heart continued his journey toward the southwest. The impartial student of history cannot but admire and appreciate the stupendous work done by those saintly religious in Tarahumara and in Upper and Lower California after the enactment of that iniquitous decree which banished the sons of the great Ignatius from all Spanish dominions in 1767. He is of necessity filled with righteous indignation when little less than a century later,[51] he finds a similar decree of secularization leveled at the missionaries of Zacatecas, and when he pictures those poor barefooted followers of Saint Francis, men who had sacrificed everything the world holds dear in order to consecrate themselves entirely to the service of God, leaving the College of Guadalupe possessed of nothing but their breviaries, and making their way southward toward the Town of Cholula.

On November 3rd Margil reached Guadalajara, where he remained for more than six weeks reestablishing peace and harmony among its citizens, preaching the word of God in the various churches, and bringing cheer and comfort to the inmates of the prison and to the sick in the hospitals. On December 20th he left this city and for more than four months gave missions in Ascatán, Piedad, Puruándiro and other towns in the vicinity of Lake Chapala. At some of these places the inhabitants swept and strewed with flowers the roads over which he was to pass; at others they erected triumphal arches in his honor, walked long distances to meet him and with bands playing accompanied him to the churches in procession. In order to escape these outward manifestations of veneration and in order to reach the numerous souls still in need of his ministrations, on more than one occasion that humble and zealous friar was compelled to leave a town under the cover of darkness. At the end of the day's journey he never failed, however, to spend long hours in the pulpit and in the confessional, although sorely in need of rest and though suffering from double hernia and from an ulcer in one of his arms and another in one of his feet,.

[51] August 1, 1859.

HIS LAST ILLNESS AND DEATH

On the night of May 1st Margil arrived in Valladolid, and was so busily engaged for the remainder of the month that he became dangerously ill, developed a malignant fever, and was confined to bed for several days.[52] Partly restored to health, he left for Acámbaro, where he opened a two weeks' mission on June 15th. On July 7th he reached the College of Santa Cruz in Querétaro. Here his condition became so alarming that the commissary general, hoping that with proper medical attention he might find some alleviation from his sufferings, suggested that he go to the community infirmary at the Convento Grande in Mexico City. One of the Fathers at Santa Cruz tried out of compassion to dissuade him from making that long journey, warning him that if he persisted in doing so he would probably die along the way, without a doctor, medicine, or Christian burial. To this Fray Antonio replied: "That is what I deserve; I am not entitled to Christian burial; I ought to die out in the wilds, where the beasts can devour me."[53]

On July 21st he left Santa Cruz, that institute from which some forty years previously he had been sent to the missions in Central America, and in compliance with the wishes of his superior, began the long wearisome journey to Mexico City. He preached at San Juan del Río on the 24th, at Cazadero on the 27th, and, burning with fever, traveled on past Ruano and Capulapa till on the 30th he came to the Town of San Francisco, sixteen leagues from the capital. The afternoon of his arrival to San Francisco he was obliged to leave the confessional because of an attack of chills and fever, but although unable to sleep that night, he went to the church on the following day, feast of Saint Ignatius of Loyola, and for the last time in his life offered up the Holy Sacrifice. A heavy rain had fallen during the night, and on the way to the church in which he was to celebrate Fray Antonio contracted a severe cold, which soon developed into pneumonia. This same day, however, he mounted a horse, rode as far as Tepeji that night, and on the following day, August 1st, reached the Town of Cuautitlán. The next morning he felt too weak to continue the journey on horseback, but having secured a carriage, he traveled on, and that evening, as the sun was sinking back of the Cordillera de las Cruces, reached the Convento Grande de San Francisco. Casting himself on his knees at the door of the convent church, he adored his Eucharistic Lord, present in the tabernacle, and then, assisted by two of the religious, climbed the steps leading to one of the cells in the community infirmary.

---

[52]The present City of Morelia, capital of the State of Michoacán.

[53]Vilaplana. *Vida portentosa*, 177. Navarro, *Oración Fúnebre*, p. 38 [*sic*], in "Láurea Funeral Americana."

Informed that there was no chance of his recovery, that saintly religious, weighed down by old age and infirmities, but happy in the thought that he was soon to be united with Him for whom he had labored so long and so faithfully, rose from his death bed, knelt down on the bare floor, and made a general confession of his whole life to Fray Manuel de las Heras, who for several years had been professor of sacred theology in the Province of San Pedro y San Pablo in Michoacán and who later on had assisted Fray Antonio on the missions. The servant of God had little of which to accuse himself before appearing before the Supreme Tribunal, however, for at the age of discretion he had placed himself in the arms of Christ Crucified and, according to the testimonies of Fray Manuel de las Heras, Fray Isidro Félix de Espinosa and his other spiritual advisers, he had modeled his life after that of Saint Anthony of Padua and had never lost his baptismal innocence.

On August 4th he received the Holy Viaticum with that same fervor and devotion that he had always manifested in the celebration of the Holy Sacrifice. On the 5th one of the friars administered Extreme Unction, and after receiving this sacrament Fray Antonio addressed a few words of parting to the brethren who had gathered in his cell, thanked them for the tender care with which they had nursed him during his illness, and begged them not to grow tepid or lukewarm in the discharge of their religious duties and never to abandon the institute. Finally, shortly before 2 o'clock in the afternoon of the following day, August 6, 1726, feast of the Transfiguration, with the words *Paratum cor meum, Deus, paratum cor meum*[54] upon his lips, and as the community intoned the canticle, *Nunc dimittis servum tuum, Domine, secundum verbum tuum in pace,*[55] he yielded up his soul in peace to its Creator.

An hour later, after the tolling of the cathedral and convent bells had announced to the people of the capital the passing of the great missionary of America, words of sympathy and sorrow were exchanged in all parts of the city, and the children in the streets and on the plazas could have been heard crying: "The Saint has died! Holy Fray Antonio is dead!" Anxious to apply medals, rosaries, and other articles to those hands that had so often been raised in benediction and to kiss those feet that for so many years had trodden the ways of peace, both clergy and laity flocked in such numbers to the small infirmary chapel in which the body was being waked that the superior, to satisfy their pious devotion, ordered that it be taken down to the convent church. On August 8th the viceroy, the judges of the *Audiencia* and many other royal officials, as well as large representations from all the religious Orders,

---

[54]"My heart Is ready, O God, my heart is ready." Psalm 107, 2 [Douay ver.].

[55]"Now Thou dost dismiss Thy servant, O Lord, according to Thy word in peace," *Canticle of Simeon,* Luke 2, 29.

repaired to the Convento Grande de San Francisco, and there, after the Solemn Mass of Requiem, which was attended by the largest concourse that had ever gathered in the capital, the mortal remains of him who during life had sought neither honors nor distinctions, and who had always styled himself *la misma nada,* were laid to rest in a vault near the foot of the altar of San Diego on the Gospel side of the sanctuary. In 1861 they were removed to the cathedral, to be placed in a niche in the Chapel of la Virgen de la Soledad, and today they repose in that of la Inmaculada Concepción. Engraved on a metal plate affixed to the coffin could have been read the following inscription:

HIC JACET SEPULTUS, VENERABILIS SERVUS DEI
PATER FRATER ANTONIUS MARGIL, MISSIONARIUS,
PRAEFECTUS, ET GUARDIANUS COLLEGIORUM DE
PROPAGANDA FIDE SANCTAE CRUCIS DE QUERETARO, SANCTISSIMI CRUCIFIXI DE GUATEMALA,
ET SANCTAE MARIAE DE GUADALUPE IN HAC
NOVA HISPANIA ERECTORTUM: FAMA UTIQUE
VIRTUTUM, MIRACULORUMQUE ILLUSTRIS.
OBIIT IN HOC PERCELEBRI
MEXICANO CONVENTU
Die VI. Augusti Anno
Dni. M.DCC.XXVI.[56]

We had proposed to present here a compendious life of Fray Antonio Margil de Jesús, but we have come to realize the impossibility of such a task. We have come to realize, perhaps more fully than any of our readers, the utter impossibility of recounting in these few pages the activities of one who spent more than forty years journeying thousands of leagues, climbing dizzying heights, crossing swollen rivers, and making his way barefoot over the burning sands of the deserts in the endeavor to win souls for God. Of his theological and moral virtues, of his power of working miracles, of his gift of tongues, and of his other *gratiae gratis datae,* so beautifully and so minutely described by Espinosa and by his other biographers and contemporaries, we have said almost nothing. We trust, however, that the ardent hope expressed at the beginning of this treatise may soon be realized, that another and a finer pen

---

[56]Here lies buried the Venerable servant of God, Father Fray Antonio Margil, Missionary, Prefect, and Guardian of the colleges *de Propaganda Fide* of Santa Cruz in Querétaro, Cristo Crucificado in Guatemala, and Our Lady of Guadalupe, erected in this New Spain. Famous for his virtues and miracles, he died in this celebrated Convent of Mexico on the 6th day of August, in the year of Our Lord, 1726.

may before long depict in a befitting manner the life and activities of this great soldier of Christ.

Shortly after Fray Antonio's death the Sacred Congregation of Rites, in answer to persistent appeals from the peoples of Central and North America, ordered that the preliminary processes, or judicial inquiries, for the cause of beatification and canonization be begun in the principal centers in which he had carried on his missionary labors, and in compliance with this order postulators were appointed for Mexico City, Guadalajara, and Guatemala. The results of these processes having been taken to Rome, several of the miracles wrought through his intercession were approved by Pope Pius VII, and it is our humble opinion that at that time he would have been beatified had not important documents relating to the processes been lost upon the entrance of the French armies into the Eternal City in 1797. These documents reappeared miraculously later on, and in 1836 the Sacred Congregation approved the introduction of his cause, the virtues of the noted missionary were declared heroic, and a decree conferring upon him the title of Venerable was promulgated by the Sovereign Pontiff, Pope Gregory XVI.

At the present time interest has been reawakened in the cause of this servant of God, with the hope that in 1936, centennial of the promulgation of the decree of Gregory XVI, he may be elevated to the dignity of our altars. It is in the belief that our readers will by their prayers hasten that blessed day that we have undertaken to publish this simple yet faithful account of the life of him who civilized nations, established pueblos, erected churches, and baptized innumerable souls, and who, nevertheless, always styled himself *la misma nada.*

FORERUNNERS OF CAPTAIN DE LEÓN'S EXPEDITION TO TEXAS, 1670–1675

Francis Borgia Steck, O.F.M.*

FOREWORD

Here are presented the results of original research pursued by Reverend Francis Borgia Steck, O.F.M., Ph.D., who is now preparing for the Commission a comprehensive and critical history of the Mission Era in Texas. The discovery of new source materials in the Archivo del Convento Grande de San Francisco in Mexico City, in the various Archivos de Guadalajara, ecclesiastical and civil, and in the Archivo de la Secretaría de Gobierno del Estado de Coahuila at Saltillo have made this study possible. Heretofore the chief authority for the Bosque-Larios Expedition has been Portillo in his *Apuntes para la historia antigua de Coahuila y Texas*. Much new historical evidence has been found which shows that approaches and reconnaissances had been made into south central Texas by the companions of Fray Juan Larios as early as 1673. These two Franciscans were Fray Francisco Peñasco de Lozano and Fray Manuel de la Cruz.

The Historical Commission and the Texas Catholic Historical Society are very much indebted to Dr. Carlos E. Castañeda, the Director of the García Latin-American Library, University of Texas, for his efforts in making these documents available. He has labored successfully in all the aforesaid archival depositories. Special acknowledgment is due also to Mr. Ernest W. Winkler, Librarian-in-Chief of the Library of the University of Texas and particularly to the staff of the Department of Archives for the many courtesies and favors to the author of the following contribution. Gratitude is also here expressed to Dr. Eugene C. Barker, who in behalf of the *Southwestern Historical Quarterly* and the Texas Historical Association has granted permission for this reprint as one of the Preliminary Studies of the Texas Catholic Historical Society. Dr. Steck gave this scholarly paper in part before the Texas Historical Association.

Paul J. Foik, C.S.C.
Chairman of the Commission and President of the Society.

---

*Vol. 2, No. 3, appeared in September 1932 as a reprint from *The Southwestern Historical Quarterly* 36, 1 (July 1932).

Forerunners of Captain De Leon's Expedition to Texas, 1670–1675*

During the mid-seventeenth century, mining enterprises and punitive expeditions against marauding savages brought Spaniards from central Mexico into northern Coahuila and across the Rio Grande into modern Texas.[1] As Professor Herbert E. Bolton correctly observes, central and eastern Texas would have been occupied sooner or later by Spain "even in the absence of foreign aggression."[2] For several decades prior to the expedition of Alonso de León into eastern Texas, the Spaniards of Mexico were pursuing friendly relations with Indian tribes in northern Coahuila and on the banks of the Rio Grande below the Pecos. Repeatedly these tribes petitioned the Spanish authorities to establish missions and settlements in their country where, they declared, material resources were rich and numerous Indians were eager to become Christians and vassals of Spain. Steps to meet their petition were finally taken in 1673, in which year also the conversion of these tribes was entrusted to the Franciscans of the Province of Jalisco some of whose members had already been active among them. Most energetic in promoting this venture was Father Juan Larios, guardian of the Franciscan friary[3] at Atoyac, about fifty miles south of Guadalajara. He is easily the leading agent in the conquest of northern Coahuila between the years 1670 and 1675.

An important turn in one's career sometimes hinges on an incident quite unimportant in itself. So it was in the case of Father Larios and his career in the Rio Grande region. In 1670, being guardian at Atoyac, he obtained permission to visit his sister in Durango. While returning to his Province, on the second day of the journey, he met two Indian warriors. Though terrifying

---

*This paper, since revised and amplified, was read in April 1932, at the annual meeting of the Texas State Historical Association.

[1]In 1665, for instance, Fernando de Azcué, *alcalde mayor* of Saltillo, led an expedition across the Rio Grande into Texas. His purpose was to chastise a band of Cataxtle Indians. See Carlos E. Castañeda, "Earliest Catholic Activities in Texas" in *The Catholic Historical Review* 17, 3 (Oct. 1931), reprint [i.e. *Preliminary Sutides of the Texas Catholic Historical Society* 1, 8 (Oct. 1931):] 9. As to early mining enterprises, see Herbert E. Bolton "The Spanish Occupation of Texas, 1519–1690" in *TheSouthwestern Historical Quarterly* 16, 1 (July 1912): 13–14.

[2]Bolton, "The Spanish Occupation of Texas," 17.

[3]"Guardian" is the legal and official title of the superior of a larger community of Franciscans inhabiting what in English is termed a friary. Guardians by virtue of their office have active and passive voice in the provincial chapters convoked at regular intervals either by the minister provincial or by the minister General. The terms "prior" and "priory" are sometimes used in connection with Franciscans, but erroneously so.

in appearance, they soon reassured the friar, demanding by signs nothing more than that he accompany them to their home in the North and convert their people to Christianity. Larios was at a loss what to do. On the one hand, his priestly heart rebelled against refusing or deferring compliance with their appeal. On the other hand, as a religious he was subject to the will of his superiors without whose express approval he felt it ill-advised to accompany the Indians. He found a way out of this dilemma, however. At his instance, one of the Indians set out the next day for Guadalajara, bearing the letter which Larios wrote to his minister provincial, Father Juan Mohedano. In this letter he told the provincial that, presuming permission, he was departing with the other Indian for the North; the provincial should please give the venture his approval and his blessing.

After traveling northeast for twenty days, Larios and his Indian guide came to a *ranchería* where they were heartily welcomed by the natives. Soon the *ranchería* had its chapel and its dwelling for the missionary. Larios began to study the language of the Indians, meanwhile instructing them as best he could in the tenets of Christianity and in the ways of civilized life. Apprized of his arrival, Indians of neighboring *rancherías* came to see and hear him, and before long the missionary was surrounded by more than five hundred Indians.[4]

From the available records it is not possible to determine where this first mission in northern Coahuila was located. Very probably it lay some thirty miles north of the present city of Monclova.[5] Certain it is that from this central mission Larios made trips to other tribes and that on one of these trips, accompanied by five Catzale Indians, he came to where in later years the Mission of the Holy Name of Jesus was founded.[6] This was at a place called Peyotes, about fifty leagues from Monclova, almost due north, between the Río de las Sabinas and the Rio Grande.[7] Here, on the very threshold of Texas, an incident occurred which shows to what dangers Larios exposed himself on such trips and to what extent he succeeded in winning the friendship of his Indian neophytes. On reaching the place called Peyotes, Larios and his five Catzale companions were stopped by three hundred Tobosos, long known as a fierce and warlike tribe. With devilish glee they invited the Catzales to take part in the *mitote* or head-dance which they would celebrate and for which they would use the head of the missionary. But the Catzales objected, eloquently

[4]Matías Mota Padilla, *Historia de la conquista de la provincia de la Nueva Galicia* (n.p., 1742), 375–76.

[5]Larios and his companion traveled northeast for twenty days. Taking six leagues as the average distance covered per day, the total distance would he one hundred and twenty leagues or about three hundred miles. Their point of departure was two days distant, apparently southeast, from Durango.

[6]This mission, named Misión del Dulce Nombre Jesús de Peyotes, was founded in 1698. See Esteban Portillo, *Apuntes para la historia de Coahuila y Tejas* (Saltillo, 1886), 142.

[7]See Portillo, *Apuntes,* 274. The present town of Peyotes is about ninety miles north of Monclova.

protesting that the unoffending friar was their father who loved them more than he loved himself; that he had befriended them in time of need, established peace between them and their enemies, and instructed them in Christianity. Then they suggested that, in place of the head-dance, five of the Tobosos challenge the five Catzales to a game of ball. "If you win, the Father will belong to you," they stipulated; "but if we win, he must go free." To this the Tobosos agreed. While these were selecting their five players, the Catzales brought Larios to a huge tree in the hollow of which they insisted that he hide himself. Thereupon they began the game of ball. Realizing after a time that he and his four tribesmen were losing, the captain of the Catzales boldly stepped forward and declared: "By the game we have lost the life of our Father; but we are determined to lose our own life in defending him." With this they hastened to the tree where Larios was hiding, seized their weapons, and prepared for the attack. Strange to say, not one of the arrows that the Tobosos now discharged at the Catzales came closer than within a few feet of the friar's defenders. Seeing that the enemy had run out of arrows and that their bows had become slack, the fearless Catzales took the offensive with deadly effect. Over a hundred Tobosos were killed, while the rest took to flight. Carefully guarding their missionary, the five Catzales departed under cover of night and reached their settlement. "So it was related to Father Esteban Martínez," Mota Padilla concludes, "to whom he [Larios] unfolded his soul and who learned it also from the mouth of the victorious Indians and of some of the vanquished who afterwards became Christians."[8]

For three years Father Larios labored successfully in this new vineyard of Christ, greatly encouraged by the official approval which the minister provincial gave the project and by the arrival of other friars who were sent to assist him. These, according to Mota Padilla, were Father Esteban Martínez and the two lay brothers Juan Barrero and Manuel de la Cruz.[9] Very probably it was also during these years that Larios founded and named San Ildefonso de la Paz, the settlement which was destined to figure so prominently a few year later.[10]

The civil authorities in Mexico realized the importance of securing northern Coahuila against the inroads of hostile tribes by cementing friendly relations with the more peaceful Indians and establishing them in organized settlements under the protection of Spain. That steps were finally taken to achieve this purpose was again due in large measure to the energy of Father

---

[8]Mota Padilla, *Historia de la conquista*, 376–77.

[9]Ibid., 376. Mota Padilla cites Manuel de la Cruz as being a priest. As will be learned later, however, it is certain that at this time Manuel was a lay brother.

[10]See n.15.

Larios. This we gather from the testimony of Father Joseph Pedruzo, procurator general of the Province of Jalisco. Late in the spring of 1673, at the bidding of his superiors, Larios left his Indian neophytes in the North and went to Parral. On his way to Guadalajara, where he was to report to the provincial, he met a band of Indians, among whom were some who had been baptized by him in northern Coahuila. Learning from these that all desired to become Christians and live in settlements and that they were now bound for Guadalajara to ask for missionaries, Larios selected twenty of the Indians and with them set out for Guadalajara, telling the rest to return to their lands and there await the arrival of missionaries. It was early in September 1673 that Larios with the twenty Indians, twelve of whom were Christians, reached Guadalajara and knocked at the door of the Franciscan friary.[11] From the official report of Father Alonso Guerrero, who at this time was visiting the Jalisco Province in the capacity of commissary visitor, we learn how cordially they were welcomed by the friars and how the Indians by their friendly and peaceful ways edified the citizens of Guadalajara. They assured the guardian of the friary, Father Diego Fregoso, that they had been sent by their captains to procure missionaries, that many of their tribesmen had been baptized by Father Larios, and that now they desired Father Larios and other Franciscans to come and settle permanently in their country.[12]

During the next three months the twenty Indians were cared for by the friars. The eight of their group who were not yet Christians received regular instructions in the faith and were solemnly baptized, prominent citizens of Guadalajara acting as sponsors. At the same time, the civil authorities negotiated with the Franciscans toward founding missions in the new frontier and settling the tribes in organized towns. The *Real Audiencia* empowered the *justicia mayor* of Saltillo, Francisco de Elizondo, to lead a detachment of soldiers to the Río de las Sabinas, receive the submission of the Indians to the Spanish crown, and in the name of the government apportion the lands among them. With the bishop of Guadalajara they sanctioned the appointment, made by the Franciscan provincial, of Father Larios as superior of the new mission field and of Father Francisco Peñasco de Lozano and Brother Manuel de la Cruz as his assistants.[13]

---

[11] "Tanto de los Auttos e información dada por la parte de la Santa Provincia de Xalisco," Archivo de San Francisco el Grande, Biblioteca Nacional de México, 1:34–58, photostatic copy at the Catholic Archives of Texas, Austin (hereafter cited as ASFG).

[12] "Informe de los Autos que se hicieron para la mission de la Provincia de Quahuila este año de 1673," ASFG, 1:1–11. The account in this report differs in some particulars from that of the Procurator General. For instance, it makes it appear that the twenty Indians were all captains and that Larios did not accompany them to Guadalajara.

[13] "Tanto de la Real Provisión, . . . Comisión del Rmo Obispo de este obispado de la Nueva Galicia, y Patente de muy R. P. Provincial de la orden de nuestro P. San Francisco en la Provincia de Xalisco,"

On November 18, 1673, the three missionaries with the twenty Christian Indians left Guadalajara and set out for Saltillo. Here they learned that in the north various tribes had again risen in rebellion and committed numerous depredations. In view of this, even the Franciscans who resided in Saltillo supported the *alcalde mayor* in his contention that for the present it would be impossible and dangerous for the friars to enter the northern regions. But the latter protested that God would protect them, since their purpose was to save souls,[14] a purpose which Larios knew from experience the mind of the Indians was able to appreciate.

Taking leave of their confrères and friends in Saltillo, Larios and his companions set out for the much-dreaded north. After traveling sixty leagues they came to a *ranchería* where they were welcomed by five hundred forty-three Indians, as Larios carefully records, and by ten Indian captains of as many tribes who were living farther north between the Río de las Sabinas and the Rio Grande. Scarcely had the missionaries begun to instruct the Indians of this *ranchería,* when they learned from the ten captains that smallpox had broken out in their settlements farther north. Without delay the friars hastened to the stricken people and on January 23, 1674, they came to San Ildefonso, fourteen leagues north of the Río de las Sabinas and twenty leagues south of the Rio Grande. Here they found numerous tribes, notably the Boboles, Guyquechales, Tiltiqui, and Mayhuam. Led by their chiefs, each of whom carried a cross, more than five hundred Indians came out to welcome the missionaries. Deeply touched, the latter chanted the *Te Deum Laudamus* and followed the Indians to the settlements where to their consternation a dwelling had already been erected for them. This, Larios tells us, was a a hut covered with reeds and in front of it stood a cross. Directed doubtless by Brother Manuel, the Indians erected a brush-wood chapel and on the following day Father Larios celebrated Holy Mass in the presence of the Indians. Thereupon, besides attending to the sick Indians, the missionaries began to instruct those who were not stricken with the disease.[15] The hardships endured by the friars during these first days at San Ildefonso are graphically described by an

---

ASFG, 1:12–26, Father Martínez and Brother Barrero, it seems, had previously returned to the Province.

[14]"Investigación sobre la erección de la Misión de Santiago por el P. Fr. Damián Massanet, Año de 1690," in "Legajos Historicos," Archivo de la Biblioteca Pública del Estado Jalisco, 1:681, 683, 689, copy at the Catholic Archives of Texas, Austin (hereafter cited as ABPJ).

[15]Juan Larios to the commissary general, Saltillo, 26 Feb. 1674, same to same, Saltillo, 2 Mar. 1674, and same to Captain Francisco de Elizondo, 23 Jan. 1674, contained in "Autos . . . de la entrada que hizo el Capitán Francisco de Elizondo a tierra adentro" ASFG 1:82–85, 111–13, 63–78. Nowhere in his correspondence does Larios say that on this occasion he named the settlement San Ildefonso. From this it would seem that the place had been previously visited and named by him, especially since some of the Indian captains were already baptized, having doubtless received, the sacrament during the earlier activity of Larios in these regions.

eyewitness, Rodrigo Morales, sergeant in the detachment of soldiers under Captain Elizondo, who reached San Ildefonso four days after the arrival of Larios and his companions. "Here," he testified, "a great epidemic of smallpox attacked them [the Indians], during which I witnessed and assisted at the baptism of more than three hundred persons, adults and children, who were in danger of death from the disease. The number of people was very great. Here I saw the friars going about, consoling the sick and serving them. Their habit was so tattered that it reached only to the knees, and from the roughness of the roads their legs and feet were covered with blood. In addition to many hardships, they had nothing to eat; and I saw them begging food from the Indians who gave them *mescal* and some roots which they ate."[16]

As previously stated, Captain Francisco de Elizondo and his detachment of twenty soldiers reached San Ildefonso on January 27. Commissioned by the governor of Nueva Vizcaya to act in the name of the civil authorities, Elizondo interviewed the Indian chiefs, received their promise of allegiance to the Spanish king, promised them in return the support and protection of Spain, and finally proposed that they select a site for their habitat, where he would place them in legal possession and where they would be expected to live peacefully in organized towns and cultivate the lands. Encouraged by the missionaries, the chiefs agreed to Elizondo's proposals and selected for their habitat the lands farther south, along the north bank of the Río de las Sabinas. Accordingly, Elizondo and his soldiers with Fathers Larios and Peñasco and the Indian chiefs proceeded to the Río de las Sabinas. Here, on February 1, 1674, Elizondo placed the Indians in legal possession of lands northward to the settlement of San Ildefonso and eastward as far as the mouth of the Río de las Sabinas. The site where the prescribed ceremonies were enacted was named Santa Rosa de Santa María. Here, too, the friars decided to establish their headquarters. Before departing for Saltillo, Elizondo exhorted the Indians to obey the missionaries who would henceforth reside in their midst and to live in peace among themselves and with the Spaniards.[17]

After the departure of Elizondo and the soldiers, whose arrival had disquieted the Indians,[18] Larios and Peñasco returned to San Ildefonso. Here they assembled all the Indians who were able to travel and conducted them to Santa Rosa. Then, on February 9, both friars set out for Saltillo. From here Peñasco continued the journey to Guadalajara, bearing the official reports of

---

[16]"Investigación sobre la erección de la Misión de Santiago," 691–92. Practically the same was testified by another eyewitness on this occasion, the ensign of the detachment, Gerónimo Juan Ramos (Ibid., 702–03).

[17]"Autos . . . de la entrada que hizo el Capitán Francisco de Elizondo," 63–78.

[18]This we learn from the two eyewitnesses, previously cited, Rodrigo Morales and Gerónimo Juan Ramos. See n.16 for references.

the recent proceedings to the commissary general. Larios, however, remained at Saltillo to solicit material aid for the new mission, making a special appeal to Francisco Barbarigo, the government protector of the Indians who had settled in the vicinity of Saltillo. Barbarigo, an ardent supporter of the northern project, eventually accompanied Larios to Santa Rosa where he took personal charge of the material affairs of the mission. "In every way and with great generosity and charity," Larios writes, "he has aided us and the Indians. He is now going with me [to Santa Rosa] in order to direct the sowing of the fanegas of corn which he has given us for this purpose and to decide on the form of the church and of the town. He does this with a love which would make him a very zealous religious."[19]

Meanwhile, at Santa Rosa, Brother Manuel was alone with the Indians. In his letter to the commissary general he informs us that seven hundred Indians were assembled at the new mission and that of these five hundred and twelve belonged to the tribe known as the Guyquechales. Because the epidemic of smallpox was still affecting their people, the Indian captains asked permission to settle temporarily farther inland, promising to return to Santa Rosa at the half-moon of March. Manuel granted them the permission and with the Obayos and some of the Boboles went to a place five leagues south of the Río de las Sabinas. We can easily imagine the dismay of Father Larios when on March 20, accompanied by Francisco Barbarigo, he returned from Saltillo and learned from Brother Manuel what had happened. Knowing the fickle nature of the Indians and realizing that the time for their return had already elapsed, Larios justly feared they would not keep their promise. Accordingly, he sent Brother Manuel in search of the Boboles. After six days, having found these Indians in an arroyo some twelve leagues distant, Manuel returned with them to Santa Rosa where Barbarigo had meanwhile begun the erection of a chapel and other necessary buildings.[20]

Gladly would the zealous Brother have joined Barbarigo in this work. But another duty, far more arduous and perilous, awaited him. "When I arrived with them" [the Boboles], he writes, "he [Father Larios] asked me whether I was resolved to go in search of the Guyquechale Indians, of whom we had information that they were on the other side of the Río del Norte [Rio Grande]. I told him that, if he commanded me under obedience, I would in

---

[19]Larios to the commissary general, Saltillo, Feb. 26, 1674, ASFG 1:82–85. See also Fray Francisco Basán to the commissary general, Saltillo, July 19, 1674, ASFG 1:129–134; and "Petición presentada a Francisco Barbarigo por Fray Juan Larios," San Esteban de la Nueva Tlascala, Feb. 26, 1674, ASFG 1:88–110.

[20]Brother Manuel de la Cruz to the commissary general, Saltillo, May 29, 1674, ASFG 1:118–25. Unfortunately, Manuel does not say expressly that he returned to Santa Rosa after finding the Boboles. There are indications, however, that it was Santa Rosa and not San Ildefonso. See below, n.23.

no manner refuse. So in obedience he imposed this upon me and the next day, after receiving the sacraments,[21] I left without fear of the dangers, of which I shall speak later.[22] Such were the circumstances under which Manuel undertook the journey that led him across the Rio Grande into what is today the State of Texas.

Apparently on March 29, accompanied by five Indians, Brother Manuel left Santa Rosa.[23] Four and a half days later, having covered forty leagues in a northerly direction, they reached the Rio Grande. Where the river formed two forks they crossed and stepped on Texas soil, probably some miles below the present city of Del Rio. The next day at sunrise they continued the journey and three days later, covering approximately six leagues a day, they came to "a mountain range which the Indians called Dacate.[24] Here they met a friendly Indian who warned them against pursuing that route. Hostile Indians, he said, were informed of their arrival[25] and were coming to capture the friar and kill his companions. They disregarded the Indian's warning, however, and continued northward until they came to an arroyo. This was probably Devil's River, northwest of Del Rio. Here they remained in hiding for three days. During this time one of the Indians whom the Brother had sent out to reconnoiter came back with the news that the Boboles "were camping in the same arroyo about six leagues farther up."

"Rejoicing over such good news," writes Manuel, "I departed at midnight and at about nine o'clock in the morning I reached the camp, where I was well received by all." From these Indians it was learned that the Guyquechales were camping at a distance of about eight leagues. Eager to get in touch with this powerful tribe, Manuel sent a messenger to their captain. The latter, to quote the Brother's report, "knowing of my arrival[26] and of the danger I was in, set out to see me so hastily that before sunset he was in my company, bringing in his own for my protection ninety-eight archers arrayed in their war paint." The

---

[21]It should be recalled that Manuel was not a priest and hence had not the faculty to celebrate Holy Mass. He could, however, receive the sacraments of Penance and Holy Communion.

[22]Brother Manuel de la Cruz to the commissary general, Saltillo, May, 1674, ASFG 1:118–25. From this letter, the only source of information, we gather the details of the Brother's memorable *entrada* into Texas.

[23]He does not say expressly that he departed from Santa Rosa. We conclude this from the fact that this place had been selected as the central settlement both by the Indians and by the missionaries. Moreover, Manuel says that after traveling forty leagues northward he reached the Rio Grande, which statement seems to indicate that Santa Rosa rather than San Ildefonso was the point of departure.

[24]Very probably these were the hills along Devils River in Valverde County, Texas. For this and other information concerning the topography of Texas I am indebted to Mr. David Donoghue of Fort Worth.

[25]"*Avisados de un demonio que se les aparece en forma visible* (informed by a demon who appears to them in visible form)," Manuel's letter reads.

[26]Perhaps it was a Guyquechale Indian of this camp who had previously warned Manuel and his companions. Naturally, on returning to the camp, he informed his captain of the Brother's arrival.

appearance of these warriors must have been terrifying. "All came," says the report, "prepared for battle, well provided with arrows, with only a breech-cloth of shammy skin over their privy parts and a large one of hide, over arms and chest many stripes of red and yellow and white; on their head some had wreaths of mesquite leaves, others wreaths of *estofiate silvestre*;[27] and over these wreaths some beautiful feathers." Having embraced the captain, Manuel told him that, being worried over the failure of the Guyquechales to return to Santa Rosa at the appointed time, he had come to find them and, if they desired, bring them back to the settlement. The captain, in turn, assured the Brother that he and all his people earnestly wished to be Christians and that consequently they would now go wherever the Brother would lead them.

Meanwhile Indian scouts reported that hostile Indians, one hundred and eighty in number, were coming to carry out their murderous design. At this the Bobole and Guyquechale captains, in their solicitude for the safety of Manuel, advised him to remain at the camp with the women and children, while they would go out with their warriors and meet the enemy. But Manuel was made of sterner stuff. "I told them," he writes, "that under no circumstances would I do this; that now I had none who were more sons and brothers to me than they; and that consequently I would not desert them even unto death. Happy over my resolve," he adds, "they said: Now we can see that you love us; and you may rest assured that we would rather die than desert you." Evidently, like Father Larios, Brother Manuel had gained the love and confidence of the Indians.

Encouraged by these mutual avowals of friendship, Manuel and the combined force of Bobole and Guyquechale warriors, one hundred and forty-seven strong, set out to encounter the enemy. It was about ten o'clock at night when they departed and before daybreak they spied the hostile camp. The next morning at sunrise they, in turn, were spied by the enemy. Both parties now prepared for battle. Being outnumbered, Manuel's defenders were seized with fear. At this point in his narrative Manuel describes a truly remarkable scene. "I told them not to fear," he writes, "since God would surely come to their aid. Taking out my crucifix, I showed it to them and said that they should not lose heart; that they were defending the law of God which their enemies refused to accept and instead, deceived by the devil whom they call their god, were persecuting this Master who died for us on the cross." Being Christians, some of the Indians with their captains evidently grasped the import of these words. The Brother having retired from the scene of the coming conflict, his Indian warriors "prepared their bows and with a horrible yell attacked the enemy so valorously that the enemy, unable to resist them, took to flight and

---

[27]This is a medicinal herb which is found in Mexico and is used as a remedy against cholic.

sought refuge in the aforesaid Dacate mountain range." Seven of the hostile band were killed in the skirmish, while many others, among them four women, were taken prisoner. "Coming back to me," writes Manuel, "victorious and happy, they kissed the crucifix and, passing their hands over head and face, said in their language: Y *taoque Dios,* which is their way of saying: O Father God." Needless to add, at the request of Manuel, the Indian prisoners were not put to death.

There was great rejoicing in the camp of the Boboles when the warriors returned and related how they had routed the enemy. On the following day, Manuel and all the Indians—men, women, and children—set out for the *ranchería* of the Guyquechales, guided by their captain who with his warriors had come to protect the missionary and the friendly Boboles. The *ranchería,* it seems, lay toward the southeast and nearer the Rio Grande. They reached it after traveling two days. Here, too, the arrival of the Brother and the news of the recent victory caused great joy. All told, six hundred and seventy-three Indians were now assembled at the *ranchería.* Agreeing to return to the lands which had been assigned to them three months before on the Río de las Sabinas, they departed the next day with Brother Manuel who at this point in his report is careful to note that he had spent twenty-one days in the region north of the Rio Grande, that is in what today constitutes Maverick, Kinney, and Valverde counties, in Texas. They crossed the river at two forks and over a wide ford, in the middle of which was an island of sand. Two days later, pursuing a southerly course, they came to a creek where they met the Pinanca and the Tiltiquemayo Indians, numbering one hundred and sixty-six persons. Taking these with them, they traveled eight days and reached the Nueces River, in Mexico. This they crossed and on the following day came to a meadow which lay between two hills and through which flowed a spring. Here they met eight-two Indians of the Babosarigame tribe, who welcomed the visitors and gladly joined them on their way to Santa Rosa. Manuel's company now numbered eight hundred and twenty-one Indians. Finally they came to a creek which was only ten leagues from Santa Rosa. Here Manuel permitted the Indians to rest for three days, he himself continuing the journey alone. "Arriving at the pueblo," he writes, "I found my dear companion, Father Juan Larios, and with him Captain Francisco Barbarigo. They were finishing the adobe church and its sacristy which with the hut for our habitation we completed the day after my arrival." It was May 2, 1674, when Manuel reached Santa Rosa.[28] About six weeks had elapsed since his departure, and of these he had spent three weeks on Texas soil.

---

[28]Manuel says he reached Santa Rosa one day before the arrival of Father Peñasco. From Basán's letter we gather that Peñasco arrived there on May 3.

It will be remembered that on February 9 Father Francisco Peñasco de Lozano accompanied Father Larios to Saltillo. From there he went to Guadalajara in order to present the official reports to the commissary general of the Franciscans.[29] Brother Manuel reached Santa Rosa on May 2 and on the following day Father Peñasco arrived. Two months later, on July 7, while still at Santa Rosa, he addressed to the commissary general the valuable letter in which he relates, incidentally, the journey he made across the Rio Grande into Texas.[30] Not being a diary, the letter unfortunately does not indicate the time consumed, the distances covered, the direction taken, and the places visited on this journey. All we know for certain is that Peñasco departed from Santa Rosa on May 8 and was back by July 7, that he crossed the Rio Grande and entered Texas, that he treated with and won over the Indians, and that some of these Indians belonged to the Tejas tribe.

One of the Indian tribes which, like the Boboles and Guyqueehales, had failed to return to Santa Rosa at the stipulated time was the Manosprietas. Perhaps it was the success of Brother Manuel, who had just returned with more than eight hundred Indians, that prompted Father Peñasco to go in search of the Manosprietas. After telling the commissary general how the missionaries were compelled to visit the Indians in the mountains and how they had "to go after them fifty and seventy leagues, suffering countless hardships," Peñasco continues: "Having arrived at this settlement,[31] I set out from there on the 8th of May in search of a tribe called the Manosprietas. I found them four leagues on the other bank of the Río del Norte [Rio Grande] and distant from the settlement about fifty leagues."[32] The Manosprietas welcomed him, regaled him with buffalo meat, and promised to set out for Santa Rosa in eight days. They also told him of another tribe, the Giorna, who lived eight leagues farther on. To these Peñasco sent Indian envoys, who should invite the Giorna to come and see him. "They told the envoys," he relates, "that they did not wish to go anywhere, because they were well off in this country, where food and necessary sustenance were not lacking to them." But the friar was not to be put off so easily. He sent another envoy, instructing him to assure the Giorna that it was not his purpose to take them from their country, but only to free them from their errors and to tell them about the true God. If what he said should please them, they could accept it. They would

[29]Juan Larios to the commissary general, Saltillo, Mar. 2, 1674, ASFG 1:111–13.

[30]Francisco Peñasco de Lozano to the commissary general, Santa Rosa de María y Valle de la Concepción, July 7, 1674, ASFG 1:126–28. From this letter we gather the details of Peñasco's journey.

[31]I.e., Santa Rosa, where he wrote the letter.

[32]Accordingly, he covered forty-six leagues before reaching the Rio Grande. The fact, gathered from another source (see n. 34), that he brought Tejas Indians back with him, seems to show that after leaving santa Rosa he followed a more easterly route and penetrated into eastern Texas, the home of the Tejas.

not be forced, however, nor would anyone molest them. "To the second envoy they listened with greater concern," Peñasco writes. "Handing over to him [the envoy] a boy of the Quezale Indians, who was a captive, they said that after two days they would come to see me."

The Giorna kept their promise. "Those of the *ranchería*. where I was staying," the missionary writes, "went out to receive them, all daubed with paint. They performed a dance for them, which is a sign of peace; and they exchanged bows and arrows for greater security of peace." On the following day, with the aid of an interpreter, Peñasco spoke to the Giorna Indians about God and told them about the king of Spain. He exhorted them to form settlements and to live in peace and friendship with their neighbors. Finally he assured them that the missionaries, to quote from his letter, "were sent by God and by his majesty in order to protect them against the Spaniards[33] and to instruct them in our holy Catholic faith."

"I got on so well with them," Peñasco continues, "that I won over more than three hundred of them, while seventy others remained with some sick in order that, when these were restored to health, they might come to the settlement, where we have at distances of two, three, five, and seven leagues more than three thousand and two hundred Indians." With this summary statement, he concludes the account of his journey. Whether the above-mentioned seventy Indians ever came to Santa Rosa is not known. The other three hundred of the Giorna, however, together with the Manosprietas accompanied Father Peñasco on his return to the Río de las Sabinas where they doubtless received a cordial welcome from Father Larios and the Indians settled there. It is important to add that among the Indians whom Peñasco met on this occasion and took with him to Santa Rosa were some of the Tejas tribe.[34] Consequently, more than a decade before Father Damián Massanet began his activity in Coahuila and entered Texas, Father Peñasco established contact with and achieved the conversion of some Tejas—Indians who were to play so prominent a role fifteen years later in the temporary occupation of eastern Texas.

---

[33]Here Peñasco adds parenthetically: "for whom they have a notable abhorrence on account of the knowledge they have of the tyrannies they [the Spaniards] practice on those in the country beyond." This is a frank statement and largely true to fact. Past abuses practiced on the Indians, in defiance of protecting laws of Spain, by unscrupulous individuals and petty government officials was one of the obstacles that hampered the work of Father Larios and his fellow missionaries in northern Coahuila at this time.

[34]This fact, not stated in Peñasco's letter, we gather from the testimony officially rendered sixteen years later at Saltillo. The occasion for this testimony was the investigation, conducted by the *alcalde mayor* of Saltillo, incidental to the controversy that arose between the Franciscan Province of Jalisco and the Franciscan Missionary College of Querétaro over Father Massanet's founding of Mission Santiago, in Coahuila, one league distant from the Jalisco Mission Caldera, some of whose Indian converts Massanet took for the new mission.

The efforts of Brother Manuel and Father Peñasco were eminently successful. By July, as stated in Peñasco's letter, more than three thousand Indians were again assembled on the lands adjoining the Río de las Sabinas. Thanks to the zeal of Captain Francisco Barbarigo and Brother Francisco Basán, the missionaries at Santa Rosa had an adobe chapel and sacristy for divine services and a large hut for their habitation, all sufficiently equipped to satisfy present needs. Four *fanegas* of corn were planted and a supply of vegetables was available. However promising the outlook, Larios and his fellow missionaries were not so sanguine as to expect their path of duty would be free from all difficulties and obstacles. To humor the petulant children of the forest and keep them in the settlements, to preserve peace and harmony among them, to travel on foot from settlement to settlement, to visit the Indians in their hovels and to witness their depraved ways, to acquire a working knowledge of their languages, to imbue their carnal minds with Christian truths and principles, to wean them from their barbarous customs and habits and win them over to clean and orderly living, to provide food and clothing for them, to teach them, and especially to induce them to cultivate the land, to protect their rights and interests against selfish and unscrupulous whites—these were tasks that involved many hardships and problems.

Brother Basán offers a vivid description of conditions as they obtained in the new mission during the spring of 1674. He tells us how disheartened the friars were when Father Peñasco returned from the South and reported that those in authority manifested little interest in the Coahuila project. "They felt this very keenly," he writes, "and it greatly disheartened them, since they have so many souls to care for and suffer want even unto hunger and nakedness. Their habits are very ragged from traveling. Since in their poverty they lack the mules to carry sufficient supplies, there is no occasion to help them often. Only when they sent for it with two mules, were two loads of wheat and ground corn and a string of sausage brought to them. This is all the luxury they possess. . . . At present they have prickly pears in abundance. This will last till November. But after that there will be no more. If they have snow and the weather is very cold, it will be fish without end. But one can not eat fried fish every day. We have seen and caught some delicious fish; they are large and palatable. If elsewhere they are good because fire, fat, and spices are available, there they are prepared merely on live coals. The number of people is large and they live in small groups. In the settlement alone, within a radius of two and three and four leagues, there are more than three thousand persons."[35] And yet, despite hardships, and privations, the friars would make merry over their lot. With a fine touch of humor Father Peñasco says of Brother Basán

[35]Francisco Basán to the commissary general, Saltillo, July 19, 1674, ASFG 1:129–34.

and the effects of his two months' sojourn at Santa Rosa: "He arrived very stout, but he left wearing, as could be seen, much more clothes than is permitted us. As to clothes," he adds in the same strain, "I judge we shall soon be wearing buffalo and deer skins. But all this is as welcome to us as the roses in June."[36]

What made the lot of Larios and his companions doubly hard was the seeming indifference on the part of those who by virtue of their office controlled the means that would lighten the labors and further the cause of the missionaries. The letters of Brothers Manuel and Basán reveal in unmistakable terms that the journey of Father Peñasco to Guadalajara had been in vain. "On the same day," writes Manuel, "Father Francisco Peñasco arrived [at Santa Rosa], in whom and with whom we were expecting Your Reverence would favor us in some way as our father and shepherd. But he returned disconsolate; wherefore . . . I had to depart for Saltillo in order to seek aid."[37] Under date of May 28, 1674, Basán warned the commissary general against accepting the information given him by those who did not know what they were talking about, adding rather caustically that it was one thing to see the conditions in northern Coahuila and another to talk about them. Some six weeks later, on July 19, Basán writes that the commissary general would not even listen to Peñasco's request for assistance.[38] On the other hand, it should be noted that under date of March 12, 1674, as we learn from Larios himself, the commissary general promised him additional missionaries, although it does not seem that Fathers Esteban Martínez and Dionisio de San Buenaventura, apparently the two appointees, came to Santa Rosa before the following August, shortly after the mission had been robbed and ruined.[39]

This indifference and inactivity of the Franciscan Superiors was in large measure due to the controversy that occupied the attention of the civil authorities concerning the form of government to be organized in Coahuila. Until this controversy was definitely settled and government aid thereby assured, the Franciscan authorities naturally withheld the generous and whole-hearted support they would have otherwise accorded the Coahuila project. On May 15, 1674, the *Real Audiencia* at Guadalajara definitely appointed Antonio de Balcárcel *alcalde mayor* of the Province of Coahuila for a period of five years, during which time according to the contract Balcárcel was to explore and

---

[36]Francisco Peñasco to the commissary general, Santa Rosa de María y Valle de la Concepción, July 7, 1674, ASFG 1:126–28.

[37]Manuel de la Cruz to the commissary general, Saltillo, May 29, 1674, ASFG 1:118–25.

[38]Francisco Basán to the commissary general, Saltillo, May 28, 1674, and same to same, Saltillo, July 19, 1674, ASFG 1:114–17, 129–34.

[39]Juan Larios to the minister provincial, San José de Parral, Sept. 15, 1674, and Dionisio de San Buenaventura to the commissary general, Saltillo, Oct. 31, 1674, ASFG 1:135–40, 141–42.

colonize the province at his own expense. There were those, however, who strenuously opposed the appointment and project of Balcárcel, declaring it would develop into another case of exploitation and thus prove detrimental to the pacification of the Indians. Most prominent among these opponents, even after the official appointment of Balcárcel, were Francisco de Elizondo and Agustín de Echevers, both public officials in Saltillo.[40]

Meanwhile the Indians of northern Coahuila had again become unruly and in July, during the temporary absence of the missionaries, had robbed the sacristy at Santa Rosa and burned most of the mission buildings. Evidently, to prevent this local disturbance from developing into a general rebellion, it would be necessary for the government to make a display of military force. Whatever the attitude of the friars toward military force may have been, it is significant that Father Larios, who had sided with the opponents of Balcárcel[41] and as late as October 15, 1674, declared that no presidio was necessary in Coahuila, changed his mind concerning the presidio. In his lengthy report of December 30, 1674, he wrote that a presidio of at least a hundred men was necessary to protect the convert Indians and to keep in check the wild tribes farther north. Moreover, he had his misgivings over the small force that Balcárcel commanded, "because," he writes, "although there is no need for conquest, it is necessary for the Indians to recognize that his majesty and his ministers have the forces needed to chastise the rebels."[42]

In September 1674 the controversy between Balcárcel and his opponents was definitely settled. Recognized now as *alcalde mayor* of Coahuila, Balcárcel began his march northward, stopping at intervals to interview the Indians and to found settlements.[43] On December 8, he reorganized the settlement of Nuevo Almadén and named it Nuestra Señora de Guadalupe. In this place, the present city of Monclova, he and the missionaries established their headquarters. For the Indians who resided in the neighborhood and for those whom the friars meanwhile assembled from the North, Balcárcel, on April 26, 1675, founded the town of San Miguel de Luna and appointed a Bobole Indian, Lázaro Agustín, its first governor.[44]

---

[40]Portillo, *Apuntes*, 45–53.

[41]Juan Larios to the commissary general, Patos, Jan. 15, 1675, ASFG 1:150–51. In this letter Larios commends the generosity of Echevers and refers to the new hardships and persecutions which the *entrada* of Balcárcel have created for the missionaries.

[42]Juan Larios to the commissary general, Guadalupe, Dec. 30, 1674, ASFG 1:141–49.

[43]On the way northward he founded San Pedro y San Pablo de Anaelo, about twenty leagues from Saltillo, Santa Isabel, ten leagues farther up, and finally Nuestra Señora de Guadalupe, thirteen leagues north of Santa Isabel. Three Franciscans took part in the founding of these places—Fathers Larios and Dionisio de San Buenaventura and Brother Manuel de la Cruz. See Portillo, *Apuntes*, 53–68.

[44]Portillo, *Apuntes*, 68–69, 98–102.

As early as December 30, 1674, Father Larios contemplated entering "in the beginning of February, the land beyond the Río del Norte which is eighty leagues distant from this town" [of Guadalupe]. Informing the commissary general of this plan, Larios says that he would take another friar with him and would send a third friar[45] to the Catujanes. The purpose he had in mind was "to see the Cacique Don Esteban who was there with all his people [notably the Guyquechales] and who told me that he would wait there for me." In this way Larios expected "also to prepare the way for the entry of the *alcalde mayor,*" who was to undertake an expedition northward "to see and explore the land and to count the Indians."[46] It is not known whether the missionaries made these advance journeys.[47] However, if Balcárcel, who seems not to have been in a hurry to penetrate farther north and eventually entrusted the enterprise to his lieutenant, set his face against these advance movements of the missionaries, we can understand why Larios begins his letter of January 15, 1675, with the statement that "with the entry of the *Alcalde Mayor,* Don Antonio Balcárcel, in the Province of Coahuila our hardships and persecutions have increased."[48] This apparent indifference of Balcárcel in a matter that mainly interested the friars may have been one of the causes of misunderstanding between them. In view of what occurred earlier and elsewhere in Mexico, Larios would have been justified in suspecting that Balcárcel's chief aim was the material exploitation of Coahuila with a minimum of attention to the spiritual phase of the conquest. On the other hand, it should be remembered that, as Larios himself admitted, the military force under Balcárcel's command was not sufficient for extensive activities in a land where formidable Indian tribes infested the forests and mountain passes. Until he was reasonably certain that the majority of these tribes were willing to live in peace with the Spaniards, Balcárcel was justified in limiting his activities to the new town of Guadalupe and its vicinity.

It was not until April 1675, shortly after founding the Indian town of San Miguel de Luna, that Balcárcel fitted out the expedition which for the third time within a twelvemonth brought the Spaniards of Mexico across the Rio Grande into Texas.[49] As stated in the official report of the expedition,[50] the

---

[45]This third friar was undoubtedly Brother Manuel, who with Father Dionisio de San Buenaventura had already been active among the Catujanes.

[46]Juan Larios to the commissary general, Guadalupe, Dec. 30, 1674, ASFG 1:141–49.

[47]Possibly, Brother Manuel went to the Catujanes, as planned, and for this reason did not accompany Bosque on the expedition four months later.

[48]Juan Larios to the commissary general, Patos, Jan. 15, 1675, ASFG 1:150–51.

[49]Portillo, *Apuntes,* 104–06.

[50]This report or diary is in Herbert E. Bolton, trans. and ed., *Spanish Exploration in the Southwest, 1542–1706,* Original Narratives of Early American History Vol. 18 (New York, 1925), 283–309,. For the Spanish text see Portillo, *Apuntes,* 106–30. After comparing the translation with Portillo's text, I followed

Manosprietas and other tribes of the Rio Grande region had asked that missions and towns be established in their country. Evidently, they presented their petition through Father Larios and the missionaries, who in turn finally prevailed on the *alcalde mayor* to explore the Rio Grande region and negotiate with the Indians. Balcárcel did not conduct the expedition personally, but entrusted its military phase to his lieutenant, Fernando del Bosque, and detailed ten soldiers to accompany him in addition to the Indian governor of San Miguel de Luna and twenty-one Bobole Indians. Two missionaries were to look after the spiritual affairs of the expedition, Fathers Larios and Dionisio de San Buenaventura, the former as commissary missionary and the latter as chaplain. As stated in the official report of the expedition, its purpose was "to reconnoiter the nations of the following of Don Esteban Gueiquesale, who live toward the Sierra Dacate and in its vicinity, and the others of their district and neighborhood"[51] and to see whether "they wish to settle in pueblos and be Christians, with religious to catechize and instruct them."[52]

On Tuesday, April 30, 1675, the expedition set out from Guadalupe and proceeded almost due north toward the Rio Grande. Practically every day the friars were given opportunity to impart religious instruction to the Indians who accompanied them or whom they met on the way. Wherever a halt was made, Bosque had a wooden cross erected and took formal possession of the region in the name of the Spanish king. On May 7, after covering about forty-six leagues, they reached San Ildefonso, where a year before Larios and his companions had tarried with the Indians and welcomed Captain Elizondo. The "ruins of two grass huts, already almost rotten," which Bosque found at San Ildefonso, were "perhaps the remains of the mission settlement established in the previous year by Father Larios."[53] The fact that the diary makes no mention of the expedition having come to Santa Rosa shows that from Guadalupe to San Ildefonso the expedition proceeded directly north. Bosque had been with Captain Elizondo the year before and consequently knew the shorter route to the Rio Grande. Furthermore, it is significant that, after crossing the Rio Grande, the expedition met only friendly Indians. This seems to indicate that, beyond the river, they traversed practically the same region which Brother Manuel had visited twelve months before. In fact, on one occasion the Indians they met said expressly that they were waiting for the return of the friars.

---

it verbatim.

[51]The reader will recall that it was this that Larios had in mind four months before, when he spoke of entering the Rio Grande region in February.

[52]"Diary of Fernando del Bosque, 1675," in Bolton, *Spanish Exploration*, 307.

[53]Ibid., 294, n.3.

On Saturday, May 11, after traveling nineteen leagues since their departure from San Ildefonso, the expedition "arrived at a very copious and very wide river, with a current more than four hundred *varas* across, which the Indians said was called Río del Norte."[54] They passed up the bank of the stream in search of a place where they could ford it. Not finding such a place, they crossed "at a place where the river forms three branches." The crossing was made very probably a little below Eagle Pass in Maverick County, Texas. Naming the river Río de San Buenaventura, Bosque continued northward about four leagues and came to "an arroyo between hills." Here they met fifty-four Yorica and Jeapa Indians. These volunteered to conduct the expedition to the Dacate mountains which Bosque was instructed to visit. After marching about three leagues farther, they met the chiefs of the Bibit and the Jume Indians, numbering more than a hundred persons. The former chief informed the Spaniards that he and some of his people had been baptized in Saltillo; that the rest of his people would also have come to Saltillo to receive baptism, if the distance were not so great and an epidemic of smallpox had not reduced them in number. In this same place, which Bosque named San Vicente, the expedition met six heathen Indians of four different tribes, all subject to Don Esteban, captain of the Guyquechales, whom Larios was doubtless hoping to meet. These Indians assured Bosque that they were "waiting to be Christians and to live under instruction in the Christian doctrine, and to settle in a pueblo."

After marching four leagues, presumably in a more northwesterly direction,[55] they came to a river called Ona which, the Indians said, meant salty.[56] "This place," the diary records, "has many groves of oak and mesquite; there are many buffalo; the country has fine pastures; and there are many fish in the river which I found unoccupied and uninhabited." Hearing of the arrival of the Spaniards, four chiefs came with their people to see them. All told, there were eleven hundred and seventy-two Indians. None had so far been baptized. In fact, as the chiefs told Bosque, they had never seen Spaniards. As to becoming Christians and living in towns, they asked this on behalf of their women and the young members of their tribes; but they themselves on account of their advanced years would prefer to remain heathen. We can imagine what the missionaries thought and felt at this naive suggestion.

---

[54]That is to say, the Indians assured them that this was the river which the Spaniards in Mexico knew as the Río del Norte.

[55]Having crossed the Rio Grande and traveled four leagues northward, the expedition, in order to avoid the arid and barren wastes of what is today eastern Kinney County, continued in a more northwesterly direction and for a time kept close to the Rio Grande.

[56]Very probably this is one of the creeks between Eagle Pass and Del Rio. The expedition was still east of Del Rio.

Bosque took formal possession of the place and named it San Isidro. Very probably because the Indians were so numerous at this place,[57] it was proposed to establish them here in a settlement. To this the chiefs agreed; whereupon, to quote the diary, "their people approached, and both men and women devotedly kissed the sleeves of the habits of the Fathers . . . Juan Larios and . . . Dionisio de San Buenaventura; and they asked permission to give them as alms something of what they possessed, as a mark of gratitude to God for having opened to them the way to the truth. And at once they began throwing things upon the ground, some a piece of tallow, others hides or skins of animals, of the kind with which they clothe themselves or cover themselves, and in which they Sleep."

On the following day, Thursday, May 16, "was erected in said post [of San Isidro] a portable altar"[58] and "prepared to say Mass; and at a signal made with a small bell the people came to hear it." Larios himself celebrated the August Mysteries.[59] After Holy Mass the Indians approached the missionaries and asked to be baptized. Larios explained to them, however, "that he could not baptize them until they knew their prayers";[60] but "to console them he baptized fifty-five infants,[61] the Spaniards acting as their godfathers." It would he interesting to know for certain where these ceremonies of Holy Mass and baptism were enacted. All that can be gleaned from the record, however, is a probability that they took place some six leagues or about a day's travel east of Del Rio, either in Kinney or in Valverde counties. It does not seem that up till now the expedition had left the Rio Grande to any considerable distance. They were heading for the Dacate mountains which, as previously noted,[62] we take to have very probably been the hills along what is known today as Devils River.

---

[57]If the Indians whom he met since crossing the Rio Grande joined his company, Bosque was now surrounded by more than thirteen hundred Indians.

[58]A "portable altar," sometimes called altar stone, is a stone slab which contains a small repository with relics of Saints. Where this slab does not constitute the entire table or *mesa* of the altar, the rubrics require that it be large enough to hold during Mass the Sacred Species of bread and wine, for which reason it is placed in the center of the table. This stone slab with its relics is to remind the faithful of the fact that in the beginning of Christianity and during the first centuries of bloody persecutions Holy Mass was celebrated in the catacombs and on the tombs of the martyrs.

[59]As far as I know, this is the earliest record of Holy Mass having been celebrated within what is today the State of Texas.

[60]That is, until they were sufficiently instructed in the tenets of Christianity and understood what obligations they contracted by baptism.

[61]The Catholic Church does not allow adults to be baptized without previous instruction in Catholic doctrine and discipline. It is different, however, with infants where the parents are Catholics and give assurance that the children will receive a Catholic education. Only in danger of death may baptism be conferred without previous instruction on adults, though even in this case they must have in some way previously expressed a desire for baptism.

[62]See n.24.

For obvious reasons also the following incident is worth recording. At San Isidro a Guyquechale Indian came and presented Bosque with a Spanish boy about twelve years old. He had "a black streak on his face running from the forehead to the nose, and two on the cheeks, one on each, like o's, and many rows of them on the left arm and one on the right." From the Indian it was learned that this boy had been captured near Parral, in Mexico, with two other Spanish children, a boy and a girl. The three were carried off to Texas, where this boy was given to the Cabesas Indians who, "although they loved him like a brother," were now eager to return him to the Spaniards "as a sign of friendship." The two other children, the Indian related, had been killed by their captors.

Having spent two days at San Isidro, the expedition continued northward eight leagues and reached a "small river which they said was called Dacate." This, we take it, was Devil's River. Though no mention of it is made in the diary, it is plain that Bosque was now where Brother Manuel had been a year before.[63] The chief of the Geniocane Indians, who visited the Spaniards at this place, related "that he was awaiting the religious with his people at another place farther on, that they might give them Christian instruction and catechize them in it." Evidently, Manuel had previously met these Indians and promised them that he would return and instruct them. It is a pity that Brother Manuel was not selected to accompany the Bosque expedition and that neither of the missionaries now with Bosque kept a diary.

On Monday, May 20, the expedition resumed the journey. After traveling several leagues, they were met by the Geniocanes who conducted them to their *ranchería,* which was situated "in an arroyo between some hills," about eight leagues north of where they reached and presumably crossed Devils River. On the following day, an altar having been erected, Father Dionisio celebrated Holy Mass; whereupon the Indians received religious instruction from the missionaries. As previously at San Isidro, so here at San Jorge, Father Larios took official possession of the place. The Geniocanes numbered one hundred and seventy-eight persons, sixty-five of whom were adults.

Several days were spent at San Jorge. During this time, Bosque and the friars treated with the Indians. On account of the distance to Guadalupe and the hostility of neighboring tribes, it was decided to form San Jorge into a settlement for the Geniocanes and other Indians who had come to see the Spaniards. On May 25 the expedition again set out and, after traveling

---

[63]It is important to recall here that Brother Manuel, after crossing the Rio Grande, traveled northward three days (probably some eighteen leagues) and then reached "a mountain range which the Indians call Dacate." This seems to show that Manuel crossed the river farther up than where the expedition of Bosque crossed it. Apparently, Manuel crossed at a point due south of San Isidro.

northward fourteen leagues, they "arrived at a small arroyo with heavy timber, between some knolls and hills." Naming this place San Pablo, Bosque instructed the four chiefs who had accompanied the Spaniards from San Isidro and who belonged to the following of Don Esteban, "to remain quiet in their country and live good lives, without killing each other, and to join with the other followers of their great chief. On hearing this they said they could comply, and remained awaiting a religious who should go to instruct them until they should settle in a pueblo."

Since crossing the Rio Grande, the expedition had traveled about forty-one leagues, made six halts, and named the following places: San Gregorio, San Vicente, San Isidro, San Bernardino, San Jorge, and San Pablo. At two of these places, San Isidro and San Jorge, the Indians were established in settlements and told to remain there and await the coming of the missionaries. From this and from Bosque's subsequent recommendations it is plain that the south-central reaches of present Texas were to become part of Coahuila under the jurisdiction of Balcárcel and that missions were to be established there in charge of the Franciscans.

Leaving San Pablo "to return to the city of Guadalupe," on May 29 the expedition "arrived at another place" on the Rio Grande. Consequently, not returning by way of San Isidro, they reached the river "evidently higher up than the place where it was crossed before," as Bolton points out.[64] If this river was the Rio Grande, it is significant that the diary fails to say a crossing was effected at the place where it was reached. Besides, the expedition reached it after less than two days' travel. This would seem to indicate that the river which Bosque took to be the Rio Grande was really the Pecos; that, without crossing it, they marched twenty leagues down the east bank of the Pecos[65] and thus finally came to "a river which they said was called the Nueces," but which in reality was the Rio Grande. On June 5 they continued in a southerly direction and a week later, having covered fifty leagues, they arrived in Guadalupe. The Indians they met during this week of travel south of the Rio Grande numbered more than eight hundred persons and belonged to such tribes, long known to the Spaniards, as the Bacoras, Guyquechales, Manosprietas, and Contotores.

Before closing his diary or report of the expedition and submitting it to the *alcalde mayor*, Antonio de Balcárcel, Bosque summarized what he had learned concerning the Indians and their lands and offered a number of

---

[64]"Diary of Fernando del Bosque," in Bolton, *Spanish Exploration*, 305, n.1.

[65]Bosque writes that after leaving the river they "traveled about twenty leagues to the west." This cannot be correct. Bosque evidently meant to say that they traveled south, not west. This may be an error of the copyist, if the diary as published is a copy of the original.

recommendations for the proposed establishment of the Indians in organized settlements. "To maintain these nations under instruction in Christian doctrine," he suggested that the entire region, including what is today south-central Texas, be divided into three distinct and mutually independent districts. Each district was to have at least four missionaries and these were to confine their activity to the Indians of their respective district. This recommendation was made in view of the fact that the Indians, as Bosque learned, "do not wish to have those of one nation attend to others, because they are of different languages, the people numerous, and their homes far apart." In this way it would be possible to convert and civilize the Indians of the north, presuming that the government would furnish "seed grain, oxen, and some families of Tlaxcalteco Indians" for the new missions and settlements.

Had conditions in Coahuila been more favorable at this time and during the ten years following, Balcárcel's project would have been carried out and central Texas made the scene of Spain's first attempt at occupation in the Lone Star State. But this was not to be. Disorders within Coahuila, disputes with Nuevo León, and new outbreaks of hostility among the disappointed Indians delayed action. A decade later, as a direct result of Jolliet's and of La Salle's exploration of the Mississippi River, France encroached upon Spain's west-Mississippi claim, thereby necessarily fixing Spain's attention on eastern Texas and furnishing the occasion for its occupation by Alonso de León.

In 1683 the Franciscan Missionary College of Santa Cruz of Querétaro was founded for the training of such friars as desired to devote themselves to the conversion of the Indians in the distant missions. A few years later a member of this college was stationed as missionary at San Bernardino de la Caldera. This was none other than the well-known Father Damián Massanet. Mission de la Caldera, as it was called, was one of the four principal missions of Coahuila, erected and supported since 1675 by the Franciscan Province of Jalisco. It was the easternmost of the Coahuila missions and lay on the border of Nuevo León. Among its Indian converts were some Tejas, doubtless those who had come with Father Peñasco in 1674. Again, it was an Indian of this mission who discovered and told Father Massanet of the presence of a Frenchman in the country beyond the Rio Grande. Being interested in this report, Massanet imparted it to Captain Alonso de León who had already entered Texas in search of the French and in 1687 had been appointed governor of Coahuila. With the new governor's connivance, but without the knowledge and approval of the Province of Jalisco, Massanet took some Christians Indians from Mission de la Caldera and with them founded at a distance of one league the Mission of Santiago.[66] There is reason to believe that, when founding this mission, Massanet had in mind the expedition which he and Alonso de León soon after made to Texas for the purpose of locating the French. At all events, it is interesting to note how Massanet, a Querétaro Franciscan in charge of a Jalisco mission, forms the link connecting the occupation of eastern Texas, achieved by Alonso de León, with the earlier *entradas* of three Jalisco friars—Manuel de la Cruz, Peñasco de Lozano, and Larios—who with Fernando del Bosque may on this account be regarded as the forerunners of Captain De León's expedition to Texas.

[66]This unauthorized procedure of Massanet was resented by the Province of Jalisco and made the subject of an official investigation, conducted by the *alcalde mayor* of Saltillo. See "Investigación sobre la erección de la Misión de Santiago," 666–734. The first and the last pages of this document are missing. See also "Letter of Fray Damián Massanet to Don Carlos de Sigüenza, 1690," in Bolton, *Spanish Exploration*, 354–56. In this letter Massanet says nothing about the founding of Mission de Santiago.

THE SIX FLAGS OF TEXAS

Carlos E. Castañeda*

FOREWORD

The following address, entitled "The Six Flags of Texas," was delivered by Dr. Carlos E. Castañeda, the Director and Librarian of the García Latin-American Library of the University of Texas. The occasion was the observance of Columbus Day, October 12, 1932, by the San Antonio Knights of Columbus Fourth Degree Assembly. These commemorative exercises took place at San José Mission, where a Solemn High Pontifical Field Mass was celebrated by His Excellency, Most Reverend Albert J. Daeger, O.F.M., D.D., late Archbishop of Santa Fe. Six permanent flagstaffs, each marked with a small bronze tablet, had previously been erected near the site of the new Franciscan monastery. The impressive ceremony of the various flag raisings was conducted by officers and soldiers attached to Fort Sam Houston. As each banner was unfurled, the speaker of the occasion summarized the history of that particular epoch.

The Chairman of the Texas Knights of Columbus Historical Commission wishes to express his gratitude and that of his associates to the Fourth Degree Assembly of San Antonio for making this publication and its distribution possible as a souvenir of the memorable historical event. He is also very much indebted to Dr. Carlos E. Castañeda, for the kind permission, privilege and courtesy extended by him to the publisher of the *Preliminary Studies of the Texas Catholic Historical Society* for this excellent contribution, giving an introductory survey of these great epochs of Texas history.

Paul J. Foik C.S.C.
Chairman of the Commission and President of the Society

---

*Vol. 2, No. 4, appeared in January 1933.

The Six Flags of Texas

Extending from the turbid waters of the Rio Grande almost to the Mississippi, and from Oklahoma to the Gulf of Mexico lies a vast expanse of territory, rich in fertile fields, large and bountiful rivers, broad plains, rolling hills, waving forests, and inviting harbors. Early in the sixteenth century, countless herds of buffalo roamed the prairies, wild game abounded everywhere, and thousands of native Americans lived in primitive savagery in these happy hunting grounds. Today, four hundred years later, this same territory has become the present state of Texas, first in size in the United States of America and fifth in population. Over its industrious citizens waves the glorious Stars and Stripes, symbol of liberty and peace.

Through the centuries there was waged, upon this privileged region on which nature lavished its bountiful gifts, where clear skies, bright sunshine, and gentle breezes seem to caress all living things and breed a spirit of unconquerable freedom, a gigantic struggle for the ultimate redemption of this great natural empire. In the struggle six mighty nations contested for supremacy. As the relentless hand of destiny moved ever forward the province finally came to form the largest, the richest, and the fairest state in the greatest democracy of our day.

Let us roll back the centuries and contemplate for a moment the mighty struggle that then took place. At that time we would see how western civilization was first brought to this vast garden spot welcoming man for his own benefit to transform its boundless resources into productivity and wealth. Soon would we behold how step by step the wilderness was reduced and the savages were led to a knowledge of God. Christian civilization gradually advanced, became firmly established and finally flourished throughout the land.

In the sixteenth century the mythical city of the Gran Quivira and the famed Seven Cities of Cíbola were thought to be located within the bosom of this great domain. Rumors of their richness and splendor spread irresistibly until they reached the mighty city of the Montezumas, Spain's seat of power in North America. The news and reports of fabulous wealth aroused the cupidity of the conquistadors and whetted their appetites for new adventures. Alvar Núñez Cabeza de Vaca, one of the four sole survivors of the ill-fated Narváez expedition wrecked upon the gulf coast, was the first European to behold the natural wonders of Texas soil, to traverse its broad plains, and to be the recipient of the spontaneous hospitality of its natives. Years before, other of his countrymen, under the leadership of Pineda had sailed along the coast from Florida to Tampico and had drawn up in 1519 the first map of the

Texas coast. After untold hardships Cabeza de Vaca, this man of iron, made his way to Culiacán on the far distant Pacific coast from where he went to Mexico City, carrying news of the country visited in his wanderings. Although he did not return to Texas as he had wished, he lived to carry the flag of Spain to remote parts of South America. This characteristic figure of the Spanish conquistador, like a herald announcing the beginning of a new era, appeared upon the stage of history as the curtain rose on the great drama, and then passed on.

Soon after the news of the mythical kingdoms had reached Mexico, other Europeans went forth in quest of them and again set foot upon Texas soil. The unfortunate Coronado expedition, which came to conquer the Gran Quivira as if going on a festive march, was sadly disillusioned and suffered the pains of the damned before its decimated survivors found their way out of the broad plains of West Texas in the Llano Estacado. Ambitious historians of neighboring states have taken the foot-sore and worn-out men of Coronado as far afield as present day Kansas, Oklahoma, and eastern New Mexico, but more recent investigations tend to confirm the opinion that Coronado and his men never left the confines of the state. But it seems that wise Providence defeated the purpose of these unscrupulous and greedy adventurers who, though accompanied by missionaries, at heart were not sincerely interested in the only justifiable cause for the subjugation of the natives: their conversion to Christianity. Texas was to wait for several years before a more serious attempt to occupy its rich lands was made.

New Mexico was formally occupied towards the close of the sixteenth century. Through its settlers new rumors concerning the Great Kingdom of the Tejas and the wealth of their province reached viceregal officials. Reports of the desire of this people to become Christians sounded as a trumpet call upon the pious ears of the worthy sons of Saint Francis in New Spain. Gradually the reports became more frequent, and at last there came news of the most singular incident in the history of missionary endeavor in the New World.

One day there came a delegation of Tejas and Jumano Indians to Spanish officials to ask that missionaries be sent amongst their people to teach and baptize them. When inquiry was made as to what had prompted them to make this petition, as to how a desire for instruction in the Christian faith had been developed, the Indians told a simple story. A lady in blue, the now famous María of Agreda, her face beaming with kindness and love as the sparkling stars of the firmament, had frequently come to them on the wings of the air to instruct them. It was she who had commanded them to go to the frontier Spanish settlements to ask for missionaries to teach all their people.

This portentous event fired the zeal of the Franciscans with an unquenchable desire to carry to this people the comforts of religion. Had not God made patent his desire? They were not to rest until the command of the Master was carried out. The woman in blue thus presaged the dawn of a new era for the Tejas Indians and was to be the determining force in the ultimate permanent occupation of this vast and immensely rich empire marked in this singular way as a chosen field for evangelization. Love of glory, of adventure, of gain, and of advantage, and other worldly passions were not sufficient. It was the simple and loving faith of the Franciscan missionaries, who, utilizing these baser motives in their noble enterprise, were at last to be responsible for the founding of the first missions in East Texas, almost upon the banks of the mighty monarch of North American rivers, within sight of the farthest French outpost in Louisiana. As a last resort, despairing of the apathy of Spanish officials, they were to recur to an unfailing source of action, the fear of foreign aggression.

We come, therefore, in the course of this rapid survey of the history of Texas, in which the endless procession of time is made to pass before our eyes like an unfolding panorama, to the first and only actual occupation of Texas soil by the French. It was the adventurous La Salle, whether by design or accident, who raised the flag of France on Matagorda Bay in 1685, while in search of the mouth of the Mississippi. In vain did he try to reach either the frontier settlements of New Spain or the mouth of the great river. Bravely he struggled against adversity, only to find an inglorious death at the hands of his own men. The leader dead, the little colony on Garcitas Creek fell an easy prey to Indian savagery. Four years later De León was to discover the charred remains of the ill-starred settlement and one of his men, moved by the pathetic figure of a half buried woman, was to write the first elegy composed on Texas soil. No serious effort was made by France to reoccupy Texas. In later years the rivalry of the two powerful pioneers was to be confined to disputes over the boundary and illicit trade. Except for a brief incursion in 1719, when the French drove the Spaniards out of East Texas, the French flag was not again to wave over the state. It was to this brief incursion, however, that we owe the establishment of this mission of San José by the saintly Margil, who, choosing this delightful spot on the banks of the San Antonio River, laid the foundations for the mission that was to become the queen of Texas missions. The Franciscans have now returned after an absence of more than a century to labor anew in Texas.

The brief and tragic episode of La Salle's futile attempt to establish a settlement in Texas marks the close of the prologue in the great drama. Spain was henceforth to occupy Texas and to hold it in order to prevent other nations from repeating the attempt of the French. As a result of this determination the missionaries, whose zeal and ardent desire to convert the natives had only been inflamed by the prolonged delay, were to have their opportunity at last.

With incredible rapidity two missions were established in East Texas within two years after the discovery of La Salle's colony. But the course of Christianization was to be rudely interrupted in 1693 and the missionaries were to be forced to abandon their beloved neophytes. Again there was a lull in Texas colonization. Again the Indians were left undisturbed by Europeans for a time. Without the paternal care of the missionaries, they soon abandoned the newly cultivated fields, forgot the lessons learned, and reverted to absolute savagery.

It was the French who again moved the Spanish authorities to occupy Texas. In 1714 a certain St. Denis, accompanied by a few companions, unexpectedly appeared on the Rio Grande to establish trade relations with the commandant at the presidio of San Juan Bautista. The viceregal government of New Spain was much disturbed when it heard of this incident. St. Denis was sent to Mexico as a prisoner, and measures were immediately taken to prevent such incursions in the future.

The zestful Franciscans now urged again the importance of reoccupying Texas and of converting the natives, making them by this means subjects of his most Christian majesty, the king of Spain, and safeguarding thereby all possibility of French aggression. Father Hidalgo, who had been forced to abandon his beloved Tejas Indians in East Texas in 1693, had patiently watched and waited from the frontier of Coahuila for an opportunity to return to his dearly beloved Tejas Indians. His love was reciprocated. When St. Denis passed through the Tejas tribe he was enjoined by these grateful Indians to entreat the Spaniards to send them missionaries, particularly to send them back Father Hidalgo, their true friend and companion.

Soon an expedition was organized under Domingo Ramón. With sixty-five men, he crossed the Rio Grande, passed by the site of present San Antonio, noting its suitable location for a permanent settlement, and proceeded to East Texas to refound the missions previously established there from 1689 to 1693. From the time of the Ramón expedition dates the permanent Spanish occupation of Texas. Two years later Alarcón, the new governor, formally established a settlement in the present site of San Antonio as a midway station, reorganizing the few scattered settlers that since two years before had taken their abode in the vicinity, and formally naming the temporary mission of San Antonio de Padua, originally founded by Father Olivares, San Antonio de Valero in honor of the ruling viceroy. From this new center of activity, destined to become with time the most important Spanish settlement within the state, the circle of influence of Spanish civilization and of missionary activity was to spread gradually to Los Adaes, Bahía del Espíritu Santo, Nacogdoches, San Sabá, the missions of the upper Nueces, and to all the eastern tribes that made up the Asinay confederacy, erroneously called the Tejas.

The history of the next sixty years is replete with the heroic sacrifices of the brown-robed Franciscans, who labored long and faithfully to bring the roving children of the plains to a realization of our Christian faith to teach them the habits and customs of civilized life. Every mission, and there were many founded during their period, became a vocational school where the Indians were gathered and taught not only the fundamental truths of religion but the rudiments of civilized life. The missionaries themselves set them an example. With plow or hoe in hand they showed the Indians how to till the soil, how to plant the seed, how to raise the crop. In the long winter days the neophytes learned manual trades, repairing the rude furniture of the mission and their own quarters. Under the direction of the kindly padres they learned to carve stone and wood, to weave, to make sandals, to sew, to mend things, and to play various instruments. Each mission had its armory, its carpenter shop, its blacksmith shop, its loom, and its amusement room where the Indians played and danced on feast days. It was in this manner that the great task of civilizing the Indians was carried on. In addition to their cultivated fields, well-kept orchards where excellent fruits were raised, and their tanneries and workshops, the Indians of the missions had their cattle, their stock, and their sheep.

But this growth was not all a garden of roses. Many were the hardships, the trials and the tribulations which the unselfish and suffering soldiers of Christ had to endure in the daily routine of their simple lives. During these sixty years they were often forced to carry on their work without the full cooperation of the officials, and frequently against their open opposition. The Indians were fickle by nature. Unaccustomed to regular work and habits of industry they soon tired, became discouraged and ran away. Sickness was a constant source of trouble for the missionaries. The Indian medicine men, who saw their power destroyed by the new order of things, naturally hinted that the epidemics were due to the waters of baptism. Against this and many other influences that were constantly undoing their work, the missionaries labored patiently, with love in their hearts, with faith and hope in their souls for ultimate success. Be it said to the honor of the sons of Saint Francis that, through it all, they never faltered. They worked with exemplary Christian resignation to bring to the fold through patience, kindness, and love the thousands of Indians that roamed the vast plains. Before their task was half accomplished, some of them made the supreme sacrifice and gladly gave their lives for the love of God. The Texas historian cannot pass in silence the heroic virtues of the saintly Margil, founder of San José Mission, nor the martyred Fray Alonso Giraldo de Terreros and Fray Santiesteban, murdered by the infuriated Comanches at San Sabá. One fell at the foot of the altar, the other at the gate of the desecrated mission. Thus "they sealed their work with their blood" affirms the illustrious historian of their order, Fray Juan Agustín Morfi.

The long Spanish period during which the real work of civilization was carried on by the Church and the missionaries lasted from the beginning of the eighteenth century to almost the end of the first quarter of the nineteenth. Early in 1810 a Struggle for independence began in Mexico, led by Father Miguel Hidalgo y Costilla, curate of Dolores. His emissary to the United States of America made his way to Texas in an effort to reach Washington and secure the much needed aid and cooperation of this great country, which had so recently succeeded in obtaining its independence from Great Britain. Unfortunately he was captured in this very city of San Antonio. In 1812 the liberals temporarily gained control of affairs in Texas; then followed the brutal and bloody days of the Gutiérrez-Magee filibustering expedition, whose short triumph ended with defeat by Arredondo on the Medina in 1814. Texas remained loyal to Spain for the remainder of the struggle. In 1821, with the proclamation of the Plan de Iguala by Iturbide, Mexico became an independent nation.

The Mexican flag was now raised over the old ramparts of the Presidio of San Antonio, where the Spanish flag had waved so long. A new era began for Mexico and for Texas. It was during this period which we are now entering that the Anglo-American colonization was to take place. Before Mexico had actually won its independence, Moses Austin, a former resident of Missouri, had applied for and obtained a grant of land wherein to establish a colony in Texas. But he did not live to carry out his enterprise. This hazardous undertaking was to fall upon the shoulders of a young man destined to become truly the father of Anglo Texas. It was Stephen F. Austin, son of Moses, who undertook to carry out the colonization contract made by his father. He thus became the first great empresario.

Mexico adopted a liberal policy towards American immigration at first. During the early years of Mexican independence the settlement of Texas was rapid. Colonies sprang up overnight. American pioneers streamed into the promised land in an endless procession. As the newcomers were brought into closer contact with the older Spanish settlers and their relations with Mexican officials became more intimate, it was only natural that differences should arise between them. The American colonists were aggressive, self-assertive, impatient of authority or of restraint. The Spanish settlers were passive, somewhat apathetic, law-abiding, good-natured. The breach consequently widened and distrust grew. The new colonists became exasperated at the repeated efforts made by Mexico to prevent an open secession and the possible loss of one of its states. The law of April 6, 1830, marked the beginning of a new era of mutual discord and suspicion. Mexico no longer favored American colonization. The American pioneer carried in his hand the ever ready rifle which he used with deadly precision, and in his pocket he placed his own law. It was not long before a cleavage occurred. The Fredonian revolt of the Edwards was a premature attempt to separate from Mexico. Austin realized the situation and wisely helped the Mexican authorities to suppress the movement. This act saved the infant colonies until a better day.

Causes for misunderstanding and friction continued to grow. By 1835 Texas was in open revolt against Mexico. The movement that began as a petition for distinct statehood ended in one for absolute and complete independence from Mexico.

The struggle that ensued was as bloody, as it was short. Santa Anna, recently proclaimed dictator in Mexico, began immediate preparations to subdue the rebels. At the head of a formidable army for those days he crossed the Rio Grande in the early part of 1836 and laid siege to the Alamo. After a heroic defense by its reduced garrison, the Alamo fell on March sixth, and every man was put to the sword. Before the smoke from the smoldering ruins cleared, came news of the Goliad massacre. Panic seized the settlers, and they fled in every direction. Houston, at the head of a small and demoralized force of Texans, slowly retreated before the overpowering troops of Santa Anna. At last he took a position just beyond the San Jacinto, near the site of present day Houston, to make one last stand and to protect, as far as possible, the retreat of the fleeing colonists. Santa Anna arrived at the battlefield flushed with victory. After burning the rebel capital, Washington-on-the-Brazos, he felt certain of ultimate success. So great was his confidence that after taking one look at the positions of the Texans, he decided there was no hurry and proceeded to take a siesta. When he awoke his troops were in full flight, victory had deserted his standards, and he had not only lost an army but his own liberty as well.

A new flag, the flag of the Republic of Texas, now waved triumphantly over the land. A new star, the lone star of the empire state, had risen from the smoke and din of battle and its banner was proudly unfurled in this domain that had heretofore successively seen three other flags displayed. From 1836 to 1845, when Texas was annexed to the Union, this new symbol of freedom was to proclaim to the world the birth of a sovereign state.

The era of the republic beheld a tremendous increase in population. In less than ten years the number of people rose from approximately thirty thousand to one hundred thousand, thanks to the unprecedented immigration from the United States. New settlements were established in the region north of the old San Antonio-Nacogdoches road, new farms began to dot the country west of San Antonio, and the areas between the Red River and the coast and between the Sabine and the Nueces were rapidly put under cultivation and many villages appeared. Amidst the attendant confusion of readjustment, of land speculation, of Indian depredations, and of the constant menace of Mexican invasion, steady progress was made in reducing the wilderness and in laying down the foundations for the future greatness of the state. Among the many matters that called for solution the question of public instruction was very important. The congress of the new republic laid the foundation for this future educational development by making the first grant of land for that purpose. The picturesque Lamar, with a facility for sonorous phrases, declared in his message of 1838: "A cultivated mind is the guardian genius of Democracy. . . . It is the only dictator that freemen acknowledge and the only security that freemen desire."

It soon became evident, however, that the infant republic could not long endure without the protecting hand of one or more of the older nations. Its immense resources, the value of its raw products to a new and rapidly developing industrial world, the threatening attitude of Mexico, and above all its proximity to the United States along with the character of its institutions, made it almost a necessity for the young republic either to join the United States or accept a protectorate that would guarantee its integrity.

The majority of the people at heart favored annexation. Thus negotiations were finally concluded late in 1845 and on February 16, 1846, "amid the booming of cannon and the mingled smiles and tears of Texan patriots, the flag of the Republic . . . was lowered" and the broad banner of the United States of America was unfurled to the winds. It was on this occasion that President Jones uttered the impressive words that marked the passing away of the short-lived Republic. "The final act in this great drama is now performed," he declared, "the Republic of Texas is no more."

After becoming a state of the Union progress was even more rapid than before. Public order was established; the Indian problem was partially settled by the establishment of reservations, the aid of federal troops, and the organization of state rangers; the land system was reorganized and liberal bounties were given to those who had helped achieve the independence of the state; large grants of land were again made for educational purposes; railway construction was actively encouraged; and the population increased from one hundred thousand to over four hundred thousand on the eve of the war between the states.

But we cannot tarry on this early period of development. In 1860 there were ominous signs of an approaching storm that was to shake the very foundations of the American Union and test all the powers of the federal government. In the great struggle that followed the election of Lincoln, Texas took her place by the side of the Confederacy, and in March, 1861, the federal troops within the state evacuated their posts. The sixth and last flag other than that of the Union now waved over the land. The five years of the war were hard and bitter years of trials and sorrows. From fifty to sixty thousand men saw service under the colors of the Confederacy. But far from the actual theater of active engagements, Texas was spared the destruction wrought by battles and the drain of marching armies.

In 1865, at the close of the terrible strife, Texas was in a chaotic state. Hungry veterans swarmed the country and deeds of violence were common. The Stars and Stripes waved serenely over the land once more. The dispossessed slave-holder, the demoralized farmer, the artisan and the tradesman, buckled down to the business of reconstruction with a stern determination during the trying days that followed the war. The spirit of the old pioneer days again stirred the people of Texas to greater efforts. Slowly, under adverse conditions, the readjustments were made, agriculture again flourished, the cattle industry developed and grew to be one of the principal sources of wealth; and West Texas became the home of the romantic cowboy and the picturesque longhorn. Railroads spread their network over the state from north to south and from east to west; irrigation made possible the cultivation of thousands of new acres; and immigration continued to pour into the state, increasing its population and furnishing the necessary man power to develop the diverse resources of the state.

But it is not the purpose of this address to outline the history of the unprecedented growth and development of the great state of Texas since the days of the Civil War. Suffice it to say that today Texas is the largest state in the Union and that its untold resources will make it the richest and most prosperous in a day not so far distant. But it is significant that the pioneers in the real beginnings of civilization in the state were the humble and pious Franciscan missionaries who almost three centuries ago, when there were no material incentives to stimulate interest in the country, braved the hardships of the wilderness, risked their lives, and gave the best they had in them to save the souls of the natives and to implant the seeds of Christian civilization in Texas, the land of God's special predilection. May the Stars and Stripes wave over the state forever, a guarantee of justice and liberty!

CAPTAIN DON DOMINGO RAMÓN'S DIARY OF HIS EXPEDITION INTO TEXAS IN 1716

TRANSLATED BY
Paul J. Foik, C.S.C.*

FOREWORD

As the expedition undertaken by Captain Don Domingo Ramón is the beginning of the activities for the permanent settlement of the Province of Texas and of the foundation and establishment of several missions in this region, it has a special importance as a document, along with the diary of Reverend Father Fray Isidro Félix de Espinosa† of which it is the counterpart. A comparison of the two records verifies the accounts given by these chroniclers of the expedition in almost every, detail, and one supplements the other with additional information.

The original documents from which the certified transcripts have been made, are located in the Archivo General y Público de México, Provincias Internas, Volume 181, and also in *Colección de Memorias de Nueva España* which forms the nucleus of the division Historia in the same national archives. The exact title of the series of source materials relating to Texas, Volumes 27 and 28, is as follows: "Documentos para la historia ecclesiástica y civil de la Provincia de Texas." Another ancient collection rich in Texas sources is the valuable Archivo del Convento Grande de San Francisco, recently made available at the Biblioteca Nacional in Mexico City. These relevant documents, most of them originals, contain various expeditions into Texas, written, signed and properly authenticated by those persons who made the reports. Reproductions by photostat have been provided by the Commission's research scholar, Dr. Carlos E. Castañeda. A comparative study has been made with the transcripts and variations have been noted.

---

*Vol. 2, No. 5, appeared in April 1933.

†*Preliminary Studies of the Texas Catholic Historical Society*, 1, 4 (April 1930), reprinted in *Preparing the Way: Preliminary Studies of the Texas Catholic Historical Society I*, Studies in Southwestern Catholic History No. 1 (Austin: Texas Catholic Historical Society, 1997), 67–89.

The translator wishes to acknowledge with thanks the valuable assistance given him in this rendition by Mr. T. L. Evans of the Domestic and Foreign Trade Expansion Department of the Houston Chamber of Commerce.

Paul J. Foik, C.S.C.
Chairman of the Commission and President of the Society

Captain Don Domingo Ramón's Diary of His Expedition into Texas in 1716

In the name of the Most Holy Trinity, in the town of Saltillo, Government of Nueva Vizcaya, on the seventeenth day of February of the year 1716, I began the diary and route of the expedition to the Province of Texas, and according to the injunction of His Excellency, the Duke of Linares, Viceroy and Captain General of this New Spain, I, Captain Domingo Ramón, started to execute the order with the company of twenty-five cavalrymen, to enter said province for the protection and custody of the missions, soon to be established. I was appointed by His Excellency, as commander-in-chief of this company, etc.

FEBRUARY

17. On this day I left the Town of Saltillo, with all my company and mule train and marched one league toward the north, where I found some bundles of cornstalks, and we pastured the horses and mules. The name of the place was Santa Ines.

18. I marched with all of the train four leagues toward the north until I reached a creek by the name of Padillas, where I stopped.

19. I remained here, because I lost some pack mules and one of the keepers, who ran away when he was most needed.

20. On this day I traveled eight leagues in an easterly direction until I reached the Rinconada Inn,* where I rested, for there was a very high mountain ahead.

21. On this day I marched five leagues in a northerly direction, where I reached the Nacatas Bridge, and here I placed my camp. Then I issued orders to the chief ensign of Yeomole, Pedro de los Santos, to leave with his horses and to join me at the inn, as it was a desirable place to gather them, and thus to afford time for the religious of the Cross to reach us, for they were to

*The Spanish here is *paraje*, which means a camp location or a recognized place.

assemble here, so that all might start the journey together. The inn was a convenient location for this purpose.

22. On this day I left my camp and at four o'clock in the afternoon reached the Town of Saltillo,* where I had sent the sergeant of this company with six soldiers to escort the religious to said camp, but as they were detained ten days in the said Town on charity, they departed on the first of March, plodded all the distance to this camp for three days, and finally reached Nacatas on the third of March.

MARCH

9. I remained at this place until the ninth, because time was necessary to gather some horses and to make preparations for the trip. On this date at night, Anna Guerra, a young mestizo girl, came to me and I asked her what she wanted. She replied that she came to see whether I desired to send or to take her to Texas, because her master had abused her, and moved by charity I placed her with my family.

10. On this day Lorenzo Mercado, a soldier of this company, came to my presence and asked me for Anna Guerra in marriage, which design put her in my company. This day I advanced about ten leagues from this place. I ordered the chief ensign of this company with three men to take the horses to the post of the Culebra and to meet me at the Piedras Corral, because the road on which I was traveling was very barren. With the rest of my company and the balance of the pack train I passed in sight of the town of Pesquería. I marched four leagues north in the middle of a canyon, crossed a river, and stopped on the plantation of Captain Francisco Quintanilla because there were some bundles of cornstalks here.

11. This day I left this place and marched four leagues to the north on the banks of the river until I reached San Martín.

12. This day I set out from this location and nearby I lost a pack mule. I marched on for five leagues to the north until I reached the farm of Captain José Villareal. Later in the same day the lost mule was recovered.

13. This day I could not leave this place on account of the fog and bad weather.

14. This day I traveled along a river four leagues to the north, crossing in front of the house of Captain José Villareal, the *alcalde mayor* of this jurisdiction, on whose plantation there is a chapel of St. James, where the religious heard the confessions of the people of the estate. I reached the place of

---

*The meaning of this statement is unclear, as De León had already traveled 18 leagues (approximately 50 miles) north, and the possibility of his making it back to Saltillo in less than a day is highly improbable.

Piedras Corral, where I awaited the horses, because I had given this order to the ensign.

15. I was notified this day that Alexander Morales and Jacinto de los Santos had deserted the cavalry, taking with them two of my horses.

16. On this day I remained in this place because the horses had not yet arrived. I was informed that two other soldiers had deserted by the names of José Cadena and José García.

17. This day the religious caught more than three hundred fish in the river which is close to this place. I sent Sergeant Augustín Félix and Marcial Sauceda on the trail of the four soldiers with a warrant for their arrest.

18. This day I stayed at this place and decided to go out and look for the horses personally; which I did, finding them six leagues from here. I issued orders that the animals be placed in the Piedras Corral at this post on the following day, and then I returned to my camp.

20. This day the horses could not arrive.

21. This day they came in the afternoon. I was advised that enemies were in the vicinity, and I went to locate them. I found two Indian trails and ordered the guards to be doubled at the end and around the horses.

22. I left this place and marched fourteen leagues on the trail to the north over a country entirely lacking in pasturage and water, until I reached the Potrero Inn adjoining the field.

23. I remained here to strengthen the horses, as they arrived in very bad shape the previous day.

24. This day I was detained at this place in order to gather some horses and oxen, which our Father Fray Antonio Margil had for me.

25. On this day I marched along the foot of a mountain crossing the realm and the Lion's Mouth River, until I reached the ranch named Juan Mendes, having traveled this day six leagues to the north.

26–29. These four days I remained in this place, because a soldier's wife gave birth to a child. At the same time I gathered some cargoes of flour and supplies that I had in the realm, and for Reverend Father Margil I collected a portion of the goats to take to Texas. The last day, the twenty-ninth, I sent the ensign in advance with the horses, because they were in bad shape. Hence they had to stop at Carrizal.

30. I marched on a rocky road, and along the way the pasturage was very scarce. Water was found nine leagues to the north at Carrizal.

31. This day I travelled on the trail four leagues to the north over a country lacking pasturage but not water. Along this road a small boy was lost in the woods and could not be found.

APRIL

1. In this location I stopped the following day, the first of April, to await a drove of mules that were about to arrive, loaded with corn from Caldera, which was a short distance away. In the evening of this day I received a paper from a religious, who was the missionary of this place, with information that the Indian enemy had taken from him all of the horses of his mission, and that there were only three men in pursuit of them. Upon the receipt of this message I mounted my steed, and accompanied by two soldiers I left the encampment in good custody and went in search of my horses. The soldiers were very cautious, for they had located the animals the night before. Here I remounted, and because I did not know of the defeat of the said Indians, I went to the mission, where they told me that they had taken the horses away from the Indians, who were under the impression that there were many soldiers.

2. This day I crossed the Caldera River and went over a plain with plenty of pasturage for a distance of five leagues, where I reached the Real del Chocolate. Fathers Fray Francisco Hidalgo, Fray Benito Sanches, Fray Gabriel Vergara and Fray Manuel Castellanos went to the Mission de la Punta to pass the Holy Week there. Two religious remained in the camp to hear confessions of all the people and to offer Mass.

3–4. I stayed at this place two days waiting for some oxen and goats from Father Margil. On one of these days there was a high wind and nothing could be done. At night two soldiers by the names of José del Toro and José de la Fuente deserted, and I sent two companions, José Flores and Jacinto Charles, in pursuit of them to take from them the two horses.

5. This day I left here and marched to the north over a good country for pasturage until I reached the Conchas River, which had been so named because there were many shells in it. I remained at this place five days, so that all of the people would have plenty of time to confess and to pass Holy Week. Here also we captured some wild horses, while in search of some mules that were lost.

11. This day I traveled three leagues to the north over good land, until I crossed the Sabinas River at the Reyneros Pass, where I remained one day to wait for the religious, who were at the Mission de la Punta with the soldiers who were escorting them.

13. This day I left this place and marched ten leagues to the north over very level and very extensive land, which was without hills or mountains, because they were lost from sight until I arrived at Fish Lake. There was no water before reaching that point. I stayed here two days to strengthen the horses, for they were in very poor condition, and here the pasturage was good.

We caught this last day two beautiful wild colts, and farther on there were horses, oxen, and goats, since the water was at a great distance.

16. This day I traveled fifteen leagues. over a very extensive country with little pasturage and less water. Crossing the Juanes Creek, I reached the Amole Creek. Here I remained the following day, because the horses, oxen and goats had not yet arrived.

18. This day I left here and marched seven leagues to the north over a good country for pasturage, crossing a creek with running water at a distance of two leagues from Presidio del Rio Grande. The captain of the said presidio, the *Sargento Mayor* Diego Ramón, my father, accompanied by other officials and soldiers, came out to receive us in two lines, and we returned the courtesy by saluting with our bows and arrows. The Reverend Father Isidro Félix de Espinosa, president of the missions, along with three religious of the same Order went to the same place. Passing close by the said presidio of the whole realm, I went to set up my camp in some cornfields adjoining a mission.

19. This day I remained in this place to secure from this presidio some provisions and other things for the trip, and this night I received advice from our Father Fray Antonio Margil de Jesús that on account of illness he was detained at the Juanes Creek, nine leagues distant from the presidio. Although it was after eight o'clock, the Reverend Father president of the missions left for said place accompanied by two religious and two soldiers who brought this sick Father to the presidio mentioned.

20. This day I marched two leagues through a marsh and a thicket of mesquites towards the East Trail on the banks of the Río Grande del Norte, which runs from west to east. We crossed at the pass called Francia, as it was the best, and we luckily found the river with very little water, which circumstance we attributed to a miracle. This day we transferred all of our things by means of a rope. More than one thousand head of goats swam over with the loss of only twelve because of the current in said river and because I personally directed the crossing to encourage the soldiers and Indians. Although I arrived late, I set up my camp on the other side of the river with extreme happiness.

21. The sergeant of this company asked permission to go to the presidio to be the best man for a soldier by the name of José Galindo, who had joined our party with the parents of the bride-to-be. I granted the same, so that it would redound to the benefit of the growth in population. For this occasion, this day and the twenty-second were spent. I therefore remained in this place four days, which time was taken up in gathering the necessary supplies from the missionary Fathers. This day all of the religious arrived. They collected all things requisite and we started on our journey. On leaving my encampment I made the following list of all the people accompanying me. First, the Fathers

Fray Isidro Félix de Espinosa, president; Fray Francisco Hidalgo; Fray Matías Sanches de San Antonio; Fray Benito Sanches; Fray Manuel Castellanos; Fray Pedro de Mendoza; Fray Gabriel Vergara; Fray Gabriel Cubillos, Religious, and Fray Domingo, Religious *Donado.* The reason that our Very Reverend Father Fray Antonio Margil de Jesús did not accompany us was on account of his illness, and it was with the great sorrow of our entire party that it was necessary for him to remain at the presidio. I, Captain Domingo Ramón; Chief Ensign Diego Ramón; Francisco de Revillar; José Guerra; Domingo Jiménez; Juan de Sertucha; Nicolas de los Santos Coy; Juan Baldes; Diego Valdes Jiménez; José Galinda; Antonio Flores; Bernardo Pruto; Domingo Flores; Agustín Telles; Marcial Saucedo; José Guerra, the servant; Manuel Maldonado; Francisco Betancour; Domingo Gonzales; all of these being soldiers in my company. In addition to this, the following persons accompanied me: Chief Ensign José Maldonado with his family; Sergeant Lorenzo García; Pedro Botello with his family; Jacinto Charles; José del Toro; José de la Fuente; Alejandro Morales; Lucas de Castro; married women María Antonia Longoria, Antonia de la Cerda, Antonia Vidales, Ana María Jiménes, Juana de San Miguel, Josefa Sanches; Ana Guerra to be married; a boy six years old; a girl four years old; Captain Don Louis de St. Denis, chief convoy, Don Jean de Medar, and Don Pierre Largen, these three of French nationality; José García; José de Montemayor Arrieres; Antonio Gonzales; Sebastián Guerra; Valentín Mendoza; Blas Jiménes; José Saez; Juan Rodríguez; Juan Pérez; Diego Miguel Pérez; Cayetano Pérez; Francisco de la Cruz; a Negro by the name of Juan de la Concepción; two Indian guides, and three in charge of the goats, making a total of sixty-five people. On the twenty-seventh day I left the said Rio Grande and marched five leagues, three to the northwest and two to the west, until I reached the Diego Ramón Pass, where we encountered a storm that night at eight o'clock. The rain was falling in sheets and the wind was very high, causing us to believe that this terrible tempest was excited by the infernal furies. Nearly all of our supplies, which were piled on the ground, were blown down. The three tents were under a mighty strain. The post of one was broken. In fact, the wind raised the animal on which the sentinel was riding and carried them a distance of three or four yards. The horses, oxen and mules were in a stampede, but it was God's wish that they were all found.

28. This day I left this place, having sent the goats and oxen ahead. I marched five leagues toward the north and east and reached a level country, where for the first time we saw green pasturage, for which we thanked God. We had experienced a difficult time with the horses until we reached Lion's Cave. On arriving here Jean de Medar of French descent fell from his horse, because the animal caught its foot in a hole.

29. This day I marched along the foot of some hills having very good pasturage. I also crossed some creeks which were very insecure for the pack train. On one of these streams, after some goats had gone through a very poor passage, the remainder were taken over at another point. When we assembled them on the other side, we found that they had used a better way, of which we availed ourselves for the transfer of pack trains and horses. This night we were short twenty head of horse stock, and this happened because some of the Indians of the Pacuaches nation had taken them to their *ranchería*; but Lorenzo Garcia followed their trail for a distance of four leagues and took them from the Indians. We did not punish them, as the fright which they suffered was considered sufficient penalty. I gave them some tobacco. I further informed them through an interpreter, that if they should repeat this act, I would hang them. This day I traveled seven leagues to the northeast.

30. This day I marched six leagues to the northeast until I reached the post of Carrizo, a well pastured country containing some mesquite thickets and much cactus.

MAY

1. This day I advanced three leagues to the east over a beautiful country and a land covered with a variety of flowers with admirable fragrance, until I reached the place of Ojo de Agua.

2. This day I left this location and marched seven leagues to the east over a well pastured country crossing two creeks, one the Caramanchel and the other the Hondo until we reached the Nueces River, where we found very little water, a very bad place, therefore, for supplying the thirsty cattle. It became necessary to dig a hole with hoes. This day I counted all of the animals, as they came up to drink and found four hundred ninety.

3. I remained in this place on this day, which was celebrated by having a cross carried in procession and saluted with bows and arrows.

4. This day I marched three leagues southwest* over level country with very many holes and open ground. There were five falls as a result, and one was the writer of this diary, who was at the point of never writing again. This was the consequence of racing with a Frenchman, attempting to reach for a hat from the horse. I arrived at Ranas Lake,† which is very fine and contains plenty of fish. Here we caught an alligator gar. This day José del Toro deserted, and I sent the chief ensign with an Indian to trail him. They found him in a tree and the chief ensign raised his arrow to scare him. The Indian

---

*The expedition was following a generally northeasterly direction. This and subsequent entries reporting a southwesterly direction are in error.

†Tortuga Creek.

begged the officer for the love of God not to shoot, which action was greatly admired by us.

5. This day I remained in this place, as it was necessary to rest the horses and because a soldier was to be married to Anna Guerra, an occasion that was celebrated with a feast prepared by his companions.

6. This day I marched five leagues to the southwest at the foot of some hills, extending down to beautiful canyons with oak trees and many strange and unknown flowers of rare fragrance, among them a great deal of wild marjoram. We reached a lake by the name of Encinos, which was very charming, and we renamed it San Juan Bautista.

7. This day we proceeded to the southwest four leagues over a country similar to that of the previous days, and we recrossed the Frio River,* which we found very dry, but with much vegetation. We camped one league from said river on a lake that we called San Lorenzo, in which region there was located an excellent variety of timber. Here we caught four turkeys which were very tasty. We met at this place six Indians of the Pataguas tribe, for they had a *ranchería* nearby.

8. This day I traveled over a land with much vegetation, where I found very good roads four leagues to the northeast to a lake situated in a grand canyon, which was named San Alexo. This location was two leagues before reaching Rio Hondo.† I remained here on the ninth of the month looking for a crossing of said river, and I found a very fine one without going around, although the channel is very deep.

10. The royal standard was advanced four leagues to the northwest, passing over said stream on the banks of which axe very large and beautiful pecan trees, however, without nuts, since it was not the time for them to bear. There was a frost. We found entwined in the trees grapevines, on which there were some bunches of grapes. We reached a beautiful lake, where the religious observed that we were in latitude twenty-eight degrees thirty-nine seconds. We gave this place, the name of Santa Rita.

11. This day I marched three leagues to the northeast at the foot of some hills with good pasturage. The country was very picturesque and pleasant. We stopped in a canyon with small lakes, because one of the religious was sick. He gave the place the name of Santa Isabel, Queen of Hungary.

12. This day I traveled in the said direction three leagues, part of which territory was a pecan grove. There were other varieties of timber, loose dirt and some pasturage, until we reached the Medina River, where we caught some fish. Here happened the most unexpected calamity, which was due to

---

*Leona River.

†Frio River.

having driven all of the horses into the lake to bathe them, which was our custom, since some of them had sore backs. A great number of them going into the water, lost their foothold. Some of them fell down. Others placed their hoofs On top of these and also fell down. They were so firmly stuck in the mud that we lost eighty-three head, a list of which I made in order to pay the owners for the same from my own pocket. I did this to encourage my people. All of them said that if all of the animals had been drowned, they would continue on such a blessed journey. Perhaps the devil had done this to hinder the conflict that was about to be made against him. To crush him a High Mass was said the following day in thanksgiving for the gift [of perseverance.]

14. On this day I marched to the northeast seven leagues through mesquite brush with plenty of pasturage. Crossing two dry creeks we reached a water spring on level land, which we named San Pedro. There was sufficient water here for a city of one-quarter league, and the scenery along the San Antonio River is very beautiful, for there are pecan trees, grapevines, willows, elms and other timbers. We crossed said stream; the water, which was not very deep, reached to our stirrups. We went up the river looking for a camping place and we found a very fine location. There were beautiful shade trees and good pasturage, as we explored the head of the river. Here we found, in the estimate of twelve ultra-marines, hemp nine feet high and flax two feet high. Fish was caught in abundance for everyone, and nets were used in the river with facility.

15. This day was spent at this place because it was very desirable to rest the horses and to celebrate the feast of San Isidro.

16. This day I marched two leagues to the northeast through some hills with good pasturage and mesquite trees. We crossed the Salado Creek, although it is not salty. We found on its banks plenty of grapes and we stopped at its edge.

17. This day we advanced five leagues to the northeast through some hills and mesquite brush. There was plenty of water and green pasturage, until we reached a creek flowing into a large lake, which we named San Xavier.*

18. This day I left and traveled to the north through some hills with good pasturage and a scattered growth of oak and pecan trees. We came to the crossing of the Guadalupe River,† which is in two branches. It is the most beautiful stream that can be imagined, because from the passage to its source it is not a greater distance than a shot with a bow and arrow. It has such an abundance of water that it can hardly be crossed without swimming, being

*Cibolo Creek.

†Comal River.

very broad. It would seem very strange without water, because on its banks and at its head were found maiden hair ferns, mulberries with leaves like the fig tree, and grapes in quantity. The rocks in the bottom of the river were transparent without any bitumen, which indicates that the water is healthful; and also it is very cold.

19. This day we went to the north one league to the other river, which until then was known as an arm of the Guadalupe, which was not the case. We learned that it was a different one and we named it San Ybon.* In both of these streams we caught plenty of fish.

20. I left this place and marched fifteen leagues in a northeasterly direction through a fine country with plenty of pecan and oak trees, grapevines and good pasturage. We crossed the San Marcos which has a great deal of good water that is very cold. We stopped at a creek, which we named San Rafael,† and found on the other side two springs, which we called San Isidro and San Pedro del Nogal. We remained at this place to celebrate the Ascension of our Lord. We caught a turkey.

21. This day I traveled nine leagues to the northeast to a creek with streams of water flowing copiously from the hills which extended beyond the wooded section. There were also springs on the land with plenty of grape-vines, pecan trees and other varieties of timber.

22. This day I marched three leagues, northeast over some barren hills, brooks and good pasturage. We reached the Colorado River which we found very swollen. Although we explored it four leagues above, we could not locate a crossing, so we stopped there that night. We experienced a heavy thunder-storm with lightning up the river, which led us to believe that the stream would rise more the following day, which was not the case, because God did not will it so. The river receded more than eighteen inches.

24. The stream was forded but the religious and women, especially Father Fray Manual Castellanos were very frightened, because the latter's horse had left the shallow water and Marcial Saucedo, a soldier, was stuck with his horse in the mud. To recite litanies was the custom after crossing the river. The whole day was consumed in transferring supplies.

25. This day the goats were conveyed and they swam through the water with great ease, even though the river was about the width of a shot with a bow and arrow.

26. I remained here this day to explore the road, as I was not familiar with the same beyond this point. This was done by sending the chief ensign and two companions as scouts, and for that reason we left on the following day.

---

*Guadalupe River.

†Blanco River.

27. This day I went three leagues southeast and four leagues to the northeast over good land for pasturage, but rough and broken, and it was with some effort that the horses advanced. Here we killed a bison, which was the first, and we were very much pleased with the fine taste of the meat and the great quantity of it. The animal at first sight is beautiful, but on closer observation it is ugly. It is larger than an ox; the hoofs are very much the same; and the horns, although very black, are much shorter and curved. The whole neck up to the forehead is ill-shaped. The bison has long hair which obstructs its view. For that reason it runs against the wind. The animal is very malodorous, does not hear well, and sees less on account of the mane of hair mentioned above. It has a tail like a hog. It runs very fast and the horse must be very quick to catch it. The bison has more meat than two steers and it is very wholesome and good. We arrived at a creek, which we named San Nicolás.

28. This day we marched six leagues to the northeast through some land with very bad holes, due to the exceedingly dry weather, which is very strange for an open and level country accustomed to frequent showers. We reached the creek by the name of Las Animas.* Here we killed four bisons, which supplied all of our people with an abundance of meat.

29. I remained in this place to explore the country, because over a period of time the water places have changed. Some dry up and others are made.

30. This day I marched three leagues to the northeast through some hills and canyons with an abundance of water and some thickets, where we found fresh tracks of Indians. I gave orders to follow them. The Indians were found four leagues from the encampment and two of them were brought to my presence. One was of the Yerbipiame tribe and the other was of the Mescal. They told me that they were near their *ranchería* and that they would act as my guides.

31. This day I traveled five leagues to the northeast over good land for pasturage and with plenty of water. I stopped at a creek which was named San Diego de Alcalá This evening there was a heavy rain, which continued during the night. This rain was very much needed, as the land was very dry. We were able to resume our journey.

JUNE

1. This day I left this place and advanced two leagues to the southeast, crossing two creeks without any water, but there were good pasturage and

*Brushy Creek.

thickets. We reached a river where we caught some fish (however, we preferred bison). We gave this location the name of San Xavier.*

2. This day I remained here, because it was such a fine day. High Mass was celebrated with great rejoicing.

3. This day I marched five leagues to the northeast; on the road were found various wild fowls. We. crossed a creek which was very difficult for the pack train. We arrived at the encampment of Santo Domingo, where an Indian caught an alligator that had come out of the water, and he killed it. This evening I sent three Indians to look for bisons, and without my knowledge and orders another Indian, a *ladino*, and Miguel Pérez, a mule driver, both servants of the Fathers, also left. The three Indians returned, but the last ones named did not, because they were lost, and even though we looked for them, they could not be found.

5–6. These days I remained here, and notwithstanding the fact that I have personally conducted a thorough search with the Indians and my company, the missing ones could not be located. The Fathers offered Masses and public prayers for their return.

7. This day I traveled through a densely wooded region of oaks. The forest was so impenetrable that we could not pass through on horseback without cutting down some trees with axes and knives. We lost two knives. We advanced seven leagues with great difficulty, arriving in the afternoon in an open spot that God had placed there for us to rest after such a painful journey. There was plenty of water and good pasturage. Here the religious saw a live bison close at hand, which was the first one that could not be killed.

8. This day I wandered three leagues without any definite direction. On the way we gathered a great quantity of wild grapes and could have procured more. We arrived at a small open space close to a lake which we named San Juan Bautista. From here I set out with an Indian who knew the country to find where the woods ended. It was at a distance of a shot with a bow and arrow. This Indian told me that he was astonished that he did not know where he was. Continuing on my course, I finally found the clearing and gave thanks to God for the discovery, as we had been misled for a period of three days.

9. This day we left this place and marched three leagues to the southeast, partly through woods as in the past, and on the road we found a quantity of wild grapes. We stopped on a plain, where we beheld very beautiful springs containing some fish. On this day a horse loaded with supplies ran away from one of the soldiers. Three soldiers, together with the ensign, pursued it, discovering that the person who always watched over the escaped animal, had also been lost in the chase.

---

*San Gabriel River.

10. This day I remained here, because it was a good camping place and because we wished to celebrate the Feast of Corpus Christi. We gave the location this name.

11. The holiday was observed as well as possible. All of the people confessed and received Holy Communion with great joy.

12. This day I marched eight leagues to the southeast and one half league to the north over a fine country, crossing two creeks, one with water and the other without. On the banks of one of these brooks forty Indians of various tribes came out to receive us, among them being four captains. The leader was of the Yerhipiame tribe, who knew me because he had done us some wrong several years before. They were delighted to meet us and served as our guides as far as their *ranchería*. Some traveled on horseback, others on foot. They gave us a house in which we could reside, and this was a bow-and-arrow shot from the said *ranchería*. I remained there some hours, where more than two thousand persons, men, women and children, most of them gentiles and very many apostates, came. We were sorry to find among them so many lost souls. They requested me to stay over the thirteenth so that the Indians could have time to exchange with my people their buffalo hides, chamois skins, and other things that they had for barter; and I legalized these trades with the said Indians in order that they would receive fair treatment and would not have a bad impression of the Spaniards. This office was performed with great pleasure.

14. This day I marched three leagues to the northeast, traveling through some canyons and creeks with water, encircled by woods, until we reached the Trinity River.* Because this river was high, we could not cross this day; but more than sixty Indians transferred the goats one by one, and I killed a steer and two goats for them for their service.

15. This way I passed over said river, taking the mules one by one. We all crossed without any difficulty, and then we reached another stream which the Indians told us was a branch of the Trinity, for the Spaniards had given it this name, when they came to this region the first time.† This river is very wide and marshy in places. The water reached to the saddletree of the horses, which made it necessary to transport the supplies on rafts, a task that was performed this evening with great satisfaction by the Indians; although they were somewhat frightened by an alligator, which the natives fear very much. I removed the peril by shooting the reptile in the eye, which is its vulnerable spot, and by this act their fright was allayed. In the afternoon the two persons that were lost at Santo Domingo presented themselves, advising me that they

---

*Brazos River.

†Also the Brazos River.

had gone into a very thick underbrush and could not find their way out for twelve days. Here they saw wild cattle that were lost by the Spaniards on their first visit to Texas, and they killed a fat cow and some turkeys, which food maintained them. At the end of this day they found our trail, and they followed the same until they reached us at this river.

16. This day I advanced to the northeast through an open country and some sparsely wooded regions, where we perceived vines in abundance with many wild grapes. We stopped at a clearing close to an old *ranchería.* Here I sent six men to kill bison and they returned with six of them. they also brought two calves with which we had a bullfight, for they were sufficiently enraged.

17. This day I remained in this place, because the saddled animal belonging to the chief ensign had run away. On account of darkness we could not look for the horse that night, but it returned later without anything missing.

18. This day I marched five leagues to the northeast through a beautiful country with fine pasturage, great pecan groves, grapevines and other admirable trees, passing by a charming brook. In the middle of the road we met four Texas Indians with two women, who were killing bisons. They were delighted to receive us, throwing their arms around us, which act is significant of friendship among the gentiles; and the same was done by the women. Thus it was apparent that they had heretofore been in touch with our people, and they were more pleased when we told them that we were coming to live in their country. They accompanied us to a river, which we named Corpus Christi,* because we arrived there on the last day of the Octave.

19. This day I traveled in company with the said Texas Indians, whom I treated in the best manner possible. We went in a northerly direction six leagues through a woodland of oaks and pecans, vineyards with plenty of wild grapes and fields for pasturage, crossing two creeks with water, one of which had it in abundance. We reached a lake which we named the Lampazos, because of the great number of burdocks nearby. We arrived at the encampment of San Cristobal on the edge of a plain in close proximity to a hill.

20. This day we marched five leagues to the northeast over some hills and plains with good pasturage and through some timbered regions and dry creeks. We arrived at a small *ranchería*, where we found seven Tejas. They received us with great pleasure and demonstrated their delight by giving us green corn and watermelons. This was the first time that we saw corn in this province.

---

*Cedar Creek.

21. This day I advanced to the northeast five leagues over a level country with some timber, as pecan, oak, and pine trees. On the way we caught fourteen turkeys. We stopped at a small creek which we named Santa Clara.

22. This day we traveled ten leagues to the northeast over a good country but without water. There were many grapevines, pecan trees, oaks, and other timber. We were very thirsty. We arrived at the bank of a river which was very high, and we were informed by the Indians that this was also the Trinity. It is the case that this branch and the one mentioned heretofore join at a great distance from this crossing. General Alonso de León passed over both of them. We traversed two dry creeks.

23. This day, after going one and one-half leagues, we found a beautiful lake with fish and the banks were very pleasant, because of the many kinds of trees on them. Close to this spot we reached a river, although the passage was not very good. The water was fine, and when we crossed the said river, we found nearby a valley with such heavy pasturage that the horses could not walk. The edges of this valley had many different trees, such as cedars, willows, elms, oaks, and many other varieties. Among these are some pines that could be used for boat making. At a short distance we found a lake, equally as beautiful as the previous one, very close to a river on the level with the land, but not with an abundance of water. With the approval of all of the religious we named this river San Fernando, the valley Linares, and the lake San Luis.

24. This day we spent in preparing a ford at said river, which was done in a short time on account of the great number of people that we had. After passing through this stream at a distance of about one league, we reached a creek, where it was necessary to build a bridge to provide a passage. In the evening, since it was the Vigil of the feast of San Juan Bautista, we shot some fireworks.

25. This day we continued to celebrate the occasion and every one enthusiastically took part.

26. This day I remained here to wait for my son, whom I had sent with Don Louis de St. Denis, chief convoy. This evening, the escort, my son and a Tejas Indian arrived with information that all the Indians of the Texas tribe were gathering to come out and meet us on the road. This day was also employed in transferring the flocks of goats to our present location.

27. This day I marched four leagues to the northeast over an excellent country, passing through some canyons with plenty of water, pine trees, and other timbers suitable for the making of light lumber. In the evening Captain Don Louis de St. Denis presented himself to me, accompanied by a group of twenty-five men, the most of them captains. He was well received among the Indians because he understands their language. I had extended for them some

sacks, where they could be seated. Before they arrived at my encampment they discharged their bows and arrows. There also came forward in single file more Indians on horseback, headed by Don Louis. These Indians carried nine long shotguns, all of French make. I ordered my soldiers to line up in single file to receive them. I went forth, accompanied by all of the religious, with a banner of Jesus Christ and Our Lady of Guadalupe. This reception was celebrated with fireworks; and the said Indians, seated on the sacks, all embraced me. They then took out a long pipe, which they had for peace only, and they filled it with tobacco, placing a fire in the center. The captains began to smoke, and the first puff was blown towards heaven, the second to the cast, the third to the west, the fourth to the north, the fifth to the south. and the sixth to the earth. This was a demonstration of true peace. The bowl of the pipe has many white feathers, which also decorate the stem from one end to the other, being more than a yard long. They then gave me the pipe to smoke, making the same demonstrations of peace; and in succession they gave it to all of the people, even to the women. Then the captains took tobacco out of their pockets, and they piled it in the center, so that I might use the same. I likewise gave them some of my tobacco. I then killed for them a young beef. All of this ceremony was performed with manifestation of joy, because these natives are a smiling, happy, and agreeable people, especially with the Spaniards. It was apparent they had been in communication with us many times before this occasion.

28. This day I marched four leagues to the northeast over land with much water. There were many grapevines, cactus, and trees of several varieties. We stopped with said Indians at a creek with running water.

29. This day I traveled five leagues to the northeast over hills with oak, pine, and pecan trees. There were vines from which we gathered some grapes as large as eggs. We reached a great open space, where we found two lakes with fish. At the edge of the same, we beheld a river with plenty of water. In the afternoon there came into my presence one hundred and fifty Indians, many of whom were captains. About one league away Don Louis went out to meet them, and they marched in three columns; the middle one displayed the captains, who carried shotguns as they approached. I went out to greet them, having ordered my soldiers to form a double column. I marched in the center, accompanied by the religious, and carried the banner. Don Louis de St. Denis fell on his knees to venerate this token. In succession he embraced me and all of the religious. He was followed by all of the captains and the other people, which ceremony lasted more than an hour. There were many shots fired by both sides, as I had given some powder to these Indians. Singing the *Te Deum Laudamus,* we went to the encampment, where they seated themselves on sackcloth. Then there came many Indians with green corn, watermelons,

cantaloupes and tamales which they piled in the center of our assembly so that we could all partake of these foods. I ordered that they be given one hundred yards of sackcloth, forty blankets, thirty hats, and twelve packages of tobacco, which were placed in a pile for them to divide among themselves. There was a very rare circumstance in connection with the allotment of sackcloth. The persons distributing the goods did not have any for themselves. Two or three of the principal captains were also victims in this shortage. They were as happy as if they had received all of the goods themselves, although they like very much the things that the Spaniards give, especially anything blue. All of the Indians having convened, I addressed them through an interpreter, getting them to understand the purposes of our coming to their country, which was for the salvation of souls; that they should recognize absolutely their only King, who is God, and their natural master, Don Philip the Fifth, who sent them these gifts as a sign of his love, through His Excellency, Señor Duke of Linares, Viceroy of New Spain, under whose orders I have come to this country; that it was, therefore, necessary for their good political government that they should elect a captain general among themselves, which should be done at their discretion. They talked for some time, and soon afterwards a young man, less than a captain, was chosen by the Spaniards because they always elect the younger in order that the government may last longer. The Indians said that they wanted this one for their captain general. To him in the name of His Majesty I delivered my cane and approved said election, giving him one of my best jackets to improve his appearance, which made the Indians very happy and contented.

30. I remained in this place to celebrate the feast of Saint Peter and also to wait for my people to arrive. In the afternoon the Indians of the Nasonis and Nacogdoches came and we had the same peace demonstration as heretofore. There was a great display of pleasure manifesting itself with an Indian dance and the beating of drums.

31. This day I marched four leagues over a beautiful country with many valleys, rich timber lands with pecan and pine trees and grapevines. I stopped at the foot of a hill because there were a spring of good water and fine pasturage. In the afternoon I went out with the religious to look for a desirable place to establish the first mission. I was accompanied by the first captain of the Indians and some others. We found a favorable location, which was decided upon by the Indians, and the Father President was very much pleased with the choice. We then returned to oar camp.

JULY

1–2. These two days were spent in building a hut for myself, which was done by all of the Indians. They were well suited for this work. They completed the abode in nine working days, due to the abundance of timber in this province.

3. This day was spent at the foundation of the first Mission of San Francisco in the pueblo of Neches, where I named a chaplain and gave possession to the religious in the name of His Majesty. The house was finished on the fifth.[1]

7. This day I reached Concepción, having traveled nine leagues through a wonderful country, for there was an abundance of water, beautiful pine trees and others. There were also vines with great quantities of wild grapes. I crossed a river, which was very high, continuing on my journey to the northeast till I arrived at the town of Asinay, where there were very many *rancherías* with their stalks of corn, watermelons, cantaloupes, beans, tobacco and a flower which they eat. We do not know the name of it. I gave possession to said religious, named a chaplain and did everything else necessary. The Indians here dedicated themselves to the same activity of building a church and a dwelling place.[2]

8. This day I arrived in the town of Nacogdoches, having traveled nine leagues to the southeast over a fertile country with plenty of pasturage, pines, oaks, and many grapevines.

9. This day I remained here to attend to such business as might arise. I named a chaplain, giving instruction to build a church and a dwelling place.[3]

10. This day I left this mission, which was founded twenty-three leagues from the place where the first one was established by the Spaniards. I passed this day in the mission of the Nasonis,[4] having traveled ten leagues to the west over land equally as fertile as that which we passed, and inhabited by the said Indians. We were entertained in their towns.

11. On the eleventh day the first steps were taken towards the building of a church and dwelling, and I proceeded to name a chaplain. All of the people referred to are of the same kind, very agreeable and generous. They are glad to teach their language and especially to those of this mission. All duties in regard to the founding of the four missions were now concluded according to the orders of His Excellency. Having finished this work, I returned to my camp very happy. I was very pleased with the manner in which the Fathers

---

[1]Mission San Francisco de los Neches.

[2]Mission Purísima Concepción.

[3]Mission of Nuestra Señora do Guadalupe.

[4]Mission San José de los Nasonis.

and our party were received by the Indians. I was the only one to reach the camp, for the horses of my companions were tired out.

I sign it: DOMINGO RAMÓN.

EARLY PLANS FOR THE GERMAN CATHOLIC COLONIZATION IN TEXAS

Paul J. Foik, C.S.C.*

The first attempts at colonization and settlement in Texas occurred at the time when the Franciscan missions were permanently established in 1716. In the years that followed, the two Apostolic colleges of Santa Cruz of Querétaro and of Nuestra Señora de Guadalupe of Zacatecas supplied the priests who were to take care of the spiritual interests of these new inhabitants and to instruct and to discipline the natives in the fundamentals of Christian civilization. These pioneering agencies were employed by the Spaniards during the entire eighteenth century, and in union with the civil power prepared the way for political and economic development and expansion in this province. The padres worked hand in hand with the military officials, and in the course of time there arose a number of frontier institutions, which became the centers for future immigration.

In 1793 the edict for the so-called secularization of the missions of Texas was promulgated, and then the Franciscans retired, leaving almost all the posts where they had labored in charge of the secular clergy. This period of transition, which occurred during the era of the French Revolution, called for a declaration of policy in the colonies along the frontiers of New Spain. Foreigners were forbidden to enter Texas, and a detachment of soldiers was placed at the pueblo of Nacogdoches to prevent incursions from Louisiana. This prohibition was very rigidly enforced until the close of the century. Several incidents that took place during the decade show that the distrust of foreigners was justified and well founded. In those turbulent days there was reason for caution, since the lure of conquest and contraband trade seemed to have attracted many intruders to the territory within the confines of Texas.

Aside from the profit obtained from this commerce and industry, there was another reason why this influx of settlers should have been made the object of vigilance and investigation. The traditional and consistent practice

---

*Vol. 2, No. 6, appeared in September 1934 as a reprint from *Mid-America* 5, 4 (April 1934).

of Spanish colonial administration had always impeded the entry of foreigners into Texas, except members of the Catholic faith, and even regarding these persons there was a searching of motives, for there were plots, deceptions, intrigues by nations for their own special advantage. These cleverly conceived plans were but the manifestations of desires for domination and the acquisition of empire. This disposition for territorial expansion was pursued first by the French, then by the English, and finally by the American government. The Louisiana Purchase, executed by the United States, paved the way for the Anglo-American settlement of Texas. Before this final contest was decided, the Spanish power and then the Mexican regime were stubborn in their control, each hoping against hope to settle the province of Texas by a thinning out of the population in New Spain. To keep the Spanish people and their influence supreme, the Catholic religion was made the bulwark by which national integrity and solidarity were to be guarded and protected. The chaos that followed the severance of Mexico from the rule of Spain sapped nearly all the energy of the revolutionary party, and this condition retarded the development of the more distant provinces in the new republic. Consequently, the growth of the ideas of independence, urged by necessity and encouraged by example, began to assert themselves in Texas. Hardly had Mexico taken over the administration of affairs, when pressure was brought to bear to settle this vast territory by the use of a more conciliatory and liberal policy; but the provision remained that immigration was permitted only to persons who professed the Catholic faith. Every promoter and later every *empresario* who received land grants from the Mexican government were instructed and ordered to choose colonists who were willing to meet these religious requirements.

With the opening of the nineteenth century, when the province was still under Spanish rule, many attempts were made to form group settlements, most of which failed to be executed because there was a lingering suspicion that duplicity and cunningness were present in many schemes proposed by the secret agents of rival nations, laboring hopefully for colonial expansion. Many foreigners, however, were admitted because they had testimonials of good character. The Spanish officials in Texas were not always of the same mind on questions of foreign policy. The governor and the commandant general were frequently at variance on the interpretation and enforcement of immigration laws. In consequence, Nemesio Salcedo was ordered to make an inspection of the eastern settlements. The governor had approved the entry of Jacob Dorst, a German, who had lived for many years at Arcos, Louisiana. He and his three sons professed the Catholic religion. In defense of these proteges, his Excellency was supported by Father José Francisco Maynes, the parish priest of the Villa de Salcedo. Thus the Texas authorities, by the application of a liberal course of action, triumphed, and certain foreigners under investigation were permitted to remain.[1]

A similar inspection was made at Nacogdoches, and here another German, Christian Hesser, is mentioned. According to the testimonials of Fathers José María de Jesús Huerta and Mariano de Jesús Sosa, he was somewhat remiss in the practice of his religion.[2] The record later showed that he returned to Louisiana, because for two years he was commissioned as a second lieutenant of militia. There is also evidence that he had engaged in contraband trade. Yet in spite of these transgressions, he secured permission in May 1815 to go to Bayou Pierre so that he might bring his family and settle again in Texas. Needless to say, there were many evasions of the laws governing immigration and commerce, and even at this early date certain non-Catholics were permanently located on ranches in proximity to the border towns of east Texas. No doubt, other German families secretly found their way into the province, but there are no available records regarding these persons.

In the year 1812 Diego Morphi, the Spanish consul general at New Orleans, proposed to the Spanish government, a colonization plan that would place in Texas German and Polish soldiers who would defend the eastern boundary against the hostile designs of Napoleon's sympathizers and supporters in Louisiana. This foreign legion, besides exercising the functions of a border patrol, was designed to engage in agriculture and the useful arts; and consequently, a grant of seven square leagues of land upon the Gulf of Mexico was suggested as a strategic location for settlement. The scheme, as presented by Morphi to the Texas authorities and to the regency in Spain, was not approved. Another less ambitious plan, containing many of the original ideas of the first proposal, was again offered to the court, but no action was taken. In fact, the Spanish government demanded "the enforcement of the law forbidding all intercourse with foreigners." This new decree even repealed the

---

[1]M. de Salcedo to N. Salcedo, March 30 and April 6, 1810, Bexar Archives; Mattie Austin Hatcher, *The Opening of Texas to Foreign Settlement, 1801–1821*, University of Texas Bulletin No. 2714 (Austin, 1927), 192–95.

[2]Sosa to Manuel de Salcedo and Huerta to Manuel de Salcedo, May 4, 1810, Bexar Archives; Hatcher, *The Opening of Texas*, 198.

order of September 24, 1803, allowing the immigration of Spanish subjects from Louisiana. These precautions were justified because of the intrigues of certain revolutionists, such as [José Antonio?] Navarro, José Bernardo Gutiérrez de Lara, and others.[3]

Another attempt was made two years later by Colonel Richard Keene, an American, to colonize Texas with Germans and Irishmen. Protection of the frontiers of New Spain was again the motive that actuated the addressing of a memorial to the King of Spain. The petitioner stressed the miserable conditions of the Germans in the Rhine region because of Napoleon's despotic rule. Keene had already received a grant of land to make the settlement, with the provision that two-thirds of the colonists should be Spaniards. The remainder could be chosen from any other country except France. All of these settlers must be Catholics. There is no official record regarding the proposed location of this settlement, but Kennedy's *History of Texas* states that twenty-one thousand acres of the richest lands in Texas had been offered to this promoter. If the political situation in Europe had not changed almost instantaneously, just as the plan was placed before the executives, the first group settlement in Texas, other than Spanish, would have been predominantly German. Thus this first empresario was one only *in petto*; the land was not distributed, and the title to it became void because the contract could not be fulfilled.[4]

Another plan of colonization proposed in 1819 by three Swiss citizens, Charles Henry Du Pasquier, P. H. Lemba, and William Wohlleben was also wrecked in that turbulent sea of circumstances. This scheme was presented to Don Luis de Onís, Spanish Minister to the United States, and the proponents requested permission to establish a settlement of Swiss and Germans on the Trinity River. A few days later a substitute petition was offered, changing the location and selecting sites either on the Sabine, the San Antonio, or the Guadalupe rivers. The colonists intended to devote their labors to farming and industrial enterprises. They expected to provide the raw materials for the

---

[3]Decree, May 6, 1819, México leg. 4, Archivo General de Indias, copy at the Center for American History, University of Texas at Austin; "Expediente sobre remisión a la Provincia Alemanes y Polacos para poblarla y otros fines," June 6, 1806, Guadalajara 103–3–17, Archivo General de Indias, Seville, copy at the Center for American History, University of Texas at Ausin (hereafter cited as AGI:G); Hatcher, *Opening of Texas*, 218–24.

[4]Ricardo Raynal Keene, *Memoria presentada a S.M.C. el Señor Don Fernando VII sovre el asunto de fomentar la población y cultivo en los terrenos baldios en las provincias internas del reyno de México* (Madrid, 1815); Hatcher, *Opening of Texas*, 241–43; Rudolph L. Biesele, *History of the German Settlements in Texas, 1831-1861*, (Austin, 1930), 22.

manufacture of cotton, woolen, silk, and linen goods. Delay was caused by negotiations regarding the cession of Florida to the United States; and soon afterwards another important event occurred, the independence of Mexico, which prevented any immediate consideration of this project.[5]

Hardly had the new government assumed control of affairs, when J. Val. Hecke, a retired Prussian army officer who had traveled to the New World, published a book entitled *Reise durch die Vereinigten Staaten von Nord-Amerika in den Jahren 1818 und 1819.* He had visited Texas and gave his impressions of this province as a fitting place for German settlement in the following words: "If there is a tract of land on the trans-Atlantic Continent that is suited for colonial possession for Prussia, it is the Province of Texas, the acquisition of which by purchase from Spain, to which it is neither useful nor of political worth, should be easily accomplished." It was his opinion that an enterprise such as the British East India Company could be formed. The only service required from the Prussian government would be military protection. The recommendation to provide six hundred acres to ten thousand ex-soldiers would supply the necessary defense. As a result of this scheme the Fatherland would receive raw materials for manufactures and foreign trade could be more easily established and developed. These far-reaching and ambitious proposals, with a magnificent portrayal of the varying physical features of the vast domain in Texas, fired the imagination of many Germans long after the enticing description had been published. Its appearance in print came, however, at a most inopportune time, when Mexico was occupied with the problems confronting a new regime, and hence no attempt was made to put the plan into execution on the grand scale with which it was conceived by the author.

The influence of Hecke's book had the effect of causing fifty-three adventurers of different nationalities to assemble at New Orleans, and the party proceeded in October 1821 to set foot on Texas soil with the expectation of making that land a place of permanent abode. The state archives in Austin preserve a report of this expedition, and among the names listed there are included the following Germans: Joseph Dirksen, Eduard Hanstein, Wilhelm Miller, Caspar Porton, and Ernst von Rosenberg. Very little is known about the careers of these daring pioneers, except that of Rosenberg. They

---

[5]Du Pasquier to Onís, May 3 and 8, 1819, Audiencia de Guadalajara 103–6–17, and Sept. 10, 1820, and April 26, 1821, Audiencia de México, Archivo General de Indias, Seville, Dunn transcripts at the Center for American History, University of Texas at Austin; Biesele, *History of German Settlements*, 22–23.

landed at Indianola and went directly to La Bahía, now known as Goliad. Here they were all taken prisoners by the Mexican soldiers. Rosenberg later was escorted to San Antonio, where he received a commission as colonel of a regiment of artillery. His fate was soon sealed in one of the military encounters during the intermittent strife that was being carried on by contending factions for the control of the government.

Some historians have given the credit to Baron von Bastrop for the founding of the first real German colony in Texas. That statement is found in Roemer's *Texas*, Koerner's *Das deutsche Element,* Eickhoff's *In der neuen Heimat,* Tiling's *History of the German Element in Texas,* and Weber's *Deutsche Pioniere in Texas.* Biesele in his *History of the German Settlements in Texas* states: "Bastrop is said to have planned an extensive colonization in Texas, when the first American settlement was made in that Mexican province." He questions "where Dr. Ferdinand Roemer, the author of the statement, got his authority for making it. It is certain that nowhere in the histories of Texas is the statement made that Bastrop was interested in bringing German settlers to Texas, and no documentary authority for the statement has been discovered." Yet Tiling cites Anton Eickhoff, saying: "Nearly all of these settlers came from the County of Elmenhorst, Grand Duchy of Oldenburg." He goes on to say: "For sixteen years, until the founding of Austin in 1839, this was the farthest northeastern settlement in Texas." According to the records in the General Land Office in Austin, under the title *Translations of Empresario Contracts,* the Town of Bastrop, the supposed center of the German colony, was founded on June 8, 1832, by Miguel Arciniega, who was appointed by the Mexican government to lay out new towns for Austin's Colony. Hence, with this information on one hand and the absence of testimony from original sources for the contrary statement, the writer is forced to conclude with Dr. Biesele that a German settlement formed by Baron von Bastrop is just another piece of historic fiction.

During the decade from 1820 to 1830 many books of travels similar to that of J. Val. Hecke's *Reise* were published. The authors of the most prominent writings were Bromme, Gerke, Arends, and Duden. The last mentioned had a great admiration for this country, and his impressions are to be found in *Bericht uber eine Reise nach westlichen Staaten Nord America's.* This work was read by thousands of Germans, especially in Baden, Hessen, Rhenish Prussia, Hanover, and Oldenburg. Many persons were stirred with the ideas of creating one or more German states in the New World.

In 1826 Dr. John Lucius Woodbury was granted power of attorney by Joseph Vehlein to secure a contract for him for the establishment of a colony in Texas. He was authorized to solicit the governor to effect this object, "offering to execute it with three hundred industrious families, professants [*sic*] of the Catholic religion and of good moral habits, part of them to be German and Swiss, and part of them from the States of North America." This petition did not comply fully with the requirements of law, and a second contract was drawn up, but it was never executed. In 1830 Vehlein, David G. Burnet, and Lorenzo de Zavala organized the Galveston Bay and Texas Land Company, which was "prepared to promote colonization on a great scale from the United States and Europe."[6]

In the same year Stephen F. Austin also conceived the idea of inducing Swiss and German immigrants to settle in Texas. This empresario preferred the Teutonic element, for "they have not in general the horrible mania for speculation, which is so prominent a trait in the English and North American character, and above all they will oppose slavery."[7]

While the Austin proposal was under consideration, Tadeo Ortiz de Ayala proposed a similar scheme and petitioned Lucas Alamán, secretary of Interior and Exterior Relations. The matter also came to the notice of Manuel de Mier y Terán, Commissioner of Colonization, who was so impressed that he reported to Alamán that "it would be very advantageous to locate about one hundred Swiss or German families in Galveston without an empresario and under the immediate supervision of the government."[8]

In April 1831 two German pioneers, Friedrich Ernst and Charles Fordtran, arrived at Harrisburg on Buffalo Bayou. They had traveled part of the way from New Orleans on the Mexican schooner *Saltillo*. Five weeks were spent in selecting a suitable location. They finally set up their new homes at Industry in Austin County. The following memoir of Mrs. Ernst With its graphic descriptions of hardships and privations in the lonely wilderness is here presented in part:

---

[6]Biesele, *History of German Settlements*, 25.

[7]Eugene C. Barker, *Life of Stephen F. Austin, Founder of Texas, 1793–1836: A Chapter in the Westward Movement of the Anglo-American People* (Nashville, 1926), 254; Biesele, *History of German Settlements*, 26.

[8]Ortiz to Alamán and Terán to Alamán, Fomento, leg. 7, exp. 57, pp. 33–36, Archivo General y Público de la Nación de México, West transcripts, Center for American History, University of Texas at Austin (hereafter cited as AGN–West); Biesele, *History of German Settlements*, 27.

> After having lived in the most primitive style for several months on our new homestead, we sold about one quarter of our grant for ten cows. Now we had at least milk and butter, which was a real godsend, for the constant monotony of venison and dry cornbread had almost become nauseating. We lived in a miserable little hut, covered with thatch that was not waterproof. We suffered a great deal in winter, as we had no heating stove. Our shoes gave out, and not knowing how to make moccasins, we had to go barefooted.
>
> For nearly two years we lived alone in the wilderness, but fortunately we were not troubled by the Indians, who were quiet and friendly. In the fall of 1833 some Germans settled in our neighborhood, among them the families of Bartels, Zimmerschreit, and Juergens. We naturally hailed their coming with great joy. In 1834 the following German families arrived here: Amsler, Wolters, Kleberg, von Roeder, Frels, Siebel, Grassmeyer, Biegel and some others whose names I have forgotten. . . . In the fall of 1834 the Indians kidnapped and abducted the wife and two children of Mr. Juergens, who had just settled at Post Oak Point, four miles from here. Through the efforts of Father Muldoon, a Catholic missionary, Mrs. Juergens was returned to her distracted husband, but of the two children no tidings ever came.[9]

Mention has just been made of Robert Kleberg in the foregoing memorandum by Mrs. Ernst Kleberg supplies a most interesting account of his journey and that of his party to Texas. The memoir here presented gives some very startling experiences:

> As soon as we decided to go to Texas, we sent three unmarried brothers of my wife, Louis, Albrecht, and Joachim (von Roeder), and their sister Valesca, with a servant, ahead of us to Texas for the purpose of selecting a place where we could all meet and begin operations. They were well provided with money, clothing, a light wagon and harness, tools, and generally everything necessary to commence a settlement. Six months after our advance party had left, and after we had received

---

[9]Moritz Tiling, *History of the German Element in Texas from 1820–1850, and Historical Sketches of the German Texas Singers' League and Houston Turnverein from 1853–1913* (Houston, 1913), 9, 18–19; Biesele, *History of German Settlements*, 42–47. See also Gilbert G. Benjamin, *The Germans in Texas: A Study in Immigration*, (Philadelphia, 1909).

news of their safe arrival, we followed on the last day of September, 1834, in the ship *Congress*, Captain J. Adams.[10]

At New Orleans we heard very bad accounts about Texas and were advised not to go there, as it was said that Texas was infested with robbers, murderers and ferocious Indians. But we were determined to risk it and could not afford to disappoint our friends who had preceded us. As soon, therefore, as we succeeded in chartering the schooner *Sabine*, about two weeks after we had landed in New Orleans, we sailed to Brazoria, Texas. After a voyage of eight days we were wrecked off Galveston Island on December 22, 1834. Among the passengers the opinion prevailed that the *Sabine* was wrecked purposely in order to get the amount for which she was insured. The wrecked boat was sold at public auction in Brazoria, and was bought for thirty dollars by a man who had come a few days afterward in the steamer *Ocean* from New Orleans. It is impossible for me to name with certainty the exact point on the island at which we stranded, but I think it was not far from the center of the island, about ten miles from the present site of the City of Galveston.

The island was a perfect wilderness inhabited only by deer, wolves, and rattlesnakes. All passengers were safely brought to shore and were given provisions partly from those on board ship and partly by the game on the island.

Two or three days after our vessel was beached, the steamer *Ocean* hove in sight, and observing our distress signal, anchored opposite our camp and sent a boat ashore with an officer to find out the situation. The captain agreed to take a few of us to Brazoria, charging a doubloon(twenty dollars) each. I, with Rudolph von Roeder, took passage on it as an agent of the remaining passengers to charter a boat to take them and their belongings to the mainland. Finding no boat at either Brazoria or Bell's Landing, the only two ports at that time, I proceeded on foot to San Felipe, where I was told I would find a small steamer, but did not succeed in chartering her, the price of one thousand dollars asked being too high.

---

[10]The party consisted of the following: Robert I Kleberg and his wife; Lieutenant von Roeder and wife, daughters Louise and Caroline, and sons Rudolph, Otto, and Wilhelm; Louis Kleberg; Mrs. Otto von Roeder, nee Pauline von Donop; Antoinette von Donop; John Reinermann and family; and many others. Passengers were nearly all from Oldenburg, and after a voyage of sixty days they landed at New Orleans.

In San Felipe I heard for the first time of the whereabouts of my relatives who had preceded us. Here I also made the acquaintance of Colonel Johnson and Captain Moseley Baker, under whose command I afterwards fought at the battle of San Jacinto. These gentlemen informed me that my two friends, Louis and Albert von Roeder, had located about fourteen miles from San Felipe on a league of land, the present Cat Spring, but that Joachim and Valesca von Roeder had died. I found Louis and Albert in a miserable hut and in a pitiful condition. They were emaciated by disease and want of proper treatment and nourishment. Tears of joy streamed from their eyes when they beheld me and my companion. After a few days of rest I continued my search for a boat. I had a letter of introduction to Stephen F. Austin and Sam Williams from a New Orleans merchant, but both men were absent from Harrisburg when I reached there. Fortunately I succeeded in chartering a small vessel from Mr. Scott, the father of Mrs. Williams, for three trips to Galveston for one hundred dollars, and immediately returned to Galveston, landing on the bay side, opposite the camp of the stranded passengers, just four weeks after I had left it. I found all the passengers in good health and spirits. They had spent most of the time in hunting and fishing. Those who could not shoot were employed to drive the deer to the hunters. There were deer by the thousands.

The next day I left with the first cargo of passengers, including my wife, her parents and Caroline von Roeder. After a stormy trip we arrived in the evening of the same day at Mr. Scott's place, where we were hospitably treated. I was fortunate to find quite a comfortable house in Harrisburg, which I rented, as we intended to remain there until all passengers had arrived from the island.

The last passengers did not come until the fall of 1835, although I had hired another small sloop from Captain Smith in Velasco, which also made three trips. The winter of 1835 was unusually severe.

We had supplied ourselves with everything necessary to commence a settlement in a new country. We had wagons, farming implements, all sorts of tools, household and kitchen furniture, and clothing which we brought with us from Germany. Early in the summer of 1835 we had finished building two log houses; one of them had even a floor and a ceiling, having sawed by hand the planks from post oak trees.

> We had also enclosed and planted a field of ten acres in corn and cotton, and we now moved the members of our family who had remained in Harrisburg to our settlement. Such of our goods for which we had no room or immediate use, we left at the house we had rented at Harrisburg. Among the objects we left was a fine piano, belonging to my wife, many valuable oil paintings, music books, etc., all of which fell prey to the flames, which consumed Harrisburg during the war that began in the following spring.[11]

Many similar stories to those related in these two memoirs could be told by hundreds of other home seekers in the vast wilderness of Texas. Courage, self-sacrifice, and perseverance were necessary to face the dangers of all kinds that lurked around these adventurous people. This condition of primeval existence is well demonstrated by the Beales Colony, which landed at Copano on Aransas Bay in December, 1833. The party was made up mostly of Irishmen, but in the group there were three German families from Bavaria, named respectively Dippelhofer, Wetter, and Schwartz. There were also some single men recorded as coming from Germany: Paulsen, Ludecus, and Talloer. From Copano, where they landed, they traveled on foot to La Villa de Dolores, where they established a settlement. In August, 1834, more colonists arrived at Copano, but they were warned that an Indian massacre had taken place at Dolores. Dr. Beales continued to bring Irish and German settlers to the region, but at last he was compelled to abandon these efforts, because the Texas revolution put an end to all his plans.[12]

During the closing years of the Mexican regime Baron Johann von Racknitz had prepared many schemes for the German colonization of Texas, which he sent to Sebastian Mercado, then Minister of Mexico in Holland. The promoter also had correspondence with Thomas Murphy, Mexican Minister to France. Racknitz believed that thousands of Germans were anxious to go to America. He next wrote to the Secretary of State for Interior and Exterior Relations in Mexico City, and enclosed with his letter the two recommendations from Mercado and Murphy, including also his plans for German settlements. After these petitions had been made, it seems that he received

---

[11]Tiling, *German Element in Texas*, 25–28; Biesele, *History of German Settlements*, 42–49.
[12]Biesele, *History of German Settlements*, 27–28; Tiling, *German Element in Texas*, 21–22.

contracts, but there are no existing records that his plans were ever carried out.[13]

Thus came to a close the Spanish and Mexican epochs of German colonization and settlement in Texas. It must be noted that during the four decades from 1793 to 1836 many ambitious proposals were presented, but the ever changing conditions of government, both in Europe and America, spelled defeat for many concerned in these undertakings. These efforts were not without some favorable results, for much German literature had been published, especially in the form of description and travel. These wonderful accounts attracted many readers. Societies like the Giessener Auswanderungs Gesellsehaft were organized. After the Texas Revolution a great number of highly educated and energetic Germans came to join the new republic. Here they readily adapted themselves to existing conditions, and by hard and persevering labor opened this vast territory to modern commerce and industry.

---

[13]Tiling, M., *German Element in Texas*, 20–21; Biesele, *History of German Settlements*, 28–31. See also Fomento leg. 1, exp. 1, pp. 58–59, AGN–West.

PEÑA'S DIARY OF THE AGUAYO EXPEDITION

TRANSLATED BY
Peter P. Forrestal, C.S.C.[*]

EDITOR'S NOTE

The Society is here indebted to the Reverend Dr. Peter P. Forrestal for this translation of the record of the Aguayo Expedition into Texas in 1722, with annotations. In rendering his translation, Dr. Forrestal has been very careful to make a critical and comparative study of all available copies of the document, and he has had the particular good fortune to have a photostatic copy of the original found in the archives of Convento Grande de San Francisco in Mexico City. This particular piece of work stands in Catholic history at the beginning of the Mission Era in Texas. The first missions in East Texas and at San Antonio had been placed in operation only a few years before, when the French incursions on Texas soil caused the viceroy to send Aguayo to Texas. Padre Peña, who kept a daily account of the advances of the expedition, tells a very interesting story and furnishes much data regarding conditions at that time.

Peña's Diary of the Aguayo Expedition

Were I as competent to carry out orders as I am happy to receive them, I might, indeed, feel confident of meriting the honor, which has been conferred upon me by the Señor Marquis of San Miguel de Aguayo, of describing, as a faithful eye-witness, the course followed during the progress of this glorious enterprise.[1] In having been chosen by His Lordship to serve Our Majesty the

---

[*] Vol 2, No. 7, appeared in January 1935 as a reprint from *Records and Studies of the United States Catholic Historical Society* 24 (October 1934).

[1] Aguayo's title in the printed copy of the "Derrotero," or diary, published in 1722, reads: "D. Joseph de Azlor, Knight-Commandant of the Kingdom of Aragón, Governor and Captain General of the Province of Texas, New Philippines, and of this of Coahuila, New Kingdom of Extremadura." At this time Texas was also called Nuevas Filipinas and Coahuila was also, known as Nueva Estremadura. The Marquis of San Miguel de Aguayo, who had been in the royal service in Spain and who continued to serve the king after his arrival to Mexico, acquired large estates and silver mines in what is now the State of Coahuila. See Eleanor Claire Buckley, "The Aguayo Expedition into Texas and Louisiana, 1719–1722," *The Quarterly of*

king (may God protect him) as chaplain of these troops I have achieved the greatest honor that could be conferred upon me.

So that peoples of all times may know what prompted this *entrada,* it may be well to state at the outset that it was occasioned by the fact that twenty-one years ago the French, instigated by their traders in Paris, had established a colony at Mobile, a port on the Gulf of Mexico, twelve leagues from our presidio of Santa María de Galve, commonly known as Pensacola. During the past twenty-one years they have extended their colonization to the Natchitoches, or Red River, that is, as far as Los Adaes, in the Province of Texas, a distance of some 300 leagues, and have also carried on their work of colonization up the Empalizada, or Missouri River, for a distance of some 400.

Taking advantage of the truce existing between the two powers, French troops surprised the garrison at Pensacola, and at the same time, June 19 of last year, 1719, invaded the Province of Texas. The padres and Spaniards, because of the superior forces [of the enemy][2] were obliged to withdraw from the six missions that had been established, and retired to the presidio of San Antonio de Béjar. This presidio is situated on the boundary of the Province of Coahuila, and is 240 leagues from Los Adaes, on the [northeast] boundary of Texas.

Apprized of these aggressions, his Excellency,[3] in order to send relief to the said province, ordered that, with the haste demanded by the urgency of the situation, there be recruited in León, Saltillo, and Parras the largest possible number of troops, and he entrusted to the Marquis of San Miguel de Aguayo the task of furnishing them with arms and supplies. The latter recruited in the three districts of Saltillo eighty-four men, and from the fifth to the twenty-eighth of September, the day on which they left, was busy furnishing them with clothing, arms, horses, and a year's supply of flour, corn and livestock. For the purpose of securing these supplies 12,000 pesos were furnished by his Excellency, and 9,000 by the marquis himself. The latter, upon hearing of the invasion, wrote to his Excellency and offered in the service of Our Lord the king (may God protect him) his estate, his life and his sword. In reply his Excellency sent him a commission in which, in the name of His Majesty, he appointed him governor of those provinces. As soon as he had received this

---

the Texas State Historical Association 15, 1 (July 1911): 20; Peter P. Forrestal, trans., "The Solís Diary of 1767," *Preliminary Studies of the Texas Catholic Historical Society*, 1, 6 (March 1931): 4, 41 [reprinted in *Preparing the Way: Preliminary Studies of the Texas Catholic Historical Society I*, Studies in Southwestern Catholic History No. 1 (Austin, 1997), 101–48].

[2]Here we have followed the printed copy, which reads: "obligando sus superiores fuerzas a abandonarla los Españoles." The word fuerzas is not found in the manuscript copy.

[3]Baltasar de Zúñiga, Marquis of Valero and Duke of Arión, was viceroy from 1716 to 1721. See Carlos E. Castañeda, *Morfi's History of Texas*, 2 pts. (Albuquerque, 1935), 231 n.14.

communication His Lordship answered that in the service of His Majesty he was most willing to go, even as a common soldier, on such a glorious expedition, and added that since the discovery of America there had never been such daring enemies and that the protection of those dominions from the imminent peril which threatened them was a matter of the utmost importance.

He set out immediately, and reached this town (Monclova) of Coahuila on October 21. Informed of existing conditions, he brought to his Excellency's attention the fact that those kingdoms (Texas and Coahuila) were open to attack, because of insufficient troops, and stressed the need of a larger force on that frontier. Acting on this information, the viceroy ordered that 500 men be recruited in Querétaro, Zacatecas, San Luis Potosí, Zelaya and Aguas Calientes, and that the sum of 450 pesos for each soldier be handed over to the marquis in order that he might pay their salaries for one year in advance, and also 25,000 pesos with which to defray other expenses of the expedition.

Knowing that Our Majesty the king (may God protect him) has manifested great zeal in the work of the propagation of our holy Faith and realizing that this work could be done most effectively through the establishment of missions, the marquis, with the approval of his Excellency, founded that of San José y San Miguel de Aguayo.[4] This mission, which is made up of three numerous tribes of Indians and which, by order of his Excellency, is to receive the usual assistance, will be a permanent foundation, because in case of attack it can obtain protection from the *presidio,* which is about one league distant.

On April 1 of the present year, 1720, the 500 men, equipped with arms and supplied with provisions for the expedition by the marquis' agents set out from the aforesaid districts. Because of the fact that the journey was being undertaken in the dry season, great difficulties were met at the very outset; and, on June 23, only 560 of the 3,600 horses that had been purchased for this *entrada* reached Coahuila with the expedition, the rest having died or become disabled along the way. Seeing that the 560 horses were very tired, the marquis realized the impossibility of continuing the journey, and decided to halt the expedition in Coahuila. By his orders, 3,400 horses were secured at the various stock farms, but as this was the driest summer ever experienced in this part of the country, those animals did not reach Coahuila until the latter part of September. In the middle of October the 600 mules that had left Mexico City on April 24 arrived with the clothing, arms, powder, and six cannon, all of which had been secured by the marquis' orders.

---

[4]This mission was established by Fray Antonio Margil de Jesús, superior of the missionaries from the College of Guadalupe in Zacatecas. The marquis, who was in Coahuila at the time, authorized the foundation.

As the supplies for which he had been waiting were now arriving, the marquis, dividing the 500 men into eight companies, formed a battalion of mounted infantry under the name of San Miguel de Aragón; and, having received from his Excellency authorization to appoint officers, he chose as his lieutenant governor and captain general Don Fernando Pérez de Almazán, and as captains Don Tomás de Zubiría, Don Miguel Colón, Don Gabriel Costales, Don Manuel de Herrera, Don Francisco Becerra Luque, Don José de Arroyo, Don Pedro de Oribe and Don Juan Cantú, and also appointed subaltern officers.

In a dispatch which arrived from Mexico on October 5, his Excellency, acting on information which he had received to the effect that a truce had been signed between the two powers, ordered that the *entrada* for the purpose of recovering for the Crown the Province of Nuevas Filipinas and of restoring the missions be continued, but that only a defensive war be waged in case the French encroached upon Spanish territory. Citing at the same time the *cédula* which he had received from Our Royal Majesty (may God protect him), in which the latter explains the manner in which the French are to be dealt with, his Excellency ordered that all of these be urged to enter the royal service, that all who cared to do so be admitted, and that they be allowed to live with the Spaniards.[5] Informed that he was not permitted to make those possessions secure, the marquis did not fail to manifest his disappointment, but stated that in this matter, also, he was ready to render blind obedience.

Due to the fact that all the clothing which had been brought at the time of the arrival of the animals had not come ready made, it was not until November 15 that the marquis could direct the battalion to begin the march. Before setting out he ordered the blessing of the standards, a solemn ceremony performed in honor of Our Lady of Pilar, to whose guidance the *entrada* was being entrusted. On one of the standards appeared the images of Our Lady of Pilar, Saint Michael and Saint Raphael, with the motto: *Pugnate pro Fide et Rege*,[6] on another those of Our Lady of Guadalupe, Saint Michael and Saint Francis Xavier; and on a third that of Saint James.[7] The artillery and all the companies were offered their first and best opportunity for practice by firing repeated salutes, Mass was celebrated, a procession took place, and the governor added joy to the festivities by supplying brandy for the soldiers and

---

[5]Elizabeth Howard West, trans., "Bonilla's Brief Compendium of the History of Texas, 1772," *The Quarterly of the Texas State Historical Association*, 8, 1 (July 1904): 32, states that the royal *cédula* was issued on May 6, 1721. According to Castañeda (*Morfi's History of Texas*, 234 n.35) it was signed in Madrid on June 23, 1721.

[6]Fight for your faith and king.

[7]Saint James the Greater, apostle of Spain.

by giving a sumptuous banquet to all the officers and to the missionaries of that province.

On November 16 the governor ordered his lieutenant general, Don Fernando Pérez de Almazán, to set out with the expedition, for he himself was unable to leave until he had issued certain instructions with respect to the government of the province, and until he had insured, by means of 500 mules that were needed for the *entrada,* the conveyance of supplies from Saltillo and Parras, a distance of 400 leagues from the Texas boundary. Besides these, 400 mules were traveling with the battalion and others (200) had already been sent ahead to San Antonio with a large store of provisions. The expedition proceeded in the following order: a picket of veteran soldiers acquainted with the country; the baggage; the companies of soldiers, according to seniority and each protecting its drove of horses; the food and war supplies; and, finally, the herds of cattle and sheep. A captain and his company covered the entire line of march.

As the route followed as far as the Rio Grande is known, we omit the daily entry for this part of the journey. At the very beginning travel became most difficult, a lagoon, which had formed on the highway, making necessary a three days' detour. On the twenty-fifth the expedition reached the Sabinas River, twenty-five leagues from Coahuila. As a result of the frequent autumn rains, which had been as excessive as the summer drought, this river had been swollen for a long time. Seeing that it was impassable and that two canoes, prepared beforehand upon instructions from the marquis, had been carried off by the current, the lieutenant general ordered that another be built. In the meantime the waters receded and, by means of a very narrow row of stones that reached to the opposite bank, a crossing was effected, though with great difficulty because of the swiftness of the current. One of the first soldiers that attempted to cross was drowned and Captain Don Miguel Colón and other soldiers fell into the river, and their lives were in imminent peril. By December 15, after a delay of three weeks, all the companies, the equipage, and animals had crossed the Sabinas; and on the twentieth the expedition, after traveling a distance of twenty-five leagues, reached the Río del Norte, commonly known as the Rio Grande. The battalion camped along this large river, which is the distance of a musket-shot in width and, near its banks, more than one and one-half rods in depth. Informed by the natives that it would be a long time before its waters receded, the lieutenant general ordered that wooden rafts be built. Three of these having been completed, the crossing began after Christmas.

At this same time the marquis, accompanied by Fray Isidro Félix de Espinosa, president of the Texas missions belonging to the Apostolic College of Santa Cruz in Querétaro, reached the aforesaid Río del Norte. A few days later Doctor Don José Codallos y Rabal, commissary and qualifier of the Holy Office, synodal examiner of the Diocese of Guadalajara, and ex-visitor and ecclesiastical notary of Mazapil and Saltillo, arrived also. Doctor Codallos y Rabal was entering Texas as vicar general, all faculties having been conferred upon him by the bishop of Guadalajara, to whose jurisdiction the said province belongs.[8] On the way north His Lordship [the marquis] had visited the missions of San Bernardino and Santiago del Valle de la Candela, located near the highway. At these places he clothed all the Indians, both young and old, as he had previously done at the missions of San Miguel de Aguayo and San Buenaventura near Coahuila.

The work of crossing the river, though very difficult, was continued, various kinds of rafts built with logs being used for the purpose.[9] One of the rafts was made from cowhide, but did not hold up for lack of resin. Several others were tried also, but of all these only one, built of ten logs and resting on barrels, proved serviceable. The work of crossing the river caused much delay, because only six loads could be taken over at a time, but especially because of the terrible frosts, snows, and rains.[10] On rainy days the weather was more tolerable, because the cold was not so severe. Fifty swimmers were occupied continuously in pulling the rafts, and they worked so hard that all but four became sick. They were encouraged and cheered on in their efforts by the fact that the marquis, who was present on the bank and who realized that they were working so faithfully, saw to it that they were kept warm with brandy, chocolate and plenty of food.

On February 2 His Lordship received from Captain Matías García of the presidio at San Antonio a dispatch informing him that he had just learned from certain Indians of the Sanas tribe that at this time Captain Louis de St. Denis and other Frenchmen were holding a convocation of many tribes about thirty leagues from the aforesaid presidio, but that he himself was ignorant of their designs. Upon receiving this information His Lordship held a council of war, in which it was determined that, without delay, a detachment of one hundred men, picked from all the companies, and sixteen veteran soldiers, that had served at the presidios and that were acquainted with the country, be dispatched to assist San Antonio, and if need be, to search for and to withstand the enemy. This determination was carried out immediately, and the

---

[8]In Spain the chaplain major had the title of vicar general and had jurisdiction, independent of the bishop, to grant to the chaplains under him faculties to hear confessions and to perform marriages.

[9]The "Derrotero" states that the expedition traveled twenty-five leagues from the Sabine to the Rio Grande, From this Castañeda (*Morfi's History of Texas*, 234 n.37) concludes that it crossed the latter in the vicinity of Eagle Pass. Buckley ("Aguayo Expedition," 30 n.3) says that the crossing must have taken place at the San Juan Bautista Mission.

[10]A *carga*, or load, is about four bushels.

detachment, divided into two companies, left under the command of the lieutenant general, Don Fernando Pérez de Almazán, and the first captains, Don Tomás de Zubiría and Don Miguel Colón. Upon reaching San Antonio the lieutenant general learned that in the meantime Captain García had sent some very trustworthy Indians to explore the country and with them Juan Rodríguez, one of the captains from the Ranchería Grande, who, with fifty families, had gone to San Antonio to ask that a mission be established for his tribe. Captain Rodríguez returned on February 25, and reported that, although he had reached the vicinity of the Brazos de Dios River, he had not found the Indians of the Ranchería Grande, who lived much farther south and were then probably attending the convocation. He stated also that he had not dared to advance any farther, but that upon his return to San Antonio his Indians had told him that a member of the Sana tribe had been there to see him and to inform him that the Indians of the Ranchería Grande and of other tribes were at the French convocation, and that they had a large number of horses and guns, and were located between the two forks of the Brazos de Dios, above the Texas road.

As soon as he had received this news the lieutenant general decided to dispatch to those parts Captain Don Matías García with the veteran troops and a scouting party of thirty men from the battalion. This captain advanced as far as the Brazos de Dios, which is about eighty leagues from San Antonio, but was obliged to return, being unable to cross a large lake which had been formed by the swollen waters of the Brazos. From smoke which he had observed on the opposite bank of this lake and from the fact that neither on going nor on returning had he come across a single Indian, he concluded that the convocation was being held at that place.

Possessed of this information, the marquis resolved to cross the river two days sooner than he had planned. On this and on the following day he distributed clothing to sixty Indians that had helped in taking the rafts and livestock across the Rio Grande; and from the day upon which the crossing of the river had begun until March 23, the day upon which the entire expedition had reached the other side, he supplied them with corn and meat.

On Monday, March 24, His Lordship and eight companies, minus the detachment already at San Antonio, continued the march beyond [east of] the Rio Grande. Each company had 350 horses, 600 head of cattle and 800 sheep (500 loads of food, war supplies, and clothing had been sent ahead) and His Lordship had with him 600 loads of clothing, provisions, and baggage.

At the Rio Grande the expedition was joined by Captains Alonso de Cárdenas and Juan Cortinas with their companies, and also by Fray Isidro Félix de Espinosa and Fray Benito Sánchez, the latter a Texas missionary who at the time had been stationed at the Mission of San Juan Bautista near the presidio on the Río Grande del Norte. From here the expedition traveled due north. As the remainder of the route is not so well known and as part of it to San Antonio is over a new road, from here on our account will take the form of a diary.

We traveled, about two leagues from the river, along the road called El Real del Cuervo. Here there is good pastureland, and various *esteros*[11] in which water can be found the greater part of the year. During the day's journey of five leagues, which ended at Las Rosas de San Juan, we had observed nothing worthy of mention. We spent most of the day crossing glens and creeks, none of which were very deep. Although we saw some tracts of land that would make good pasturage, most of the country is densely covered with bushes called mesquite. Five leagues.

Tuesday, 25. In order that the troops might not be left without Mass on this solemn feast (of the Annunciation], the march was interrupted at Las Rosas de San Juan. His Lordship saw that it was necessary to remain here on the twenty-sixth also, as many horses and trains had been lost. All of these were found later.

Thursday, 27. We left Las Rosas de San Juan. It had been announced that, because of the dense fog that morning, a soldier traveling with one of the droves of horses had become lost, and His Lordship dispatched two soldiers to search for him. Advancing directly northeast for about two leagues, we left the old road, which is rough and hilly, and we followed another running through a flat and open country for a distance of three leagues. We again struck the old road, which runs east-northeast as far as a place called El Ojo de Agua de San Diego,[*] nine leagues from Las Rosas de San Juan. The day's march was fatiguing for such a long train, but the lack of water along the ordinary route made the detour necessary. Along the way another soldier that had gone after a runaway horse became lost, and His Lordship sent two other soldiers to find him. Nine leagues.

Friday, 28. We traveled northeast about half of the day, and then went east until we came, at the end of our journey of about five leagues, to Caramanchel Creek.[†] Here there is excellent pasture-land, and in autumn and winter plenty of water. Along the banks of the creek there are many turkeys, and along the way thither quail, rabbits, and hares can be found in large numbers. Five leagues.

---

[11]Pool of water resulting from an overflow of a river or creek.

[*]Comanche Creek.

[†]Downstream on Comanche Creek.

Saturday, 29. We set out, and after traveling east-northeast for a distance of two leagues, came to the Nueces.[12] This river was crossed by means of a bridge made from trees, branches and dirt. Earlier in the day we had crossed a very deep creek. This creek carried no water at the time; but whenever it overflows its banks it forms many *esteros* in which water remains most of the year. From the Nueces we traveled northeast as far as La Tortuga, where we ended the day's journey of five leagues. At this place there is a very large *estero,* which contains water all year around and which is well supplied with fish. In the vicinity the land is flat and very good for pasturage, and there are many turkeys, peacocks, quail, and rabbits. Five leagues.

Sunday, 30. We journeyed east-northeast six leagues until we came to a place called Los Encinos del Río Frio, vulgarly known as Los Muertos. During the day we had traveled through a very open country with fields carpeted with various kinds of beautiful and fragrant flowers, and along the way had seen a great number of turkeys and quail. Six leagues.

Monday, 31. We turned east-southeast two and a half leagues in order to find a way of crossing a canyon called Río Frio, which carried water at the time.[13] On one side of the Frio Canyon, for a distance of about a league, there are dense woods, and on the other, for about the same distance , there are briers and bushes. At this place a soldier became lost, and His Lordship sent after him. Upon leaving this canyon we passed through beautiful pastures until we came to Los Gatos. Here we found nothing but a few pools, containing such a small amount of water that it was necessary to take the droves of horses and mules to other pools a league and a half distant. During the journey of six leagues we saw deer, quail, rabbits, and turkeys. Six leagues.

Tuesday, April 1. We went east-northeast, and, after traveling two leagues and a half, came to a dry gorge, and a half a league farther on reached Arroyo Hondo, which was deeper than the latter and which carried water. Before we crossed Arroyo Hondo workmen went ahead to clear the way. In the vicinity of the gorges there are many walnuts and other trees, and the road leading to them is rough. From Arroyo Hondo the entire country is very flat and beautiful, and the rich pasture-lands are covered with various kinds of flowers. We went past Las Cruces, where we found several groves and where there is water the year round; and after traveling on for two leagues we arrived, at the

---

[12]See Mattie Austin Hatcher, "The Expedition of Don Domingo Terán de los Ríos into Texas," *Preliminary Studies of the Texas Catholic Historical Society*, 2, 1 (Jan. 1932), entry for June 6, 1691 [reprinted above, p. 12].

[13]"The Frio is perhaps the best known of the several Texas canyons. Its rugged, varicolored walls, adorned with Nature's whimsical carvings, stretch across two counties. All but 22 of the 88 miles between that scenic wonder and San Antonio are over paving, and that stretch is well graveled." H. R. Riegler, *San Antonio Express,* April 4, 1932.

end of the day's journey, at a place called El Tulillo, where water can also be found in various pools at almost any season of the year. During the entire day's march we found deer, wild goats, turkeys, rabbits and quail in large numbers. Seven leagues.

Wednesday, 2. The marquis was delayed in starting the march, for on the previous night there had been such a violent storm and such a heavy rain that the droves of horses and mules became frightened, many of these animals ran away, and all the beasts of burden were missing from one of the companies. After they had been rounded up we set out in a rain, and traveled northeast for three leagues until we reached El Charco de la Pita,* where water can be found the entire year. We realized that it would be impossible to find water at any suitable place farther on, and decided to remain here. The country through which we had passed is somewhat broken, but most of it is good for pasturage, and throughout it there are many turkeys and deer. Three leagues.

Thursday, 3. We journeyed east-northeast about three leagues, and the rest of the day traveled between north-northeast and northeast. We were delayed in starting, because the preceding night had been very stormy; the wind, rain, and thunder had frightened the droves, and in the morning all the horses and mules of two companies were missing. Although these were not brought back until 9 o'clock in the morning, we traveled on as far as the Medina River, a distance of nine leagues. The march was very difficult, but we had to continue it, for we found no water along the way. One of the new recruits became lost in trying to round up the horses, and the marquis left two of the veteran soldiers to look for him. For about three leagues we traveled through woods in which we saw walnuts and oaks, and some vines that already were covered with clusters of grapes. One of these vines was three feet in circumference [*sic*]. During the remainder of the day we passed through a flat country and found a great many deer. We saw around us, almost at the same time, as many as three or four hundred of these animals, and the mounted soldiers that covered the line of march, riding at full speed, captured two by driving them in toward the droves of horses. They could have caught several had they not been afraid of throwing into disorder the line of march. Here also we found a great number of turkeys and quail. Nine leagues.

Friday, 4. The lost soldiers were brought back. We set out after High Mass and several Low Masses had been celebrated in commemoration of the feast of the day, Our Lady of Sorrows, and entered the province of the Texas Indians, or Nuevas Filipinas, which is separated from the Province of Coahuila, Nueva Estremadura, by the Medina River. We traveled east-northeast about three leagues until we came to León Creek, in which water can

*San Miguel Creek.

be found the greater part of the year, and in several *esteros* all year round. From here we advanced northeast along a beautiful plain until we came to San Antonio. On most of the route from the Medina River to León Creek we had crossed low hills and fertile valleys and had found a great quantity of flint stone. This kind of stone can be found at several places between the Rio Grande and San Antonio. That same day we reached San Antonio, which is six leagues from the Medina River. Six leagues.

To our great joy and also to that of all who were awaiting us in order to join the happy expedition, that same day, April 4, feast of Our Lady of Sorrows, we reached the town and presidio of San Antonio de Béjar. The governor (after his men had crossed the river) proceeded with the entire battalion to the San Antonio de Valero Mission, dedicated to the glorious Saint Anthony of Padua, in order that all the soldiers might offer their hearts to God from the time they took their first steps in the Province of Nuevas Filipinas. With the chanting of the *Te Deum*,[14] in keeping with the versicle *benedictus qui venit in nomine Domini*[15] all the padres received Our Lord the king (may God protect him) in the person of the governor. Reciting the prayers of holy Church, they implored and blessed the success of His Majesty's arms in the spread of the Catholic religion, a matter in which His Majesty is so deeply interested. The missionaries that awaited and that joined the expedition here were the following: Most Reverend Fray Antonio Margil de Jesús, commissary of the Holy Office, founder and ex-guardian of the apostolic colleges of Santa Cruz in Querétaro and of Cristo Nuestro Señor in Guatemala, prefect of the missions, and actual president of the Texas missions belonging, to the Apostolic College of Nuestra Señora de Zacatecas;[16] the apostolic preacher, Fray José Rodríguez; and the lay brothers, Fray José Albadadejo and Fray José Pita.[17]

Although the governor had planned to continue the march on Holy Saturday, upon learning that the horses were exhausted as result of the severe winter and that they could not stand such long journey unless given time to regain their strength, he decided to postpone his departure. In this decision he was actuated also by the desire to celebrate Holy Week in a place so suitable for the purpose. Harkening to the persuasive and weighty arguments advanced by the padres, His Lordship realized that it was not only expedient but

---

[14]Hymn of thanksgiving.

[15]Blessed is he that cometh in the name of the Lord.

[16]For the life of this great missionary see Peter P. Forrestal, "The Venerable Padre Fray Antonio Margil de Jesús," *Mid-America*, 3, 4 (April 1932), which appeared as *Preliminary Studies of the Texas Catholic Historical Society* Vol. 2, No. 2 (April 1932) [see above, pp. 67–94].

[17]Fathers José Guerra and Gabriel Vergara seemed to have joined the expedition here, although their names do not appear in the original manuscript copy of the "Derrotero."

necessary that all the soldiers should, as good Christians, cooperate by their example in complying with the precept of the Church before attempting to establish the holy Catholic Faith among so many pagans. Furthermore, most of the men had not gone to confession the previous year, because during that time some of them were being levied and others were already in active service. In order to minister to the spiritual needs of those men a mission was given, and during the mission many of the padres preached the word of God. The expedition delayed for some time in this town; and, to the great consolation of all, the padres reaped abundant fruit through their sermons as well as through their kind and continuous labors in the confessional.

In the meantime, in order that the troops might be active in the service of the king and in the welfare of these provinces, His Lordship issued several orders, all of which were very important. As these two provinces lacked salt, he sent a company of forty soldiers to discover certain *salinas* which the Indians had reported as being very close by. The soldiers did not succeed in finding the principal *salina,* for after they had traveled fifty leagues some of the natives whom they met informed them that the deposits were still about forty leagues distant. They assured them that the discovery of these would be unprofitable because of the great distance and also because the country in which they lay was inhabited by very warlike tribes that had repeatedly resisted as many as fifty, and even sixty armed men from the New Kingdom of León that had gone there to gather the salt, many deaths having resulted on both sides. Although the twenty-two days spent in reconnoitering this country were not profitably employed, they were not altogether wasted. The soldiers, when returning, found at a distance of four days' journey from San Antonio, and one from the Rio Grande highway, two *salinas* very close to each other. These were under water at the time, as a result of the unusual rains that had fallen this year, but the Indians of those parts assured the soldiers that in dry seasons excellent salt could be found there. That this was true was evident from a sample which the Indians brought and which, according to their own assertion, they had gathered the previous January.

Being worried because of the fact that he had not received news of the company of forty soldiers that he had sent from the Rio Grande with the detachment under Captain José Ramón, and that on March 10 had left San Antonio to take possession of Espíritu Santo Bay, on Good Friday His Lordship dispatched four trustworthy Indians [to investigate the results of that mission].[18] On April 18 a lieutenant and four soldiers dispatched by Captain José Ramón, arrived at San Antonio with the joyful news that Espíritu Santo

---

[18]Castañeda (*Morfi's History of Texas,* 234 n.40 and 241 n.112) says this was Domingo Ramón and that his full name may have been Domingo José Ramón.

Bay had been taken possession of in the name of Our Lord the king, and that the holy cross and the royal standards had been raised there on the feast of Our Lady of Sorrows. Due to the fact that the Indian guide had lost his way and to the fact that two swollen rivers had to be crossed, the journey from San Antonio had taken thirty-two days.[19] In six days, however, the lieutenant made the journey back to San Antonio, and there reported that La Bahía was not more than sixty leagues distant [from San Antonio], that it was said to be very beautiful, and that this bay, which had not as yet been sounded because of the lack of wood with which to build a canoe, was said to be sufficiently large to float many vessels. This news was celebrated with joy befitting the announcement of so necessary and so important a discovery, for, as this bay is the key to the province, if it be defended the entire province can be discovered and within a few days any necessary assistance can be obtained from Vera Cruz.

On April 26, His Lordship, after having received this news from La Bahía, sent a dispatch to the viceroy, acquainting him with these facts and informing him that he was ready to continue the journey. He also called to His Excellency's attention the fact that although the soldiers' wages were very good, they would not be sufficient for their support if the food supplies continued to be transported by land. He informed him also that there was danger of running out of supplies, because of the time lost in crossing the rivers and because of the distance of 400 leagues to Los Adaes from Saltillo and Parras, from where they were then being conducted. In view of all this, he begged of His Excellency permission to bring the supplies from Vera Cruz to La Bahía; and he offered, if this permission were granted, to purchase or charter a bilander in which to transport whatever supplies are at present necessary for the province, and stated that in this way an important maritime route would be discovered. He stated also that, presuming His Excellency would grant the request, he was then writing to his agent in Mexico City, instructing him to purchase or charter a bilander and to ship him without delay a supply of flour, corn and other things.

As soon as His Lordship had sent the dispatch he visited the Mission of San Antonio de Valero, located near the presidio, and on another day visited that of San José y San Miguel de Aguayo. The latter, which he had established a year previously and at which he had congregated three tribes of Indians, is about a league and a half down the river from the presidio. At both of these missions he distributed among all the natives clothing and other articles which they value highly. At the San Antonio de Valero Mission he clothed 240 of both sexes and of all ages, and at that of San José y San Miguel de Aguayo 227.

---

[19]From a reading of the entire diary it is evident that the trip to La Bahía and back again to San Antonio took thirty-two days.

Afterwards he clothed in like manner fifty men, women, and children that had accompanied Captain Juan Rodríguez from the Ranchería Grande. This captain had come [to San Antonio] to request that a mission be established for these and for other Indians of said *ranchería.* The marquis learned that over the road to the Texas heretofore followed he would encounter insuperable difficulties with such a large train, because of lagoons and swollen rivers, and because of the great amount of brush in the Monte Grande, through which there was no road and which was so called because of the fact that it was twenty leagues in extent. Moreover, the Indian Juan Rodríguez had just volunteered to lead the expedition through a good country, one that was open and level and through which many rivers and creeks, which branched off into various forks, would be crossed, and which on the lower road reunited to form rivers that would be impassable as a result of the torrential rains of the previous winter. The Indian stated further that they would avoid the Monte Grande, crossing only the edge of it. The marquis, after considering these points, convoked a council of war, in which it was decided that this new route should be discovered and that the said Juan Rodríguez and other Indians should act as guides.

At various times during his stay at San Antonio the marquis sent out detachments of soldiers to check certain Indians that were infesting that neighborhood. Two days before His Lordship reached San Antonio they attacked some of our animals within three leagues of the presidio, and in the encounter that ensued [between them and our men] they killed a muleteer and wounded one of the soldiers. In ordering the aforesaid incursions His Lordship was actuated also by the belief that the aggressors might have been Apaches, and he gave instructions to the effect that an effort be made to bring back alive as many as possible, so that he might manifest kindness toward them and consider with them the important confederation of their great nation, that extends as far as New Mexico.[20] On May 10, finding that the horses were rested, His Lordship announced that the march would be resumed on the thirteenth; and as he was now about to enter a country infested with enemies, he ordered that during the remainder of the journey whatever company happened to be on guard act as a picket, that the baggage and droves of animals continue in the order previously followed, and that another company cover the entire line of march.

---

[20]In the conflicts between the Apaches and the Texas the Spaniards took sides with the latter. Had they been neutral, the work of settling this territory would probably have been much less difficult. See Castañeda, *Morfi's History of Mexico,* 235 n.49; William E. Dunn, "Apache Relations in Texas, 1718–1750," *The Quarterly of the Texas State Historical* 14, 3 (Jan. 1911): 204.

On Tuesday, May 13, we continued the march toward Texas, traveling in a northeasterly direction for one league, and from there turning still farther to the northeast until we reached the water-ditch at the San Antonio Mission.[21] Here there are vines that look as if they had been planted by hand and that at the time bore beautiful clusters of full-grown grapes. We then turned east-northeast, and later traveled to the northeast as far as Salado Creek, where we ended the day's journey of four leagues. As some pack mules and horses had become lost, His Lordship remained here the following day. This part of the country is hilly, but very wooded and beautiful. All the lost animals were recovered. Four leagues.

Thursday, 15. We set out, and traveled over a country thick with live oaks, and also with thorny mesquite bushes that produce a fruit eaten by the Indians. But we found clearings at several places along the route, all of which is very level. Later we advanced northeast, a quarter to the east-northeast, until we came to some low hills from which we were able to see a long stretch of flat, open country, very suitable for pasturage. From there we went northeast about a league, then two leagues due east, and finally, traveling a little toward the east-northeast, we ended our day's journey of five leagues at Cibolo Creek, along which there are several *esteros* the year round. We remained here the following day also, because a soldier and some pack mules had been lost. Both the soldier and the mules were found on the second day. Five leagues.

Saturday, 17. We continued the journey, traveling through woods which, though passable, were thick with mesquites, evergreen oaks, and other species of trees. We advanced north one league, and then northeast a league and a half until we came to a little hill called La Loma de las Flores. This name was most appropriate, for at the time all the plants were in bloom, and they were of so many varieties and so close together, without any intermixture of weeds, that they looked like one bouquet or as if placed together in a flower-pot. The meadows were beautiful and seemed to be carpeted with fragrant flowers. From this hill is visible for a long distance and in every direction a very delightful, level and beautiful country. From here, traveling over land covered with mesquite trees, we went northeast, a quarter to the east-northeast, about two leagues along a plain, and then crossed a number of hills. Later we came to a creek which bore no name, and as we crossed it on the feast of Saint Pascual Baylón, the governor called it after this saint. Although the creek is not very deep, it carries water the entire year, and about it there are junipers, poplars, walnuts, mulberries, and many vines. The country is wooded as far as

[21] At this time Texas comprised only the territory between the Trinity and Red rivers and part of what is now the State of Louisiana.

the Guadalupe, a distance of a quarter of a league.[22] At this season of the year the latter river is usually very low, but at the time of our arrival its waters, as clear as crystal, were about three feet in depth and covered the stones. The Guadalupe has its source in three large springs, only a fourth of a league from the crossing; it is rather wide, its vicinity there is a great variety of very beautiful trees. These are so shady that the sunlight cannot penetrate the foliage, in which several species of song birds warble. Here also innumerable vines twine about towering trees and unite them in most artistic fashion. The river contains very good water, for at its source His Lordship found ceterach and maidenhair.[23] Although at the crossing we found no irrigation ditches, it seems these could be built farther down the river. If they were built this section of the country would be suitable for settlement, for even at this season, when most parts of the kingdom are arid and dry, the plains here look beautiful, and the soil must be very fertile. From the Guadalupe we continued on in the same direction for three-fourths of a league until we reached the San Ybón.* This river has a deep bed, and at the time of our arrival its waters were as high as those of the Guadalupe and, due to the rains and storms, its course was very rapid. The San Ybón, which is impassable most of the year, flows down from some hills located to the north, but its source has not as yet been discovered. On its banks can be found the same kind of trees, although not so luxuriant, as those along the Guadalupe. His Lordship stopped on the north bank of this river, having made a journey of very close to eight leagues. All those days we found, as the asp among the flowers, chigres, that annoyed us more than mosquitoes, and also many ticks and snakes. Eight leagues.

Sunday, 18. We set out, and advanced toward the northeast, a quarter to the east-northeast, and again turned northeast before we reached Peñuelas Creek, where there is water in *esteros* all year round. We moved on, and crossed a plain covered with mesquites, before ending our day's journey of four leagues. The Apaches live in Lomería Grande, a very broken country about a league to the north. Four leagues.

Monday, 19. After following for about two leagues, and over a flat country here and there dotted with clumps of mesquites and live oaks, the route taken on the previous day, we came to a woods covered with the same species of trees as we had found at the Guadalupe. On the preceding day workmen had gone ahead to these woods to clear a way for the trains. Later we reached the Inocentes River, which was as swollen as the Guadalupe and which is two and a half leagues from the Peñuelas. The northern bank of this river is not so

---

[22]The present Comal.

[23]Kinds of fern.

*Guadalupe River.

wooded, but it is also beautiful, and so shady that the sunlight cannot penetrate the foliage. From here we traveled one league to the northeast, a quarter to the east-northeast, and then a league and a half almost directly north over a flat country, covered here and there with trees. This brought us to San Rafael Creek. Without consulting Tobias, we knew that its fish was good, as is true of all the rivers we had crossed since leaving San Antonio. Deer and turkeys are the most abundant game found at this place, there being but few rabbits or quail. At San Rafael Creek we met a squadron of Sana Indians that, riding on horseback and armed with spears and arrows, came forth, dressed in the clothes which His Lordship had given them at San Antonio, to renew their fealty to Our Lord the king (may God protect him). The San Rafael, which has quite a number of trees along its banks, carries water the greater part of the year, and in its large *esteros* water can be found at all times. From this creek, where we camped after a journey of five leagues, a small detachment was sent to look for a soldier that was missing from one of the squadrons. On the previous day footprints left by Castilian cattle had been observed, and His Lordship, wishing to procure for the battalion something more than the daily ration of food, had sent the said squadron after these animals. But, as the soldier had become lost, the effort to bring back the cattle was unsuccessful. Five leagues.

Tuesday, 20. We continued the march due northeast, and, after traveling a quarter of a league, came to the San Isidro Spring, which is surrounded by trees. The rest of the day we traveled over an open country, with low hills and beautiful valleys, and found such an abundance of deer and turkeys that, without interrupting the march, we captured a great number. That day we covered six leagues, and camped at a small creek, which had no name and which His Lordship called San Bernardino. Six leagues.

Wednesday, 21. Although the weather looked threatening we set out, following the same route. As a matter of fact, we had gone only a quarter of a league when it began to thunder, lightning, and rain so much that the horses became unmanageable and broke away from the line of March. Only with great difficulty did we succeed in rounding them up, it being impossible to do so in the case of the cattle, that became so frightened that we were unable to make any progress. It was impossible, likewise, to advance with so many trains, and these were left behind with a good escort of soldiers from the company that covered the line of march. As the rain kept up half of the day we stopped on the banks of a river called Las Garrapatas.* Part of the day's journey of only one league took us past five deep gullies, all of which were

*Onion Creek.

covered with rain-water; the rest of the journey was through a very level and open country. One league.

Thursday, 22. This being the feast of the Ascension, there were six Masses and a sermon. We spent the day here in order to celebrate the feast, and also to wait for the animals. These reached the Garrapatas River this same day, without any injuries to the men, some of whom had been thrown from their mounts. In the afternoon, to the great joy of all, the party of soldiers that had been dispatched from San Rafael Creek arrived with the soldier who had been lost. The latter had fallen into the hands of pagan Indians, but had made use of the provisions and tobacco with which His Lordship had supplied the soldiers in order that these might distribute them among the Indians.

Friday, 23. Continuing the march toward the northeast, we immediately crossed the Garrapatas River, which, because of a storm on the previous evening, was impassable save by means of a row of stones that stretches to the opposite side and that during the entire year causes a beautiful waterfall.[24] From here as far as the San Marcos River,[*] both banks of which are covered with a great variety of shady trees and vines, the entire day's journey was through an open country dotted with low hills. As this river was swollen to twice the size of those we had already passed and as it was very wide, we were obliged to lighten the burdens of the pack animals. Because of the consequent delay and because we had spent practically the entire day in taking the livestock to the other side, we had to halt about three-fourths of a league beyond the river, where we found a good camping ground at a creek covered with shady trees, and with many mulberries and blackberries, double the size of those in Spain. Tracks of bison were found here, and a party of soldiers that had been dispatched to hunt these animals brought down a very large one. The bison is what the first Spaniards called the Mexican bull. It is a monstrous animal; its horns are crooked, its back humped as that of a camel, its flanks lean, its tail short, and hairless as that of the pig, except the tip, which is covered with long hair. The entire skin, which is of a dark tanned color, resembling that of the bear, though not so fine, is also covered with long hair. It has a beard like that of a goat and, as the lion, its neck and forehead have hair a foot and a half long that almost covers the big black eyes. Its feet are cloven, and its forehead is armed [with horns] as that of the bull, which it imitates in ferocity, although it is much more powerful and swift. Its meat is as savory as that of the best cow. After the day's march of three leagues we observed that we were at thirty degrees. Three leagues.

---

[24]McKinney Falls on Onion Creek. See Buckley, "Aguayo Expedition," 38. After reading the "Derrotero" we visited the falls and found the description to be exact.

[*]Colorado River.

Saturday, 24. We set out over some beautiful plains, and at various intervals crossed some very low hills. Along the entire route we found good pasture land and a variety of flowers, until we came to a creek covered with trees and with such thick brush that the approach to it was difficult. As this creek had no name it was given that of Santa Quiteria, whose feast was celebrated on the previous day. We came to another creek, and, because of the time that had been lost in crossing the Santa Quiteria, and especially because no good camping ground was to be found at a suitable distance farther on, the day's journey of four leagues ended here. This creek also lacked a name and was now given that of San Francisco, whose feast fell on the following day. As we arrived here at an early hour a company of fifty men was sent to hunt for bison. Travel in this country was dangerous, for it borders on the Lomería Grande inhabited by the warlike Apaches. If any of these were found efforts were to be made to establish peace with them. Four leagues.

Sunday, 25. The company, bringing back three bison, returned during the morning. It had been forced to halt the previous night, because in pursuing these animals, that are very fleet, it had gone off six leagues. When night came on, everything became so dark and there was so much thunder, lightning, and rain that it was impossible to continue the journey.

Monday, 26. The baggage and supplies were loaded and the order to mount was given; but, as it commenced to rain, the hour for departure was postponed in hopes that the storm would blow over. But the rain, instead of ceasing, began to pour down in such torrents that orders were given to dismount, and to cover the supplies as rapidly as possible. Had this not been done a great quantity of flour would have been ruined, and the corn also would have been in danger of becoming wet, and of burning later on, because it would have been difficult to dry it along the way. In like manner, that is, as a result of continuous rains, 500 bushels of corn, which the governor had bought on the Rio Grande, had been ruined. This morning the rains had been so heavy and the wind so strong that some of the tents were blown down and much clothing had become wet.

Tuesday, 27. We set out, and traveled northeast as far as Las Animas Creek, a distance of two leagues. The entire country as far as said creek, both sides of which are very wooded, is covered with flat hills. A quarter of a league farther on we crossed another small creek, along which there are also many trees, and which, from all appearances, has its source very close by. From here we journeyed still farther to the northeast, until we ended the day's journey of five leagues at the San Xavier River.* We had left behind us, at a distance of half a league from this river, a large creek with trees along its banks. The trees

*San Gabriel River.

and vines along the San Xavier, while of the same species, are more numerous than those along the rivers we had already crossed. The San Xavier is not deep, but usually it carries a foot and a half of water. Not far from this river three bison were killed. Five leagues.

Wednesday, 28. We crossed the two branches of the San Xavier, both of which were of equal width, and, after traveling about the distance covered by a musket-shot, came to an *estero*. As it was necessary to make our way through a dense thicket, it was only with great difficulty that we managed to get the animals across. Because of the delay, we were unable to cover more than four leagues, and we camped at a creek which bore no name and which, because of the fact that it is close to the San Xavier, the governor called San Ignacio. After crossing the river we made our way over several hills, some of which were high, others low, through many miry places, and past a creek shaded with trees. The first league of the journey was to the northeast and the last three to the north-northeast. Four leagues.

Thursday, 29. We spent the day at San Ignacio Creek, for on the previous afternoon tracks of bison had been discovered. Twelve of these animals were killed, although some of them, that had been brought down far from the camp, were not utilized.

Friday, 30. We set out toward the northeast, and during the day at times turned toward the north. After having crossed twenty creeks we finished our day's journey of five leagues at another which carried an abundance of fresh water and was shaded with trees. This creek was given the name San Fernando. Five leagues.

Saturday, 31. We continued our journey, traveling about two leagues north-northeast, then two more to the northeast. A league and a half from San Fernando we crossed a very shady creek, which carried a large amount of water. We traveled on for one league, as far as a mesquite grove, over a flat country, covered with small hills and carpeted with various kinds of flowers. The day's travel of four leagues ended here, because we came to a river which was impassable at this point. As we arrived at this river on the eve of Pentecost, it was called Espíritu Santo. With stupor all of us, likewise, witnessed the signs of the coming of the Holy Spirit, although His coming was not accompanied by tongues of fire, but by a bolt of lightning that fell within the camp and that left unconscious two of the soldiers. One of them regained consciousness immediately; but the other, whose hat had been pierced as if by a very fine auger, did not recover his senses until more than an hour later. The bolt split the pole of the tent in which the latter happened to be with his wife and two children, but without causing further damage. We learned afterwards that this river is the first [branch] of what is known as the Brazos de Dios, which is crossed on the route to Texas followed on previous *entradas,* and that south of the place at which it is crossed there flow into it the San Xavier River, Las Animas Creek and all the other creeks that we had already crossed.[25] As a result, there below it is impassable the greater part of the year. Because of the continuous and incessant autumn and winter rains, it would have been so at present; and with so much baggage it would have been impossible also to cross the Monte Grande, for even the Indians, that carry but little, that take the shortest cut and are well acquainted with the road, have to travel a distance of from eighteen to twenty leagues in crossing it. Four leagues.

Sunday, June 1. On Pentecost Sunday, Monday and Tuesday we remained at Espíritu Santo, not only because this river was very high and impassable, but because in the council of war which the governor had convoked it was decided that a party of soldiers be dispatched to reconnoiter the country, to look for the Ranchería Grande, and to find out the designs of the French, for thus far we had not been able to ascertain their motive in having congregated so many tribes in the vicinity of this river and had not met a single Indian. In the meantime the river was explored, and it was learned that two leagues farther up it divided into three forks. The march was to be resumed on the following day, Wednesday after Pentecost.

Wednesday, 4. We traveled toward the northwest until we passed the first fork. This fork, and also the second, which was more swollen, offered a good crossing. As much time was lost in taking over the cargoes and the stock, and as news had been received that the third fork was very high and that it would be necessary to fell the trees in order to clear an entrance to it, this day we were able to advance only two leagues. Two leagues.

Thursday, 5. Seeing that the third branch had risen considerably, we remained at the same place.

Friday, 6. We left, traveling toward the northeast as far as the third fork, and about a league from it came to a creek which was deep, though easily crossed. From the very outset this day's journey was through a country that is broken, hilly, and thickly wooded, especially along the banks of the river and creek. The task of crossing the third branch, into which some of the soldiers and some pack mules fell because of stones and deep holes, presented great difficulties and detained us half of the afternoon, and we had to halt three quarters of a league beyond it. After crossing we turned north and ended our day's journey of two leagues at a suitable camping place close to a creek. The creek had no name, and it was now given that of San Norberto, on whose feast we had arrived. Two leagues.

---

[25]Both Peña and Morfi state that this was the first fork of the Brazos. Buckley and Castañeda claim that it was Little River, which was crossed, between Cameron and Belton.

It was decided that we should remain here for the next seven days, for the corporal of the party that had gone to look for the Indians [of the Ranchería Grande] had been told to meet us at this place in case his party were delayed. At a matter of fact, it did not return until the following Thursday. Its mission, moreover, had been fruitless, because, although the men had journeyed more than thirty leagues, they had not come across a single Indian, but found only huts that had been abandoned long since.[26] From the swamps and ponds which they found and the great quantity of water in the river, they concluded that they had arrived at one of the forks of the Brazos de Dios, and they learned from the Indians that the river was broader here because Las Animas Creek and the San Xavier River enter it at this point. During these days 128 mules arrived with provisions and other things that were needed. A great number of bison were found near by, and the march, which was to have begun on Friday, was suspended in order that the meat, with which the entire battalion had been supplied, might be dried. But, due to the rains, the effort to dry the meat was not entirely successful.

Saturday, 14. We traveled to the northeast over some barren, flat hills which were divided by some rather deep streams and from the top of which we were able to view all the surrounding country. After advancing two leagues we journeyed northeast until we crossed a creek, whose beautiful trees we had observed from a distance. At this creek, which we named San Antonio de Padua, we concluded our journey of five leagues. Five leagues.

Sunday, 15. Following the route toward the north, in order to avoid the swamps and creeks that had already been observed, we traveled along a beautiful plain which was covered with grass and flowers, and whose attractiveness was enhanced by the presence of bison at a short distance from us. Three of these, scared by the battalion, entered the camp and were quickly consumed. Later we came to a creek which we called San José. Its banks were covered with white soil and, washed by the current, seemed to form a series of terraces. Although tempted to remain on its shady banks, we traveled on to the northeast, and ended our journey of seven leagues at another beautiful creek, which we called San José de los Apaches. It was so called because of its proximity to the country of the Apaches, and also in the hope that under the patronage of the saint these Indians might be brought into the fold of the Church. This day many bison were killed and one, tied to a rope, was brought alive into the camp and served as a diversion as well as food. We observed that we were now at thirty-one and one-half degrees. Seven leagues.

Monday, 16. Traveling through a country much like that we had left, we advanced toward the northeast, turning at times toward the north-northeast

---

[26] *Barancas* which appears in the original, was evidently meant for *barracas*.

and, perhaps, toward the north. After marching five leagues we entered a woods covered with thorny trees, which in these parts are called mesquites and which produce fruit of which the Indians are very fond. Later we came to a creek, which we called San Joaquín y Santa Ana.* The great heat this day made its thickly wooded banks seem more pleasant. Our journey of seven leagues ended without any mishap. Seven leagues.

Tuesday, 17. The baggage had been prepared for the march, but, as word arrived that the nearby river had become rough the previous night, the journey was postponed. Taking advantage of the delay, the governor dispatched a scouting party to investigate certain fires that were thought to have been lit by some Indians; but, upon investigation, it was learned that they had been kindled by members of the battalion that, with permission, had gone off to hunt bison.

Wednesday, 18. We remained at this same place, because the river, which was given the name Jesús Nazareno, and which is the second main branch of the Brazos de Dios, was still swollen. It was observed that at a distance of half a league it was joined by another branch that flows from the west. Both form a mighty river, on the banks of which are tall, shady trees.

Thursday, 19. The river subsided, and after the ford had been examined the animals approached and crossed without difficulty. Traveling toward the north, and later toward the east-northeast, along a shady and very beautiful road, we stopped at a lake which was called Santa María. This last, a quarter of a league in extent, is not very deep, but its water is sweet. In order to allow the animals to pass and because a heavy rainstorm was threatening, this day we covered only two short leagues. Two leagues.

Friday, 20. We marched east-northeast about a league through a somewhat wooded country, with beautiful clearings at various places; and after traveling eastward, finished the day's journey of three leagues on a spacious plain. There was, however, no water close by, nor did we know of any suitable site where it could be found. At this place, which His Lordship named San Silverio Papa, five young bison were captured. This was the last time that game of the kind usually hunted by soldiers was killed. From the time we had come across big game more than one hundred had been brought down. Both the soldiers and the captains killed a large number of bison, thereby showing their agility and skill, and the governor killed four in the three times he went out hunting. There were no accidents to the men. Only one horse was killed; two were wounded, but were cured later. Three leagues.

Saturday, 21. We traveled a league to the west, and later to the southeast through a sandy country, covered with mesquites and many evergreen oaks.

---

*Brazos River.

At times we passed creeks that carried no water, and went through some gullies. We crossed a running creek, on the banks of which we found beautiful trees, and ended the day's journey of five leagues at a small *estero,* which was given the name of San Jorge. Five leagues.

Sunday, 22. Striking out toward the southeast, and turning at times toward the lateral winds, we advanced through a country that was covered with trees; but these were not so close together as to render travel difficult. We crossed some high hills, covered with a variety of flowers, and after a day's journey of about four leagues halted at a creek, which, because of the proximity of the feast, His Lordship called San Juan de los Jumanes. Four leagues.

Monday, 23. We remained at this place to await the scouts and to look for two soldiers that had become lost. Some others, who went off to look for a camping place, found the two soldiers and brought them back very happy to the battalion.

Tuesday, 24. Although its solemnity demanded that we remain to celebrate this feast [Nativity of Saint John the Baptist], it was decided that we should continue on so as not to prolong the journey. We took the route followed the preceding day, and made our way through some woods, which, because of their density and the unevenness of the ground, made travel quite difficult and occasioned the loss of some pack mules. After a close search the mules were found, although two of the cargoes were lost. Later we came to a muddy creek, and at a short distance from it had to build a bridge in order to cross another creek which, because of the mud, we were unable to ford. The battalion, after a day's march of six leagues, camped near this creek, although the site was not well cleared of trees. His Lordship called the place El Real del Patrocinio de Nuestra Señora. Six leagues.

Wednesday, 25. We continued to the southeast, and, after traveling three leagues through a mesquite woods, came to a plain that spread out before us for more than a league. We kept on till we came to a wood covered with very tall trees and through which there flowed a creek, the ascent from which was very steep. Later we came to an oak woods, parts of which were very dense. During the rest of this day's journey of seven leagues we made our way among clumps of mesquite shrubs and over a broken country until we reached a long and narrow clearing close to a marsh that contained rather warm water. This place was named El Angel de la Guarda. Seven leagues.

Thursday, 26. We turned to the east-southeast, and, after crossing a small creek, entered a woods in which were many walnuts, some oaks, an abundance of plums and green medlars, and a variety of vines bearing very large grapes. After journeying on for about a league we came to a running brook, and, traveling down its banks, now on one side, now on the other, we advanced two leagues to the southeast. Here there is a clearing for a short distance. On the banks of the creek, which was named Nuestra Señora del Camino and along which there are poplars, willows, and a great many vines, we ended our journey of three leagues. Three leagues.

Friday, 27. Traveling to the east-northeast and then to the cast about a league and one fourth, we made our way through a woods thickly settled with walnuts and oaks, it being necessary to level the road and clear the way at the creeks. After we had crossed the latter we came to a lake situated in a beautiful plain. Later we entered an oak woods that shortly opened on to an extensive and beautiful plain partly covered with oaks. Here we found three old Indian huts. At the close of the day's journey of four leagues we camped at a creek along which were some pools of rain water. This place was named Nuestra Señora de Guía. Here, for the first time, we were greatly pestered by ticks and chigres, and the animals were annoyed by gad-flies. Four leagues.

Saturday, 28. The march was suspended, because at daybreak rain was falling and a strong wind was blowing from the north. At nightfall a messenger announced that a ship had brought the good news that their Majesties were well, and a joyful salute was fired. Earlier in the day we had observed that we were at thirty-two and one half degrees.

Sunday, 29. Traveling eastward and at times turning to the east-northeast, we advanced four leagues, having crossed a wood thinly settled and three muddy creeks before reaching a clearing in which we found a few trees and an abundance of plums. We camped at this place, which was given the name San Pedro y San Pablo. Four leagues.

Monday, 30. As the scouts had not returned on the previous night we remained here. Other scouts were dispatched over a different route, and all returned with the information that we would be able to continue the march on the following day.

Tuesday, July 1. Moving along in an easterly direction and through a sandy country, we went through a woods sparsely settled with oaks and crossed two muddy swamps and two creeks, the approaches to which were very steep and slippery. We then advanced southeast along a marsh, and, after crossing a creek over a bridge which we had built, traveled for the remainder of the day through a very wooded country, in parts of which we found volcanic rock and many nettles that, because of their poisonous properties, crippled the horses, some of which had to be left on the road. We stopped at a shallow creek, which, however, was unsuitable for a camp because of the small oaks along its banks. This creek was named Nuestra Señora de la Estrella. Five leagues.

Wednesday, 2. Traveling southeast for a distance of a league, we went through a woods thinly covered with tall trees, and through another thick with oaks. After passing several miry places we came to a running creek, the crossing point at which had been prepared. A short distance farther on we crossed a muddy creek, and afterwards came to places so miry that we were obliged to retrace our steps and to seek a route over the hills. Traveling along in much the same manner and in the same direction, we came upon some old huts, sheltered by very tall and beautiful trees. Shortly after leaving these huts we came to a small creek, to cross which we had to build a bridge, and to our right we found a large marsh covered with grass. Thus far we had marched six leagues, but as the scouts had reported that we would soon reach the plains, and the road to Texas ordinarily traveled, His Lordship decided to continue onward. We did so only with great difficulty, and for the three leagues we were still to cover the road, as a result of the rains that had fallen the previous night and that morning, was so heavy that the soldiers could not manage to cover this part of the journey on horseback and were unable to keep the line of march or to travel in order. The animals avoided, as known precipices, the tracks of those that went before them and that became embedded in the mud. And as they lacked the courage and strength to complete the journey through the swamps, some of the men were obliged to lead them. In order to give the companies of the battalion an opportunity to reunite it was decided that the rest of the day should be spent in bringing across some beds and tents, which, moreover, comprised the least part of the cargo. The animals and the baggage remained behind at various places, for none of these had been able to advance more than three leagues before the battalion, after having advanced nine, came to a halt. In honor of the feast of the day, the place was named Visitación de Nuestra Señora. Nine leagues.

Thursday, 3. His Lordship ordered that the animals be conducted over a southern route. This route was different from that followed by the battalion, and, as it was higher, the animals were brought to the aforesaid place without serious mishap. This afforded us great joy, because we had feared that the cargoes might be damaged if they were not brought over a safer route.

Friday, 4. The day was employed in looking for a place to ford San Buenaventura Creek.[27] As the creek was then very high, preparations to bridge the narrowest part of it were made, and work on the bridge was begun on the following day.

Saturday, 5. His Lordship detached a still larger number of men [for the building of the bridge], and he himself assisted personally. The bridge, twenty-four *varas* in length and three in width, was completed and the approaches on the near and far sides of the creek were cleared as far as the old road to the Texas. The bridge was made of tall trees that had been cut down along the banks of the creek and of some small pieces lain crosswise and covered with

---

[27]The present Navasota. See Buckley, "Aguayo Expedition," 41; Castañeda, *Morfi's History of Texas*, 236 n.53; see Forrestal, "Solís Diary," entry for April 27.

branches and dirt in such a way that the ingenuity of the builders solidified the weakness of the branches. At this place two little tiger cubs were found. Their eyes were still closed, and their fur, that in color resembled that of a lioness, was pretty to behold.

Sunday, 6. Our course was now to be northeast, a quarter to the east-northeast. The first companies began to cross the bridge, but through negligence on the part of a soldier one of the horses with a cargo fell into the water, and though he reached the other side, the cargo became very wet. It was noticed that the bridge had given way somewhat, due to the fact that one of the props on the right side had slipped down, and another bundle of branches and more dirt were necessary in order to block up the openings that were appearing. The governor was present at the bridge the greater part of the day, and with his assistance the crossing was effected without any risk. We continued our journey along a cleared path, leaving to our right the Santa Ana Lake, also known as Las Cargas, because in 1719, in the woods opposite this lake, were concealed for eight months the supplies being conveyed to the needy religious in Texas.[28] Having passed three clearings, a thinly settled wood, and two running creeks, we stopped after a day's journey of four leagues at another creek, on the banks of which were some trees. His Lordship called the place Nuestra Señora del Rosario. Four leagues.

Monday, 7. Traveling to the east and a quarter to the eastnortheast, we advanced about two leagues through woods thinly settled with oaks, and during the remainder of the day marched over an open and level country. We crossed Carrizo Creek, but the ascent from it was so steep that it delayed the crossing of the companies and so slippery that it had to be fixed several times. The entire expedition, after having covered eight leagues, halted at Santa Clara, also known as Las Cruces, because of the fact that many crosses had been carved on its trees during the previous *entrada*. Eight leagues.

Tuesday, 8. Continuing east-northeast, we traveled over a broken hilly country and through a woods thinly covered with trees and in which we found some clearings. A bridge was built over San Fernando Creek. The battalion marched on till, after leaving an extensive plain six leagues from Santa Clara, it came to a small creek, which His Lordship named Nuestra Señora del Buen Suceso. Here it halted in order to search for huts of Texas Indians, that were said to be close by. Six leagues.

That morning His Lordship had dispatched a party of soldiers, and, as interpreter, President Fray Isidro [Félix de Espinosa], accompanied by two other religious. Leaving the highway and following a path, these went south three leagues until they came to some fields planted in the Texas fashion. As

---

[28]Forrestal, "The Venerable Padre Fray Antonio Margil de Jesús," 24.

they did not notice any huts, they called out in the language of the natives, and a response came back from the direction of the woods. Having crossed a small creek they met some Indians, most of whom were from the Ranchería Grande. Juan Rodríguez, captain of this *ranchería* was traveling with the party of soldiers, and all the Indians received him with great joy. The soldiers advanced to the aforesaid huts, which were nearby, and observed that there were assembled with all those of the Ranchería Grande some Indians of the Vidays and Agdocas tribes. At the same time the picket, having noticed fresh tracks of Indians and having heard the war whoop, halted, and the captain sent an ensign with this news to the governor. His Lordship, who at the time was marching at the head of the battalion, set out in great haste with one of the companies and instructed the others to follow. Upon reaching the place where the picket was stationed he ordered a halt; and, following the tracks left by the Indians, he traveled along a much beaten path, until, at a distance of about a league, he found the Indians and with them the party he had dispatched that morning. At the sound of the trumpet and upon the unfolding of the royal banner the Indians marched forth, carrying a white silk flag with blue stripes, which they had received from the French, and with their guns, which many of them carried, fired a salute. As they kept marching toward the governor with manifestation of submission and reverence, the latter ordered them to place their flag under the royal standard as a mark of obedience to the king Our Lord (may God protect him), and which among them is a sign that His Majesty receives them under his royal patronage. This made them very happy. Without dismounting, His Lordship, complying with a custom prevalent among these Indians, placed his hand on the head of each as a sign that all of them, men, women and children, in number about 200, rendered obedience. Afterwards he alighted at the hut of one of their captains and, by means of an interpreter, he told them that his mission was one of peace and explained whatever he deemed proper with regard to the motives for the *entrada.* He then returned to the camp, which was a league distant, and where he expected that the Indians that were then absent in the hunt would come to see him. Accompanied by the others, these came to the camp and with a discharge of their guns saluted our royal standard. The governor received them with great kindness and sent them away very happy with bundles of tobacco. These they were to distribute among their wives and children.

Wednesday, 9. Several captains with their Indians from the *ranchería* called on the governor, who, after repeating to them flattering words, gave them a head of cattle so that their people might have something to eat. He admonished them to keep the peace, assured them that they would be happy under the protection of the Spaniards, ordered them to retire to their old home beyond the Brazos de Dios, and promised that upon his return from Texas he would erect for them a mission near San Antonio. They replied that they would do as commanded. Informed by the said Indians that the Trinity, about five leagues away, was on a rampage, His Lordship told them to go to that part of its banks where the crossing was to be effected and that there he would give them clothing and many presents. So that out of motives of love and fear they might remain faithful to the Spaniards, the order to mount was given with a trumpet and the battalion was commanded to fall in line in the form of a square. The governor, having been requested to maneuver his horse in the Spanish fashion in order that the Indians, who had never witnessed such horsemanship, might be favorably impressed by its advantages, did so with the greatest skill and in so many different ways that they marveled greatly. He then put himself at the head of the battalion in order to continue the march, and the companies, according to rank, began to file out. We set out toward the east-northeast through a woods thinly settled with tall trees and at times passed through some clearings. After crossing two muddy creeks, into which many of the cargoes fell, we reached the Linares Valley. Here we turned to the northeast, traveled on past two lagoons, the running Santa Rosa Creek, and went through some clearings and some woods covered with oaks, walnuts, and pines. Finally, we arrived at the Trinity River, and about a musket shot from its banks pitched camp among some trees, having covered five leagues that day.[29] Five leagues.

Thursday, 10. As it was observed that the river was greatly swollen and that it would remain so for some time, the governor ordered that two rafts be built, one by the Indians of the Ranchería Grande. The latter, built in the customary way, of dry logs and reeds, was finished in two days. But, because of the rapid current it did not prove serviceable, and after their first attempt to cross on it the Indians became exhausted and realized the impossibility of doing so. The soldiers made a very large one out of trunks of trees and barrels; but, as this proved very cumbersome, it was found that its use would occasion great delay and that the cargoes, clothing, and provisions would become wet on crossing. Informed by the missionaries that upon leaving the province at the time of the French invasion they had constructed a canoe and had left it at a creek about a league distant on the other side of the river, the governor sent some soldiers to find out if it were still there. After spending two days in the search they found it on the banks of the creek. When the governor learned this he sent to the creek a number of soldiers, oxen that he had brought for

---

[29]Bolton and Buckley maintain that Aguayo crossed the Trinity at the first bend in the river above Randolph's Ferry, that is, directly east of Centerville. See Herbert E. Bolton, "The Native Tribes about the East Texas Missions," *The Quarterly of the Texas State Historical Association*, 11, 4 (April 1908): 263; Buckley, "Aguayo Expedition," 42 n.2.

the purpose, and also some carpenters, who were to make rollers and yokes. But, such was the difficulty experienced in bringing the canoe overland that four days were spent before it was launched in the river. Immediately three companies crossed, and afterwards all the trains, the animals and the rest of the battalion crossed also. During the delay of sixteen days the captains of the Ranchería Grande and some Indians came here. His Lordship, besides supplying them with food all the time they remained, gave them clothes and other things; and, after fitting out in a special manner the captains, he sent clothes, knives, and other articles which they prize highly to all those at the *ranchería.* Two mule loads of these things were taken to the said *ranchería.* by Nicolás de los Santos. This soldier, who was accompanied by the captains and who was well acquainted with the Indian language, learned that the natives were very grateful.[30] There visited the place four Texas and Ygodosas Indians, and these also, before they again left for Texas, the governor clothed in a special manner in order that they might spread the report that the Spaniards had entered [that country] in a friendly manner. All the companies having crossed the river, we camped one league from its banks. Along the way we had come to the San Juan Creek, and, as the horses had to swim it, the governor arranged that a bridge fifteen *varas* long and three and a half wide be built [so that the rest of the expedition might cross]. One league.

Friday, 25. It was necessary to remain here in order to put away the canoe. This was taken upstream to a creek, where it was pulled up on the banks so that it would not be washed back by the freshets. The same day the cacique of the Hasinai,[31] whom all Texas tribes recognize as their superior, arrived with eight Indian chiefs and four Indian women. Among the latter was Angelina, who had been brought up on the Rio Grande and in Coahuila and who acted as interpreter, being acquainted with the Spanish as well as the Texas language.[32] For a while the cacique sobbed so bitterly that he could not speak, but finally broke out saying that, having heard of our arrival to the Trinity fifteen days previously, he was impatient because of our long delay and had come forth to welcome us, and that he had missed so much the Spaniards and the padres and Captain Ramón after their departure from Texas and had regretted so much our tardiness in complying with our promise to return that he would have gone willingly to seek us in San Antonio had we delayed any longer.

---

[30]Castañeda (*Morfi's History of Texas*, 236 n.57) says, "it is well known that the Indians were extremely proud of European articles of clothing and the impression these would produce on the Texas was well calculated to cause a favorable reaction."

[31]Variously spelled: Hasinai, Asinai, Assinais, Hainai, Aynay.

[32]Bolton tells us that the Angelina River was probably called after her.

In reply the governor showed that he appreciated his good will and told him that His Majesty (may God protect him) had manifested his love for the Texas by sending the Spaniards to preserve peace among them and to defend them from all their enemies, and had sent missionaries to instruct them in the Catholic Faith. He then gave him a long coat, a jacket, and woolen breeches, presented him with a silver-headed baton, and named him captain and governor of the Texas Indians. He clothed, in like manner, all the other men and women that accompanied the cacique.

Saturday, 26. We continued our journey, traveling northeast through a woods thinly settled with pines, walnuts, oaks, and vines, crossed two creeks, and ended our march of four leagues at the Santa Efigenia Creek. The captain of the Texas and the rest of the Indians followed us, surprised on seeing so many Spaniards and so many cargoes and cattle. Four leagues.

Sunday, 27. Continuing the march, we advanced east-northeast through a broken country and through woods of pines, walnuts and chestnuts, crossed two running creeks, and finally reached that of Santa Coleta, where we ended the day's journey of seven leagues in a beautiful clearing. That afternoon President Fray Isidro Félix de Espinosa, accompanied by the captain of the Texas, went ahead, desirous of preparing with his Indians the reception [of Aguayo] at the site on which the first mission had stood. Seven leagues.

Monday, 28. Continuing the march east-northeast and through the same kind of country, thinly covered with trees, we traveled on as far as San Pedro, the place where the presidio and mission had been built in 1690, the year of the first *entrada,* and beyond which the Spaniards had not penetrated. As the site was suitable for a camp and as there was no other such west of the Neches, we advanced only three leagues. On this same day there came to the camp Indian men and women from the neighboring ranches, accompanied by their children and carrying presents of flowers, watermelons, pinole[33] and beans. The governor received them kindly and clothed them completely, and they returned very well satisfied and grateful. At the same time the captain of the Neches and sixty Indian men and women of his tribe entered the camp and fired a salute. They were received affably by the governor. After the usual signs of peace, all using the same pipe after mixing their tobacco with ours, the captain stated that he was greatly pleased because of the arrival of the Spaniards; he said that he hoped they would remain, and promised that he and his would continue to manifest gratitude for the benevolence that had been

[33]Pinole: a drink made from parched corn, mixed with sugar and water. In the printed copy we find elotes instead of flores. Peña probably meant the former, meaning "ears of corn." At several of the missions the natives brought these to the Spaniards.

shown them.[34] By means of the interpreter Angelina, the governor assured them that the Spaniards would remain, and he explained to them the motive for their coming. He decided not to clothe them until after he had arrived at the San Francisco Mission, in the vicinity of which they live, and he gave them only an abundance of meat and corn so that they might have food that night and the following day. At dusk a Frenchman sent by Captain Louis de St. Denis from the capital of Texas, where the Concepción Mission used to stand, came to inform the governor that if he [St. Denis] were granted safe conduct he would come to lay before him the orders which as commandant of the French force on this frontier he had received from Mobile. The governor replied that he might come with all security. He dispatched the messenger immediately, but the latter was unable to leave until the following morning. Three leagues.

Tuesday, 29. Moving along to the northeast, we went through a woods thinly settled with the same kinds of trees and crossed some hills and gullies. We then marched over the plain in which, in the year 1716 the presidio was first built, beside a lake fed by a fresh water spring, and we ended the journey of four leagues on the banks of the Neches. As we found this river greatly swollen, the governor ordered a bridge built. This bridge, the construction of which took six days, was thirty-two *varas* in length and four in width, and it was so well made and so durable that it was given the blessing of the Church.[35] Four leagues.

Wednesday, 30. A hundred Indians, including women and children, came from their home in Nacono, five leagues from our camp. They were accompanied by their captain, who is also chief priest of the idols and who is blind, having presumed, after acting as captain for many years, to follow the Indian custom of tearing out the eyes in order to become their high priest. With the greatest power, with natural eloquence and with signs he addressed His Lordship at great length, and expressed the utmost joy upon the return of the Spaniards. To manifest his love he stated that what his people most esteemed was God, the sun, the moon, the stars, and the Spaniards, and that the air, water, earth and fire could not compare with these. Through the interpreter Nicolás de los Santos, one of the soldiers who had come on the

---

[34]In the ceremony of smoking the peace-pipe the first puff of smoke was blown toward the heavens, the second toward the east, the third toward the west, the fourth toward the north, the fifth toward the south, and the last toward the earth. See West, "Bonilla's Brief Compendium," 26.

[35]*Vara*: unit of measure, 33⅓ inches; 36 *varas* equal 100 feet. [The 33⅓-inch *vara* is a Texas measure, devised during the Mexican era by Anglo American surveyors to standardize and facilitate their calculations, in part because no standardized *vara* length was available to them, Mexican measures varying between 32.9 and 33.4 inches. See Virginia H. Taylor Houston, "Surveying in Texas," in *One League to Each Wind: Accounts of Early Surveying in Texas*, Sue Watkins, ed., (Austin, 1964), 20–48.]

Ramón expedition and who was very well versed in their language and signs, the governor answered that he was most grateful for the kind remarks. He told them that the reason why His Majesty had sent so many Spaniards was to establish peace in that large province and to fortify it with the large number of soldiers that were to remain there, and that if need be, many more would come to defend them from all their enemies. He stated, further, that by means of missionaries that accompanied them they were now about to establish among them the Christian religion, and that no longer was there reason for them to fear any invasion. On hearing this the captain manifested great joy, and, having risen, in a lengthy and touching discourse repeated what His Lordship had said and persuaded his people that they should live on friendly terms with the Spaniards and that in their company they should be ready to go to any wars that should be waged. He told them also that they should hunt turkeys, deer and bear for the Spaniards and that they should bring them all the foods they themselves use.

Thursday, 31. They brought the governor tamales,[36] watermelons, ears of corn, pinole, and beans. This same day His Lordship clothed all the men and women in coarse woolen garments, and small cloaks with ribbons, and presented them with glass beads, knives, earrings, finger rings, mirrors, combs, awls, scissors, chain-links, and blankets, all of which things they treasure highly. To the captain he gave a silver-headed baton, a suit in keeping with his office and made in the Spanish style, and to his wife he gave double the quantity he had given the others. All were very much pleased and very grateful. This same day Captain Louis de St. Denis, who had swum his horse across the river, arrived at the camp and was received by the governor with the proper courtesy and gravity. He remarked that he was very tired from the heat of the sun and from the hard journey, and His Lordship granted his request that he be allowed to rest and to spend the night with the missionaries.

Friday, August 1. The governor heard Mass and then sent for Captain Louis. Having received him, with the lieutenant general and captains, he asked him to state the reason for his visit. To this the latter replied that the object of his visit was to announce that, if His Lordship were willing to do likewise, he, as commandant of the forces on that entire frontier would observe most amicably the truce which had been published in Spain between the two powers and which according to letters that he had received from France, had probably already been established. His Lordship replied that, in compliance with orders which he had received, he would observe the truce, provided that the French commandant would immediately evacuate the entire province of Texas and

---

[36]Tamales, which are common throughout Mexico and along our southern border, are made of a ground maize and highly seasoned meat, boiled in a corn husk.

withdraw with all his soldiers to Natchitoches, and provided that he would not impede or try to impede, directly or indirectly, the restoration which at all costs was to be made to the Royal Crown of all it had possessed, including Los Adaes. Don Luis accepted these conditions unreservedly, but although he tried to dissemble his feelings, his disappointment over our determination to recover Los Adaes was evident. The French had always coveted this territory, because it offers communication with the presidio which they have among the Cadodachos and which facilitates entrance to New Mexico. The captain stressed the unhealthfulness of the Adaes country and its uselessness for farming purposes; but as we had had there the San Miguel Mission, which they had invaded, we could not be ignorant of the condition of its soil. Finally he took leave, promising that without delay he would retire with his people to Natchitoches.

Saturday, 2. The governor dispatched a detachment of soldiers to the Mission of San Francisco and another to that of Concepción with instructions to rebuild the churches and dwelling-quarters at these places. The soldiers of the former detachment, whose horses swam the river, were accompanied by Fray José Guerra, and those of the latter by Fray Gabriel Vergara and Fray Benito Sánchez. Up to this day, on which the padres separated, each morning during the entire journey seven, and on feast days eight, Masses were celebrated and each Sunday, to the great edification of all the troops, there was a mission sermon, preached alternately by the presidents of the two colleges. Crosses were erected in order that this sign of salvation might be exalted among so many idolators and in order that this emblem of peace might be left among the Apaches, who consider it as such and who know by the crosses that Spaniards have been there.

Sunday, 3. After the bridge had been finished all the companies, baggage, and animals crossed without difficulty. We traveled on to the east-northeast for only two leagues and camped close to the San Francisco Mission, on the site to which the presidio was moved, for the second time, in 1716. Two leagues.

Monday, 4. So that on the following day it might be possible to celebrate the reestablishment of the Catholic Faith, the practice of which had been discontinued in Texas, the governor sent new reinforcements to complete the work on the San Francisco Mission.

Tuesday, 5. Seeing that the church and the dwelling-quarters of the missionaries were ready, the governor, with the entire battalion, went to reestablish the Mission of San Francisco de los Neches, vulgarly known as de los Texas.[37] This solemn function consisted of a High Mass sung by the Reverend Fray Antonio Margil de Jesús. During the ceremony there was a general salute by all the companies accompanied by the pealing of bells, blowing of trumpets, and beating of drums. After the ceremony the Indians, who also assisted, knelt down at the request of Fray Isidro Félix de Espinosa, president of the mission of the Apostolic College of Santa Cruz de Querétaro. In the presence of the Indians who were congregated in the dwelling-quarters of the padres, and in the presence of all the captains and officers of the battalion, and in the name of Our Lord the king (may God protect him), His Lordship appointed as captain of the Neches, one whom all the Indians had already unanimously acclaimed as such, and he presented him with a baton and with a full suit of Spanish style. He also fitted out completely 158 men, women and children, all of whom were extremely pleased, because they had never received so much. Through the Father president, who acted as interpreter, he informed them that the principal motive which actuated his coming was His Majesty's zeal for the salvation of souls, and that His Majesty received them under his royal protection and favor in order to defend them from all their enemies. His Lordship showed them that the latter [the French] had made them presents only because they were interested in their chamois, bison, and horses, and especially in their wives and children, whom they wished to enslave, while Our Lord the king (may God protect him) not only made no demands of them, but, as they had just observed, gave them an abundance of presents and desired solely that they enter the fold of the Church. (The governor had refused to accept so much as a single buckskin so that it would not appear as if he had received anything by way of recompense). He explained to them clearly His Majesty's will and told them that, in keeping with a practice introduced by the Spaniards, they would have to congregate, and establish a pueblo at the said Mission of San Francisco, which he called San Francisco de Valero. He warned them that their pueblo was to be permanent, and not merely temporary as heretofore. Finally, informed of all this by the said Father president [Espinosa], who is well versed in the language, all replied that they would willingly do this as soon as they had gathered in their corn crop; and they asked, in order that they might be able to carry out these instructions while His Lordship visited Los Adaes, that they be granted possession of the lands and be given sufficient water for irrigation. His Lordship, in the name of His Majesty, granted their request, gave them full title of possession and left with them Fray José Guerra of Santa Cruz College. After the latter had been presented to them as missionary by the Father

[37]Bolton ("Native Tribes," 262) says that this mission was located at the Neches village, close to the mounds and from two to four miles from the crossing.

president of Santa Cruz, the governor stated that he hoped that the newly appointed missionary's zeal would bring about their conversion in the shortest possible time. We then continued the march between northeast and east-northeast, traveling through groves thinly covered with tall oaks and mulberry trees, and we crossed two creeks and two plains before coming to a running creek that flows along another plain, larger than those we had left behind. We had spent more than half of the day at the mission, and as we reached this creek, which His Lordship named Nuestra Señora de las Nieves, at a very late hour, we decided to camp here, after a day's journey of four leagues. Four leagues.

Wednesday, 6. Continuing along the same route and along the same kinds of groves and plains, we crossed a creek, and after traveling over a level country for about two leagues came to another small, permanent creek. Most of the year the latter is so high that the Indians keep there a canoe in which to cross it. We were not obliged to use one, however. This creek, which had no name and which is located less than half a league from the Mission of Nuestra Señora de la Concepción, was now called Santa Barbara.[38] The governor, in order not to damage the planted fields on the neighboring farms advanced another league and camped, after a day's journey of five leagues, on the site occupied by the presidio of Domingo Ramón at the time the missions were abandoned. In the afternoon the governor sent another detachment of soldiers to repair the church, the only one at any of the missions that had not been completely ruined, and to construct two dwelling houses for the padres. As soon as His Lordship arrived [at the Concepción Mission] the Indian Juan Rodríguez reported that he had learned that Captain Louis de St. Denis, after returning from his interview with His Lordship on the Neches, had for three days remained about seven leagues from this mission. Here he had been visiting the Cadodachos and other tribes of the province, who during the previous winter he had convoked in order to go to take possession of La Bahía del Espíritu Santo and to proceed from there to San Antonio. He reported, further, that with the arrival of the Spaniards this cloud had cleared away. Five leagues.

Thursday, 7. Learning that the governor had threatened to mete out severe punishment for any damage done to the sown fields, the Indians were very much pleased, especially when, later on they observed that his orders were being obeyed. This same day the church was finished, and the artillery was prepared for the ceremony [of reestablishment].

Friday, 8. The governor, with the entire battalion and the two companies of Don Alonso de Cárdenas and Don Juan Cortinas, proceeded to the

---

[38]The present Angelina.

mission. As soon as he had arrived he presented the captain of the Texas with the best suit which he had and which was of a blue color and beautifully braided with gold. He gave him a jacket trimmed with gold and silver cloth and everything else necessary to make a complete suit. The ten companies were ranged in three files in front of the church, and between these and the battalion the cannons were placed so that three general salutes might be fired during the Mass, which was sung by the Reverend Fray Antonio Margil. The sermon was preached by the Reverend Fray Isidro Félix de Espinosa, who delivered a very eloquent and touching discourse, for he rejoiced to see the reestablishment of the mission and of the Catholic Faith. The ceremony was attended by many Indians of various tribes, and among them were about eighty Cadodachos. The latter, who are subjects of the French, had come with the Texas, whose governor lives here, to the aforesaid convocation. All of them marveled greatly and were extremely pleased on hearing the volleys from the artillery and companies and on seeing so many Spaniards. After Mass all the captains of the tribes that had assembled here entered one of the dwelling quarters of the padres in order to meet His Lordship, and each of the Texas women brought him the kinds of food they use: beans, ears of corn, pinole, and *tamales*. The governor showed that he appreciated highly their good will, assured them of the love which the Spaniards had always had for them, and promised that this time many of the latter would remain in Texas. Of this the Indians had misgivings, fearing that they would be abandoned, as had happened after other *entradas*. But, His Lordship dispelled their fears, assuring them that the Spaniards would defend them from an their enemies. Aware of the fact that Cheocas, captain of the Texas, had a large following, His Lordship told him to bring together all his people, men, women and children, so that he might distribute among them clothing and other things and so that he might explain to them His Majesty's designs in having sent so many Spaniards. The captain replied that his followers were then scattered at distant ranches, but that he would assemble them, leaving at their houses only such as were needed. Later His Lordship, to celebrate the day, gave a sumptuous meal to the padres and captains. After the meal the Father president [Espinosa] requested title of possession for his college and for the Indians. His Lordship, with all solemnity, made to him and to Governor Cheocas this grant, the said religious and the apostolic preacher Fray Gabriel Vergara remaining there as missionaries. In the afternoon His Lordship, with all his companies, returned to the camp.

Saturday, 9. To build the church and dwelling of the padres, both of which were in ruins, His Lordship dispatched a lieutenant and a body of troops, with the apostolic preacher, Fray Benito Sánchez who was to be stationed at the San José de los Nasonis Mission, eight leagues to the north of Concepción.[39] Eight leagues.

Sunday, 10. The governor sent another detachment with the very reverend Fray Antonio Margil de Jesús, president of the missions of Nuestra Señora de Guadalupe, and two other religious to build the Mission of Nuestra Señora de Guadalupe de los Nacogdoches, which was eight leagues distant and of which no vestige of either the church or the dwelling of the padres remained. Eight leagues.

Monday 11. After the captain governor of all the Texas had assembled the Aynais who attend the Concepción Mission and the eighty Cadodachos, he brought them, many of them carrying their guns, to His Lordship's camp. His Lordship told them, as he had told the other Indians, that they should congregate into pueblos, and they in turn promised to do so as soon as their crops were harvested. He then clothed, completely and after their fashion 400 of these Indians, and to each one gave gifts which they prize highly: knives, combs, awls, scissors, mirrors, *belduques*,[40] chain-links, *chochomites*, belts, necklaces, earrings, glass beads, and finger rings. He clothed also two captains that accompanied the Cadodachos and gave them a bundle of clothing and articles of merchandise to distribute among their Indians. He did this in order that they might become fond of the Spaniards and because they [the Cadodachos] were allies of the Texas. Upon receiving these presents all of them were very contented and grateful.

Tuesday, 12. In order to give the horses a rest the governor left the battalion at this camp and went with only one company to the Mission of San José de los Nasonis. The Indians of this mission, which is located eight leagues distant [northeast of Concepción], welcomed him with great demonstration of joy.

Wednesday, 13. The restoration of this mission was celebrated with High Mass and repeated volleys from the company; and after Mass the grant of possession was made, with the same solemnity as at the other missions, to the Father president and to the captain of the Nasonis. In the presence of the assembled Indians, men, women, and children, His Lordship named as captain the one whom they had recognized as such, and, as insignia of office, gave him a silver-headed baton. By means of an interpreter he explained to the natives the reason for the *entrada* and, as he had done at the other missions, insisted that they establish a pueblo. He then clothed the captain in a complete suit of Spanish cloth and of the Spanish style, clothed all the rest in the same kind of garments as he had distributed at the other missions, and, as he had done at

---

[39]The Espinosa diary entry for July 9th, states that this mission was seven leagues to the northeast.

[40]Large knives.

other pueblos, gave to the missionary Fray Benito Sánchez clothing for the Indians who at the time were absent guarding their cornfields and houses. The natives, 300 of whom were clothed here, were happy, and all day long they brought pumpkins, watermelons, ears of corn and pinole.

Thursday, 14. His Lordship returned to camp to join the battalion.

Friday, 15. After the Feast of the Assumption had been celebrated, very early in the morning, His Lordship left at the [site of the] old presidio the company of Captain Don Juan Cortinas, composed of twenty-five men. This company was to be a guard and a defense for the mission [Concepción] from which the presidio is one league distant. His Lordship then set out with the whole battalion. We traveled east-northeast, crossed woods sparsely covered with walnuts, pines, and oaks, and came to a large clearing in which we found a creek fed by large springs. Here we ended our day's journey of four leagues. As the creek had no name, it was now called La Asunción de Nuestra Señora. Four leagues.

Saturday, 16. We continued our journey east-northeast[41] through the same kind of country and woods until we reached the site on which had stood the Mission of Nuestra Señora de Guadalupe, belonging to the College of Zacatecas.[42] This day we covered four leagues. Four leagues.

Sunday, 17. The church and dwelling of the padres were finished by fresh reinforcements from the battalion that had been sent by His Lordship.

Monday, 18. The new church was blessed, Mass was celebrated, and during the Holy Sacrifice a sermon was preached by the very reverend Fray Isidro Félix de Espinosa, president of the Santa Cruz missions. The nine companies of the battalion and that of Cárdenas, drawn up in rows in front of the church, fired the general salutes, as had been done at the other missions. After Mass the reverend Fray Antonio Margil de Jesús, president of the missions of Nuestra Señora de Guadalupe, asked of His Lordship the title of possession for his college and for the Indians. This was granted, with the usual ceremonies, and Fray José Rodríguez was left there as missionary. The Indians of all ages being assembled, His Lordship clothed their captain in a complete suit of English cloth and with everything corresponding, gave him a silver-headed baton, and conferred upon him the title of captain. He likewise clothed all the rest after their fashion, and as had been his custom at the other missions, distributed among them many gifts, persuaded them to congregate into pueblos, and explained the reason for his coming. In a very long discourse

---

[41]Buckley, quoting other diaries, says that the march was east-southeast ("Aguayo Expedition," 49 n.1).

[42]This mission was located on the site occupied at present by the town of Nacogdoches. See, Castañeda, *Morfi's History of Texas*, 239 n.88; Bolton, "Native Tribes," 258; Buckley, "Aguayo Expedition," 49.

and with expressions of joy and gratitude, they promised to do as requested. The governor celebrated the occasion by tendering the padres and captains a splendid banquet. Three hundred ninety Indians were clothed here.

Tuesday, 19. The march continued east-northeast, although at places the road was crooked and took us in a somewhat different direction. We made our way through gorges, woods sparsely settled with oaks, pines, and walnuts, crossed some creeks, and were obliged to build two bridges. On a plain near the last of the aforesaid creeks, and in the vicinity of a small lake, which His Lordship named San Bernardo, we ended our journey of six leagues. Father Margil went ahead with a detachment in order to build the next mission, that of [Nuestra Señora de] los Dolores. Six leagues.

Wednesday, 20. Continuing along the same route and through the same kind of country and woods, we crossed a river which when on a rise,becomes very turbulent and which was already known as Todos Santos. The battalion camped on its banks, after a day's journey of eight leagues. Eight leagues.

Thursday, 21. We continued the march toward the east-northeast, through a broken and wooded country, until we had advanced one-fourth of a league beyond the spot on which had stood the Mission of Nuestra Señora [de los Dolores] de los Adaes, of which not a vestige now remained.[43] To Father Margil this new site for the mission seemed preferable, because it is on the banks of a stream that has its source near by, and because it is on an elevation, without trees, and near a large tract of level land that can be used for cultivation. This day we covered six leagues. Six leagues.

Friday, 22. The day was spent in building the church, all the men necessary being employed.

Saturday, 23. The occasion was celebrated with the same solemnity as at the previous missions, and after the High Mass and the salute from all the companies Fray Antonio Margil and the captain of the Indians were granted title of possession. The captain was clothed as other Indian captains had been, and the Indian men and women were clothed also as at the other missions. His Lordship added joy to the occasion by offering the padres and captains a splendid meal. One hundred and eighty Indians were clothed at this mission, and Father José Albadadejo remained here.

Sunday, 24. The governor having left a detachment to finish the church and to build the dwelling for the padres, we set out toward the east. Later we turned east-northeast and went through a country covered with walnuts and

---

[43]This was not the Adaes, but the Ais mission. The expedition did not reach the former until the twenty-ninth. The Ais Mission was located on the site now occupied by the Town of San Augustine. See Isidro Félix de Espinosa, *Chrónica apostólica, y seráphica de todos los colegios de Propaganda fide de esta Nueva-España,* (Mexico, 1746–92), 1:443; Forrestal, "Solís Diary," 33.

pines, crossed ravines, clearings, and some permanent streams, and ended our day's journey of five leagues at a lake which was now named San Bartolomé. From here His Lordship sent a messenger to San Antonio with various instructions, and with special orders to hasten the convoy of supplies. At the hour for prayer, a general salute was fired in honor of the Prince's birthday.[44] This same day the messenger that His Lordship had sent to San Antonio returned with an answer from the viceroy. In his reply his Excellency thanked His Lordship for the discovery which, at his own expense, the latter had offered to make of the route from Vera Cruz to Espíritu Santo Bay (which the French call San Bernardo) for the purpose of succoring this province through said bay. He informed His Lordship that he had already ordered that the bilander leave Vera Cruz, that the agent had chartered it for the voyage at a cost of 3,500 pesos, and that during the month of July it would, without fail, set out from Vera Cruz, conveying all that had been requested. Five leagues.

Monday, 25. We continued the march east-northeast through a broken country, and over high hills and through gullies, all of which were covered with trees. Later we came to a number of creeks, which were so muddy that in order to cross we had to build bridges; and, about a league from the ford of the Sabinas River, we halted at a lagoon, which we named San Luis. This day we covered seven leagues. Seven leagues.

Tuesday, 26. We continued in the same direction and crossed the San Francisco de las Sabinas River, although its waters were so high that they reached the horses' girths. As it was necessary to fix a long stretch of muddy road on the opposite side, more than half of the day was spent in crossing. The remainder of the afternoon was spent in crossing pools of water and some miry places that we found also on the other side of the river and that in winter are impassable. After a day's journey of three leagues we camped on a hill, not far from a creek which His Lordship called San Nicolás Tolentino. Three leagues.

Wednesday, 27. We followed the same route, which took us over hills and gullies, and through woods of pine, walnut, oak, chestnut, and medlar trees. We crossed several creeks and finally came to one which flows through a very open plain and which was given the name of Santa Rosa de Lima. We crossed this also and camped on its banks, after having traveled six leagues this day. Six leagues.

Thursday, 28. We continued the journey in the same direction, crossed hills and gullies, made our way through pine and walnut woods and went through some clearings. We then came to some creeks, to cross which we had to build bridges, and camped, after a day's march of eight leagues, between a

[44]Birthday of the Prince of Asturias, heir to the throne of Spain.

lagoon and another creek. The latter was given the name San Agustín. Eight leagues.

Friday, 29. Before setting out His Lordship increased the picket so that it might be possible to clear the dense brush at the approaches to the creek on both banks and to build a large bridge. As soon as he was informed that this had been done the march was continued in the direction followed the previous day. We traveled along over open plains, in places sparsely covered with walnuts, medlars, pines, and oaks, until we reached the site on which had stood the San Miguel de los Adaes Mission. Observing that the place was not suitable for a camp, because it was so low that it might be flooded in case of rain, and finding no running water in the creek, the governor sent out scouts in various directions. Half a league away these found a spring that flowed through an extensive plain, and here we ended our journey of three leagues. Three leagues.

Saturday, 30. His Lordship, not having found a single Indian in Los Adaes, dispatched parties of soldiers in various directions. On the following day these returned with the news that at about ten or twelve leagues from the camp they had come across the nearest *ranchería.* They stated that, following orders, they had informed the Indians of the arrival of the Spaniards, and reported that the former were greatly rejoiced and that the Indian captain had said he would assemble his people and would come to see His Lordship.

Monday, September 1. A Frenchman, bearing a letter from Monsieur Rerenor, commandant at Natchitoches, arrived at the camp. The letter, which His Lordship sent later to the viceroy, merely congratulated His Lordship on his coming and stated that Captain Louis de St. Denis, immediately after his return from Los Texas in the middle of August, had gone to Mobile by way of the Natchitoches or, as the French say, the Red, River, in order to inform its governor of the arrival of the Spaniards, that the commandant had received no order to permit us to settle in Los Adaes, and that because of this His Lordship should refrain from doing so until after the return of Captain Louis. In view of this ambiguous proposal His Lordship convoked forthwith a council of war, in which it was decided that, since the French had seen what force His Lordship had at his command, Lieutenant General Don Fernando Pérez de Almanzán and Captain Don Gabriel Costales should on the following day set out for Natchitoches in order to observe the location of the island on which their presidio stood and also the kind of fortress, so that we might be prepared in case war were declared. In his letter to the commandant he replied that since affairs of war could not be discussed satisfactorily with the pen, he was sending there his lieutenant general with instructions to explain clearly the course he was determined to follow. In the conference held with the commandant the lieutenant general explained in detail the letter of

His Lordship and stated that the purpose for which the latter had come was to reoccupy Los Adaes, as he had already done in the case of Los Texas, and that he was determined to restore the San Miguel Mission and to build on that frontier a presidio at whatever place he saw fit. To this the commandant answered that he had no express orders either to agree to this or to prevent it, and that, aware of the truce existing in Europe between the two powers, he would maintain this truce in America if His Lordship agreed to do likewise. With this was concluded the conquest or recovery of that entire province. According to the terms of agreement reached by the two parties, to Our Lord the king (may God protect him) will be restored whatsoever the arms of his Catholic Majesty had possessed in that province, and the governor will be at liberty to fortify wherever he may see fit.

Whereupon the marquis set about immediately to select a site on which to build the presidio. But, although he sent scouts to all parts of that country and although he himself went out to explore it, he found no place more suitable or with more conveniences than that on which he was then camped. This was on the highway leading to Natchitoches and seven leagues from Natchitoches itself. He favored this site because, while all the rest of the country is closed in and covered with shady trees, there are here, close to the presidio, suitable ravines in which to erect the mission, and sufficient land with a spring of water along the hillside for Spaniards and Indians to cultivate separately. On this site, which commands a view of all the surrounding country, His Lordship drew the lines for the fortress. Work on the fortress, which was to be hexagonal in form, was begun immediately;[45] three corners were not fortified, but the other three were built in such a manner that each covers and defends two curtains. Each of the curtains is fifty-five *varas* in length. After the number of bastions had been reduced the fortress, to defend which there will be only six cannon, fitted within the section that had been marked off and was sufficiently large to accommodate the garrison of one hundred soldiers, thirty of whom will always be busy taking care of the horses and other livestock. The distance from the fortress to the spring is half that covered by a musket-shot, but an effort will be made to dig a well within the plaza. The foundation for the fortress had to be opened with crowbars, and the site, as well as the ground around the fortress, had to be cleared of very numerous and large trees. These trees were felled so that the enemy might not approach unseen and so that, as is proper, the stockade might have the best possible defense.

[45]The portion of the original manuscript from here to the end of this paragraph has been damaged, and is illegible. Through the kindness of Carlos E. Castañeda of the University of Texas we have been able to secure the printed copy of 1722.

On the first of September the cacique of the Adaes and a great number of Indians, all of whom manifested great signs of joy because of the arrival of the Spaniards, came to the camp. After the governor had welcomed the cacique and had given him presents, as he had done in the case of the other captains of the Texas Indians, the latter explained that he rejoiced greatly at the coming of the Spaniards and that all the Indians of that country wished to live under their protection, because the French, on invading the Mission of San Miguel de los Adaes, and also the Indians from Natchitoches, were guilty of many hostilities toward them and on retiring had carried off as captives some of their men, women, and children, merely because their tribe had expressed regret at the withdrawal of the Spaniards. He explained also that because of this his people had found themselves obliged to abandon that territory and to seek refuge in a more remote and more broken part of the country. From their new abode more than 400 of them, men, women, and children, had now come to see the governor. The latter made them very happy by distributing among them clothing and gifts, as he had done at the other missions. He assured them of the protection of Our Lord the king, and told them that he would leave on the frontier a presidio garrisoned with one hundred soldiers and would rebuild close to it the mission of San Miguel. The Indians promised to congregate at this mission. Part of the information which the governor had gathered with respect to this country was furnished by the Indians, who had informed him that certain *salinas* were located nearby. As the discovery of these was both useful and necessary, His Lordship sent there a lieutenant and twenty soldiers. These men brought back from deposits fifteen leagues distant from the presidio twenty-five mule-loads of salt-earth of such an excellent quality that when worked it yielded fifty percent.[46]

The ceremony for the restoration of the mission, which is to be erected a quarter of a league from the presidio, was celebrated in the presidio chapel on the feast of the Archangel Saint Michael; and on October 12, feast of the Apparition of Our Lady of Pilar in Zaragoza, whom His Lordship had chosen as patroness and column of defense on that frontier, was celebrated the dedication of both chapel and presidio.[47] The two feasts were solemnized with the greatest possible rejoicing, and volleys were fired by the artillery and companies, which formed on the military plaza during the Mass sung by Doctor José Codallos y Rabal, During the ceremony of blessing the chapel and fortress the image of Our Lady of Pilar, whose cult the reverend Father Margil

---

[46]Morfi (*Morfi's History of Texas*, 219), says that this amounted to one *arroba*, or what would be equivalent to about twenty-five pounds.

[47]"It is to be noted that the mission was not actually built until later. The celebration held on this day was to observe the feast day of the titular saint and officially declare the determination to build a permanent mission at this site" (ibid., 240 n.98).

extolled in an eloquent sermon, was carried in procession. At the close of the ceremonies His Lordship gave an excellent banquet to the padres and gave brandy to the soldiers, who in various kinds of dances, comedies, and farces showed their joy.

In the middle of October His Lordship received the good news that the bilander which at his orders had been chartered at an expense of 3,500 pesos for the purpose of discovering a route from Vera Cruz to Espíritu Santo Bay, had on the feast of the Nativity of Our Lady happily put in at the latter port, bearing 350 loads of flour and 150 of corn, as well as other provisions for the soldiers.

This news was celebrated in a manner befitting both the discovery of so important a route and the arrival of the supplies. The governor, knowing that there was only a sufficient amount of corn in Los Texas and Los Adaes for the Indians and fearing that his men would be without supplies in case anything happened to the convoy, ordered that the 200 loads of flour and of other things that had just arrived be forwarded by a number of mules which he kept in readiness at San Antonio for the purpose of hauling these provisions. Forty loads of supplies arrived on October 20, and the rest, together with 400 sheep and 300 cattle, that had been brought from the borders of the Kingdom of León, 340 leagues from Los Adaes, arrived at the beginning of November.[48]

The Great Lake of the Adaes, ten leagues in circumference, is located a league from the presidio, and through it flows the Cadodachos River. This river goes to Natchitoches, and covers sixty leagues, the distance between the two presidios.[49] In the lake, the nearest point of which is four leagues from Natchitoches, there are all kinds of fish, and a great variety of ducks can be found there all winter. In the Adaes country there are bears, deer, walnuts, and medlars. Of these, and of bear lard, which is very tasty, the Indians lay up a large supply for the winter.

The fortress and the soldiers' quarters having been completed on All Saints Day, the governor dispatched a message to the viceroy, acquainting him with this fact and informing him that he was leaving at this presidio one hundred soldiers, thirty-one with their families, and that he was supplying it with six cannon, provisions of war, and everything necessary for the proper maintenance of the soldiers. Although only ninety loads of flour remained, he expected, in the course of the journey, to send one hundred more from the

---

[48]"Both De León and Terán brought some cattle along, but this is the first recorded herd of cattle ever driven across Texas, and should be regarded as the forerunner of the cattle droves that were to play so import a role in the later history of the State" (ibid., 241 n.102).

[49]Both the presidio of Cadodachos and that of Natchitoches were located on Red River. See ibid., 76 n.80.

second convoy that was coming from La Bahía and that, as he had learned, was already on the way to Los Texas.

After he had attended to all these matters, the governor ordered that everything be in readiness for the retreat to begin on November 12. But, on the day preceding that set for the retreat there began a violent storm accompanied by sleet, and icicles so heavy and so large hung from the trees that their weight broke off the branches of some and uprooted others. This continued for so long a time that within twenty-four hours probably more than 200 trees fell within the camp and more than 2,000 in its vicinity. In falling they killed many horses and mules, but, thank God, the only man injured was one of the officers, whose life was in imminent danger when a tree fell on his shoulder while he was asleep. Although after three days the storm let up somewhat, it was impossible to round up the horses and mules before the seventeenth. On this day the march was resumed; but, from the very outset travel was very difficult, and the horses, having become extremely exhausted as a result of the cold, began to fall dead, and already from the Dolores Mission, thirty leagues distant from that of Nuestra Señora del Pilar, many of the soldiers began to travel on foot. When we reached the following mission, that of Nuestra Señora de Guadalupe, there arrived from Mexico a reply to the letter which the governor, on making the *entrada*, had from this place dispatched to the viceroy. In this communication his Excellency acquainted him with the royal *cédula* which he had received and which was dated, Aranjuez, May 6, 1721.[50] The *cédula* stated that Our Gracious Lord the king (may God protect him) was pleased to approve of all the preparations which his Excellency had made for this *entrada* and that under his direction it be undertaken by the governor; and it again ordered that in recovering this province war was not to be made on the French. This news, particularly the portion of it referring to the health of their Majesties, was celebrated with several general salutes. His Majesty commanded also that this province be fortified with presidios at the most strategic points, especially at La Bahía del Espíritu Santo. For a year this bay had been occupied by forty soldiers, but his Excellency ordered the governor to increase the number and to place here fifty of the best men he had at his command.

On the 29th His Lordship arrived at the Texas presidio and here, in the form of a square, but with only two bastions, delineated a fortress for a garrison of twenty-five soldiers. The bastions were to be built on diagonal corners so that each might defend two curtains, each of which, including the demigorge, was to be sixty *varas* long. The fortress will occupy a good site on

[50]A delightful little town on the banks of the Tagus, about forty-nine kilometers from Madrid. It has beautiful gardens and a royal palace begun by Philip II and finished by Charles III.

a hill that overlooks the surrounding country, and all year round can count on water from Nuestra Señora de la Asunción Creek, which passes close by. Here His Lordship remained only three days, fearing lest the return journey might be delayed by the swollen rivers. Learning from scouts whom he had sent out that the Santa Barbara River, situated between the San Francisco and the Nuestra Señora de la Concepción missions, was very high, he ordered a bridge thirty *varas* in length built; and, as a result, the river was crossed without any delay.

On December 9th His Lordship found at Santa Efigenia the second convoy which he had been expecting from La Bahía; and that same day he sent from this convoy to Los Adaes one hundred loads of flour and other provisions, taking with him what was left so as to have supplies for the journey. He decided to return by the old road through the Monte Grande, for he had noticed that the Trinity carried only about half a *vara* of water, and he had learned from soldiers whom he had sent out that the Brazos de Dios also offered a good crossing. With the help of an Indian guide, and making its way through clearings and places sparsely timbered for a distance of seventeen leagues, the battalion crossed the Monte Grande. We shall not make a daily entry of the retreat because this was over a route already known and because the days' marches were irregular. Due to the heavy rainstorms and terrible frosts, to the lack of pasturage, and the excessive mortality that continued among the mules and horses, each day we were able to advance only two or three leagues, and sometimes only one. The weather was so severe that from the Texas presidio nearly all the men traveled on foot, and the governor was obliged to leave at the San Juan Evangelista Creek, shortly before entering the Monte Grande, eighty cargoes, guarded by an escort of twenty soldiers. When he reached the Trinity His Lordship sent a party of ten soldiers after provisions, for he was aware of the fact that he would be delayed in reaching San Antonio and feared lest he might run out of supplies on the march. At El Encadenado, four leagues from the San Marcos River, the party met him with a second convoy of thirty-two loads. Having learned that sixteen soldier huts, as well as the granary with 700 bushels of corn and the supply of flour, had been burned and that not even one ear of corn had been saved, His Lordship ordered that the animals he had asked from Saltillo should with all haste bring the 200 loads of flour and the 1,000 bushels of corn which he had ready on the Rio Grande, and which he had planned to use in case anything happened to the bilander. As the mules brought these provisions with all possible haste, there were enough supplies to stock that presidio [of San Antonio] and to feed the troops, and also to warrant our continuing the journey. His Lordship sent to Guadiana and to other places urgent orders that a fresh supply of 800 horses be sent him for the march.

The journey was continued, and along the route the men endured great hardships; even the officers and captains walked, and at times the governor did likewise in order to share their sufferings. On January 23 the expedition reached San Antonio, and all were greatly rejoiced and consoled, because only mules and horses were included among the mortalities. Among these, however, the mortality was so great that of almost 5,000 horses that had entered with the expedition less than fifty returned, and about 100 of the 800 mules. Not one of the soldiers had been lost, and even those that had left Los Adaes in a sickly condition were well when they reached San Antonio. His Lordship dispatched a message to the viceroy with all this information.

Informed, through several letters, that the horses he had requested would not arrive for more than a month and a half, and that the presidio of San Antonio was defenseless, and as had been observed but a short time previously, exposed to fire because of the fact that the soldiers were living in thatched huts, His Lordship planned to build of adobe brick a fortress which would not be in danger of burning. And, having ordered that timber be cut with which to put up a church, storehouses and barracks, he selected a site between the San Pedro and San Antonio rivers. This site was preferable to that on which the [old] presidio had stood, although some trees had to be felled in order to clear a place for the buildings. His Lordship put men to work on adobe bricks, and he himself began to delineate the fort. This he planned in form of a square and with four bastions, so that if the soldiers chanced to be absent and an invasion took place a few men, stationed on opposite corners, could hold the fort, defending from each bastion two curtains, each of which, from bastion to bastion, was to be seventy-five *varas* long. He proposed also that with irrigation facilities from the water-ditch, which at his own expense he had made from the San Pedro River, a large crop of corn be raised with which to supply the presidio and also the friendly Indians that each day come to see the Spaniards. The water-ditch will be able to irrigate the two leagues of very fertile land which make up the small valley formed by the San Pedro. The latter enters the San Antonio a short distance below the presidio, forming, between the two, a sort of island. The presidio, which is to be built on this island, will be about thirty *varas* from the San Pedro and about 200 from the San Antonio.

On March 8 the messenger that His Lordship had dispatched on November 4 with letters to the viceroy returned with a communication from his Excellency. The latter expressed his most sincere thanks to the governor and approved whatsoever had been done in Texas for the recovery of that province and for its safeguard by means of the fort erected in Los Adaes.

On the 10th of this same month, a good site having already been selected between the San Antonio and San José missions, the governor proceeded to grant to Juan Rodríguez possession of the mission which the latter had asked for himself and for those who had come with him from the Ranchería Grande. The Indian captain promised and assured him that, although he had with him at the time only fifty families, his many followers from the *ranchería* would come there as soon as they learned that a mission had been established for them. His Lordship granted full title of possession to Captain Rodríguez, and also to Fray José González. The latter accepted the mission, under the title of San Francisco Javier de Nájera and in the name of the College of Santa Cruz de Querétaro.[51] The captains of the battalion were present at the ceremony; and this same day His Lordship clothed in a complete suit of English cloth and in the Spanish style the Indian Juan Rodríguez.

With the first drove of horses that arrived His Lordship dispatched, under the command of Captain Gabriel Costales the fifty soldiers destined for La Bahía. These men, all of whom were volunteers, were selected from each of the companies in the battalion and formed a very brilliant troop. As a sufficient number of horses had not as yet arrived, His Lordship was unable to leave until the sixteenth of the said month. On this date he set out with forty men detached from all the companies and with Doctor Don José Codallos y Rabal and Captains Don Tomás de Zubiría, Don Miguel Zilón y Portugal, Don Manuel de Herrera and Don Pedro de Oribe. As far as the Mission of San José y San Miguel de Aguayo, a distance of about two leagues, we marched toward the south, and the rest of the day's journey, as far as the Salado River, traveled to the southwest. This day we covered four leagues, traveling through a level country sparsely covered with evergreen-oaks. Four leagues.

Wednesday, 18. We journeyed south about two leagues and east the rest of the day. The march of eight leagues, as far as the Cibolo River, took us through a hilly and sandy country and through woods thick with oaks and mesquites. The only water, we found along the way was a small stream. Eight leagues.

Thursday, 19. We traveled toward the east-southeast over a level country in which we found the same kinds of trees and mesquite shrubs, and also some clearings. Our march of seven leagues ended at San Cleto Creek. Seven leagues.

Friday, 20. We set out in the afternoon, for in the morning there had been a bad storm accompanied by thunder and lightning, and many of the horses became lost and were not rounded up until midday. After traveling toward the east for two leagues, over a country similar to that covered on the previous

---

[51]Data on this mission can be found in Herbert E. Bolton, "The Mission Records at San Antonio," *The Quarterly of the Texas State Historical Association* 10, 4 (April 1907): 297–308.

day, we came to a creek, which had no name and which His Lordship now called San Joaquín. Here there is an opportunity to hunt turkeys. Two leagues.

Saturday, 21. Continuing our journey, we traveled east-southeast three leagues through a very rough oak woods, three leagues to the east-northeast over a very flat country without trees or bushes, and then turned east for three more leagues through an open country. We finally ended our day's march of nine leagues at a creek which His Lordship called San Benito. Nine leagues.

Sunday, 22. We set out toward the west and traveled about six leagues through an untimbered and somewhat broken country. Then traveling east for three leagues over very flat land, we kept along the banks of the Guadalupe until we came to a point where a crossing can be made over some rocks. The river, whose bed is very wide, was more than a *vara* in depth, and we had to carry the supplies across on our backs. We camped on the south side of the river, after a day's journey of nine leagues. Nine leagues.

Monday, 23. Continuing our journey we traveled for half a league through a woods sparsely covered with oaks and the rest of the way over a very level country. After we had covered four leagues we turned east, and ended our journey of seven leagues on the banks of the San José River.* Seven leagues.

Tuesday, 24. We continued eastward, still traveling through an open country covered with a variety of flowers. We crossed two rather deep creeks and after a march of five leagues turned to the southeast and came to the presidio of Nuestra Señora del Loreto at Espíritu Santo Bay. This day we covered nine leagues. Nine leagues.

During the first eight days nothing could be done, because the governor, who had suffered a physical breakdown as a result of the hardships of the journey, was confined to his bed. Moreover, those were days devoted to the celebration of the Holy Week services of the Church. To all this afforded great consolation, because it was the first time that the sacred ceremonies could be carried out with becoming solemnity, Our Lord being present in the Repository.[52]

On Easter Monday, which fell on April 6, His Lordship, in compliance with orders from His Majesty (may God protect him), began to draw lines for the presidio on the site where the French under La Salle had occupied it from 1684 to 1690. In the latter year the Indians massacred the French, taking alive three men and one girl. The French buried the artillery, but later on it was recovered by the Spaniards and carried off to Vera Cruz. The hole in which the artillery had been buried and in which the powder had been burnt is within the lines of the new fort and can still be seen. On opening the ditch in order

---

*Garcitas Creek.

[52]From Thursday until Saturday of Holy Week the Blessed Sacrament is reserved on a special altar.

to lay the foundation of the fortification nails, pieces of gun locks and fragments of other things used by the French were found. The foundation for the fort, which is to be in the shape of an octagon and which is to have a moat and covert-way, was ready in fifteen days. The governor drew the lines for only four bulwarks (because for the present the garrison will consist of only ninety men; but, as this is an important fort and as its garrison is to be increased, he planned four *lenguas de sierpe** in place of the four bastions) and in the rear, on the angle formed by the two curtains, each of which is to be forty-five *varas* long, he planned a large tower or cavalier.

After this His Lordship proceeded to grant the right of possession of Espíritu Santo de Zúñiga Mission, which was established close to the presidio. This mission was founded because during these days there came from the three tribes many families that had promised the governor that the others would join them as soon as they learned that members of their tribes had remained. As a matter of fact these families did remain at the mission; and they will not abandon it, for they were very well pleased with and grateful for the gifts of clothing and other things which His Lordship distributed among them, just as he had done at the other missions. It was evident that these Indians were very docile and that they would, more readily than the others, devote themselves to the cultivation of the land and of their souls, because they experienced greater misery, living on fish alone and having no clothes, and also because of their own will they brought to the governor three babies and asked him to be their sponsor in baptism. The governor acted as sponsor, and after the children had been baptized by Fray Agustín Patrón, missionary belonging to the College of Nuestra Señora de Guadalupe in Zacatecas, he once more, to the great joy of all, presented gifts to their parents.[53]

Everywhere in the vicinity of the presidio there are beautiful, untimbered fields, which, during our brief observation of one year, we found to be very fertile. There are also beautiful strips of land on which horses and all kinds of stock can be raised. In these parts, particularly along the road from La Bahía to San Antonio, deer and turkeys are plentiful.

Entrusting to Don José Ramón, captain of that presidio, the work of building the fortress, the governor set out for San Antonio, and arrived there on April 26. He was still sickly, but he remarked that he felt very happy to have enjoyed good health as long as he had had duties to perform in the service of the king and that now all that remained for him to do was to accompany his men back to Coahuila. His Lordship could not leave for

---

*Salient extensions.

[53]Bolton says that later events show Peña to be a poor prophet. We cannot agree with him in this, for in 1767, when Solís visited it, the mission was quite flourishing. See Forrestal, "Solís Diary," 15–17.

Coahuila until May 5, because, although some of the horses that he had been expecting reached him at La Bahía, the last of them did not arrive until the thirtieth. In the meantime the new presidio at San Antonio would have been almost finished had it not been for the fact that as a result of continuous rains it was not possible to work more than three weeks, and that 30,000 adobe bricks which had been made before His Lordship left for La Bahía had been ruined. But, 25,000 more bricks were made, much of the presidio was built, and a large supply of material was placed at the base of the new structure. His Lordship paid for the services of forty Indians that had worked on the fortress all this time, and that still continued to work on it.

We left on the 5th, but one very stormy night at a place called La Pita, two days' march from San Antonio, the horses became frightened and made such a stampede that it took all the following day to round them up, and eighty of them became lost. We continued the journey and without being delayed crossed the Rio Grande, which carried a little more than a *vara* of water. We traveled on, and the night of the second day, at a place south of the presidio of San Diego, it also rained heavily and the horses stampeded again. It took four days to gather them together, and forty of them were lost. We left behind us the Sabinas River, which on entering we had experienced much difficulty and delay in crossing, but which now carried less than half a *vara* of water, and on May 25th arrived at Coahuila. On the 31st His Lordship disbanded the troops, for he had received from his Excellency orders to do this at the end of the expedition, that is, as soon as he returned to this town [of Monclova]. He ordered that the men be given their pay for the last two months of the second year; and these, having been supplied with what food they needed for their journey, left [for their homes] on June 12th.

The arms of Our Lord the king (may God protect him) have been covered with glory on this expedition, because merely by a threat they have brought back under His Majesty's loving sway all that the French had dominated in that extensive province. There have been brought under his dominion the many, various, and numerous tribes that inhabit that territory in the 200 leagues that lie between the villa and presidio of San Antonio and Nuestra Señora del Pilar de los Adaes, and in the eighty leagues that lie between San Antonio and Espíritu Santo Bay. During this undertaking had they been called upon to do battle, the captains, subalterns, and soldiers would have performed their duty, for by undergoing hardships of every description on such long and painful marches, battling against the rampages of rivers and enduring defiantly the inclemencies of the weather, now the burning heats, now the biting winter frosts, traveling onward and subjected to the sudden changes of the torrid and frigid zones, they have displayed the second part of a soldier's valor, which is constancy and the spirit of endurance. It seemed as if hell had conjured up all its powers in such unprecedented storms in those regions, because so many souls were about to be wrested from its satanic empire and were to be brought into the fold of the Church, and because the cult of the Holy Catholic Faith was to be restored after it had been abolished and vilified and after the temples had been profaned and demolished. If this outrage has not been repaired, it has at least been compensated for in part by the many old people, of all tongues and nations that are predestined, that have lately asked for baptism at the hour of death and by the infants for whom parents, realizing that the little ones were in danger of death, have urgently requested baptism. At the nine missions which the governor established, besides that of San Antonio de Valero, the Indians continue to do this.

All the kingdoms of New Spain are protected by the defense which has been added in that extensive province, by the presidios that have been built in Los Adaes, Los Texas and La Bahía, and by the fortifying of the presidio at San Antonio. To the latter town, which is situated at the entrance to the province, the Spaniards had retired at the time the French took possession of the rest of the country, there being no fort there [at Los Adaes] previous to this. In the recent *entrada* the governor, carrying out the instructions and orders of the viceroy with the most scrupulous exactitude and vigilance, has for twenty-six months showed his zeal and his innate love for the royal service. Of no less importance is the care he used and the measures he took that the troops might be supplied with food in those far off deserts, to which it was necessary to transport the provisions a distance of 400 leagues. And, realizing that Our Lord the king (may God protect him) considers as more important than the extension of his dominions that Christ, the Sun of Justice, be seen throughout the world, he has with the greatest complacency not only left the entire province under the command of its legitimate owner, but has made every effort that the light of the gospel may shine in as many souls as live in the hapless shades of paganism. In this undertaking the governor's aurora has been Our Lady of Pilar. He had chosen her as his guide and patroness, and as a shield of defense has left this Tower of David on the border of Texas in order that she may take it under her protection. For, even as the Most Blessed Virgin had placed the *Non Plus Ultra* of her mercies, with her image and column, in Zaragoza, remaining there as protectress against the paganism of Spain, then the end of the known world, so too she has placed [here] the Plus Ultra, coming to protect the most remote regions which the Spaniards have discovered in America. Yesterday His Lordship brought the expedition to a close with a most beautiful and solemn feast in honor of Our Lady, in order to return her thanks and in order to implore, not only the conservation of that province, but also that there might be added to the dominions of Our Catholic Philip all upon which the sun rises, for thus all shall be of the kingdom of God, to whom be given praise by all creatures and for all eternity.

Santiago de la Monclova, capital of the province of Coahuila, Nueva Estremadura, June 21, 1722.

BACHILLER JUAN ANTONIO DE LA PEÑA

I, Doctor Don José Codallos y Rabal, Qualifier and Commissary of the Holy Office, Ex-Visitor General, Apostolic and Synodal Examiner of the Diocese of Guadalajara, Vicar General, Ecclesiastical Judge of Real y Minas of San Gregorio, of Mazapil and of Saltillo, Vicar General of the Province of Texas, Nuevas Filipinas, etc., etc., do certify, in so far as I am able, that the diary written by and bearing the signature of Bachiller Don José Antonio de la Peña, Vicar General of the battalion of San Miguel de Aragón, concerning the journey and expedition which the Marquis of San Miguel de Aguayo has directed into the province of Texas for the purpose of recovering this province, restoring the missions and establishing a defense by the construction of presidios in Los Adaes, Los Texas and Espíritu Santo Bay, and for the purpose of protecting these dominions of New Spain, is correct, true, and in every detail written with the most scrupulous exactitude. I have been an eye-witness of all these events, having accompanied the marquis from the time he left the Río Grande del Norte until he returned to this town of Santiago de la Monclova, capital of the Province of Coahuila; and in order that credence be given the said Diary I have affixed to it my signature in this town of Santiago on June 23, 1722.

DOCTOR DON JOSEPH CODALLOS Y RABAL
In my presence,
ANTONIO DE ESPRONZEDA,
Notary Ecclesiastic

SILENT YEARS IN TEXAS HISTORY

Carlos E. Castañeda*

FOREWORD

The following contribution to the early history of Texas is the result of critical research by Dr. Carlos E. Castañeda, who has explored and discovered new source materials in the San Francisco Grande Archives, located in the Biblioteca Nacional, Mexico City. As the title indicates, the account here given attempts to throw light on the period from 1694 to 1716, which no historian heretofore has successfully treated in a way that would bridge the gap by the record of happenings between the date of the abandonment of the first missions established on Texas soil and the permanent settlement made by Captain Domingo Ramón near the eastern frontier, during the second decade of the eighteenth century. The general impression among scholars seems to have been that these years were silent ones, when there was a suspension of activities everywhere throughout this vast region once occupied by the official representatives, the sons of St. Francis and other loyal subjects of the Spanish Crown.

Here in this narrative is found the connecting links that furnish the background to subsequent events which cannot be completely or clearly understood without a knowledge of the facts contained in these pages. Here may be traced from their origins the movements that shaped the destinies of rival nations for the control of colonial empires in America.

The Commission and the Society wish to give grateful acknowledgment to the Texas State Historical Association, to Dr. Eugene C. Barker, the managing editor of the *Southwestern Historical Quarterly*, and his associates for permission to republish this contribution for the *Preliminary Studies of the Texas Catholic Historical Society*.

Paul J. Foik, C.S.C.
Chairman of the Commission and President of the Society

---

*Vol. 2, No. 8, appeared in April 1935 as a reprint from *The Southwestern Historical Quarterly* 38, 2 (October 1934).

Silent Years in Texas History

Like a blinding flash, like a bolt out of a clear sky came the news of La Salle's colony in Texas. It electrified Spanish officials both in Spain and in America. The daring of the French attempt called forth superhuman efforts. The little settlement on Garcitas Creek was considered "a menace which threatened the safety of the Indies and of the whole Spanish empire."[1] No sooner was the news transmitted to the viceroy in Mexico by special courier from Vera Cruz than an expedition was immediately ordered to search the gulf coast and find the intruders. Within three months after the capture of the French corsair in 1685, off the coast of Campeche, when, through the declaration of one of the prisoners, it became known that an attempt to establish a settlement in Texas had been made by the unfortunate La Salle, a maritime and a land expedition were ordered to find the French settlement. Before a year passed three different expeditions were undertaken by land and sea to search for the little colony. Then followed in rapid succession the De León and Terán expeditions and the first official occupation of Texas became an accomplished fact with the establishment of a presidio and several missions.[2]

Up to this time casual reference to Texas and the various tribes that roamed over its vast expanse is all that we find in the documents and accounts of that time, but from the appearance of La Salle the history of Texas becomes audible. The woods resound with the activity of the missionaries and the soldiers, and a new era is noisily heralded, as it were, by the ill-starred La Salle and the followers of De León

For five years, from 1689 to 1694, the story is filled with details, with dramatic interest, with the sorrow and pathos of the survivors of the little French colony, with the patient, nay, heroic efforts of the missionaries against adversity and against the indifference of the natives, who soon tired of ordered life and restrictions and threatened the very existence of the men who had come at their bidding out of love for humanity. Then one night, the small band of disheartened missionaries and soldiers steal away, after burying the mission bells and small cannon, and silence reigns once more over the wilderness. For twenty years, until St. Denis appeared unexpectedly at Presidio San Juan Bautista on the Rio Grande, this silence seems to reign supreme.

---

[1]"Consulta de la Junta de Guerra," Audiencia de México, 61–6–20, Archivo General de Indias, photostats of Dunn Transcripts, Catholic Archives of Texas, Austin (hereafter cited as AGI:M–Dunn).

[2]For a detailed account of how the news was obtained of the La Salle expedition and the strenuous efforts made by Spanish officials to locate and drive out the French from Texas see William E. Dunn, *Spanish and French Rivalry in the Gulf Coast Region of the United States, 1678–1702*, Studies in Texas History No. 1 (Austin, 1917).

Until very recently it was thought that in reality there had been a complete lull; that during these years all interest and activity in Texas ceased; that these were silent years in the history of our State.

Contrary to this general impression, interest in Texas continued, activity went on, although greatly diminished, and far from being silent years, these two decades are replete with interest because of the mystery that envelops the activity of the French in the region occupied by the Asinai. In the subdued light that filters into the unexplored region, in the all-enveloping silence, there stealthily moves the shadow of a man who for more than forty years was to play an important role in the history of the Franco-Spanish frontier in America, a man of whom Governor Boneo y Morales said in 1744 "St. Denis is dead, thank God! Now we can breathe easier."[3] In the stillness of the forest a voice is heard calling to the Indians, expressing a hope for an early return. Fray Hidalgo kept his eyes fixed constantly on his dearly beloved Tejas, as he waited patiently on the outposts of Coahuila for an opportunity to return to Texas, and on two occasions made bold to write to the French themselves to inquire after the welfare of the Indians.[4]

In the course of this short paper it is the intention of the writer to bring out as many of the meager details as he has been able to find concerning the activities of St. Denis during this apparently sterile period and to point out other indications of both Spanish and French interest in the area occupied by the Asinai confederacy in the hope of arousing interest among those who love to delve into the obscure corners of history that the silent years may at last tell their story and that our history may be continuous instead of broken by this gap.

Aside from the activities of St. Denis, it will be shown that there was at least one expedition which set out from Mobile in 1707 for the purpose of establishing trade with the Indians of Texas, Nuevo Reino de León, and Nueva Vizcaya This expedition had a definite relation to the hitherto almost unknown expedition into Texas in 1709, whose diary was only recently published in English for the first time by the Texas Catholic Historical Society.[5] It had puzzled the writer, until the discovery of the French expedition of 1707 why this little band of Spanish missionaries under the leadership

---

[3]Herbert E. Bolton, *Texas in the Middle Eighteenth Century: Studies in Spanish Colonial History and Administration*, The University of California Publications in History Vol. 3 (Berkeley, 1915), 41.

[4]"Resumen general de los autos sobre noticias, informes y escritos desde 1688 a 1716," Archivo de San Francisco el Grande, photostats, 8:126–63, Center for American History, University of Texas (hereafter cited as ASFG).

[5]Gabriel Tous, trans., "The Espinosa-Olivares-Aguirre Expedition of 1709," in *Preliminary Studies of the Texas Catholic Historical Society*, 1, 3 (March 1930), reprinted in *Preparing the Way: Preliminary Studies of the Texas Catholic Historical Society I*, Studies in Southwestern Catholic History No. 1 (Austin, 1997), 67–89.

of Father Espinosa and escort of Captain Aguirre had come into Texas in 1709, traveled as far as the Colorado River, and returned to Coahuila. It is thus that we see how one incident leads to another and how piece by piece the connected story of these silent years is evolving as the old records are more carefully studied.

If La Salle's incursion was the flash that first lighted the way and aroused interest in Texas, St. Denis may be said to have been the long rumble that echoed through the wilderness for years and kept the Spanish officials in constant fear of the approaching storm. The biography of this remarkable man has yet to be written. Considerable confusion exists in the data now available between Louis de St. Denis and Juchereau de St. Denis, and the coming publication of a semi-fictional biography will no doubt only add to the confusion. Juchereau was the father of Louis de St. Denis. He was lieutenant general of Montreal and in 1700, while in Paris, offered his services to the king to colonize the mouth of the Mississippi. "After twenty-five years of experience I should be able to establish a flourishing colony," he confidently declared to the aging Sun King. But others more influential in the court circles of France, however, had won the ear of the king and Juchereau was only able to get a concession to establish a tannery on the Mississippi. This grant was made to him on June 4, 1701. The *Compagnie de Canada* remonstrated loudly against the concession, but Juchereau ably defended his rights. Soon thereafter he returned to America, going to Canada again. Little is known about his activities from this time on, although it seems that after his arrival he went to the Missouri, probably with a view of continuing from there to the mouth of the Mississippi. In a letter dated September 6, 1704, Bienville informs the French Minister that word has just been received of the death of Juchereau de St. Denis, who died during the preceding autumn (1703) in the region of the Missouri. He never came to Louisiana.[6]

It was the son, Louis de St. Denis, sometimes called Louis Juchereau de St. Denis, who came to Louisiana down the Mississippi from Canada, probably with Tonty, in 1700. Almost from the day of his arrival he became an active and important member of the colony. D'Iberville must have recognized at once the natural ability of the young Canadian, because, when the new fort built on the Mississippi early in 1700 was completed, he left his brother Bienville and M. de St. Denis as joint commanders of the important post.[7]

---

[6]Pierre Margry, *Memoires et Documents pour servir a l'histoire des origines francaises des pays d'outre-mer: Descouvertes et etablissements des Francais dans l'ouest et dans sud de l'Amerique Septentrionale*, 6 vols. (Paris, 1876–1886) 4: 399. The data for this sketch is found scattered throughout this volume of Margry.

[7]Ibid., 399.

Just when he became commander of the fort of San Juan on the Mississippi, situated about 40 leagues west of Mobile, is not known, but he was its commander by 1705, according to his own statement made in Mexico City on June 22, 1715.[8] It is from the declaration made at this time that we gather much information about his activities in Texas from 1705 to 1715. He declared that he had been among the Texas Indians ten years before. If we are to believe his statements made under oath, he went at that time (1705) from Mobile to the Choctaws, a populous tribe, according to St. Denis, numbering about 18,000 members. After a visit with them he went to the Natches, a nation that lay 30 leagues west quarter-northwest from the Choctaws and consisted of eleven pueblos, all of which had sworn allegiance to his most Christian Majesty the king of France. From the Natches he traveled 40 leagues in a southwesterly direction to the Nachitos. This nation also traded with the French ever since 1701, the chief article of exchange being salt. According to St. Denis the salt secured from these Indians was whiter and purer than the salt that came from France. The Nachitos were neighbors of the Asinai, with whom they traded also. It was thus through the Nachitos that the French traders introduced their merchandise among the Tejas in the early years. After a short stay with the Nachitos St. Denis went on to visit the Tejas Indians and from there—mark this statement—he proceeded, over the same route as in 1714, to the Presidio of San Juan Bautista on the Rio Grande. This fact has not been brought out before and the general belief has prevailed that he appeared on the Rio Grande for the first time in 1714.

He not only declared he had visited the presidio ten years before but he goes further and explains that the distance by land from Mobile to the Rio Grande is 280 leagues. Let us quote his exact words. "There are from Mobile to the said presidio 280 leagues over good and passable ground and the routes so run that they come together at the Nachitos. No mines have been discovered over the entire land route, but there are numerous groves of shade and fruit trees to be found along the road."[9] The two routes referred to here are the all land and the water and land routes from Mobile to San Juan Bautista on the Rio Grande. It was the last of these two that was followed by St. Denis in his expedition of 1713–1715, at which time he traveled by water in canoes from Mobile to the Asinai and from the Asinai to the Rio Grande over land. It is worth noting that at the time he made this declaration he also gave the viceroy a map which he had made of the country over which he traveled. If this map is ever found, it will be of great interest not only in

[8]"Declaración de St. Denis y Medar Jalot sobre su viaje hasta el presidio del Capitán Diego Ramón," ASFG 8:27–32.

[9]ibid., 32.

helping to locate the first route from the Mississippi to the Rio Grande but also as the earliest map of Texas drawn from actual observation.[10]

Although he did not state that he had visited the Tejas on other occasions, it seems he was in the habit of spending as much as six months at a time among them frequently. One of the dispatch carriers of Diego Ramón declared on being asked to give testimony of what he had observed and learned from the Indians "that St. Denis knew their language because he had lived among them on various occasions."[11] This statement is further borne out by the declarations made by Father Olivares who said "Don Luis de St. Denis was the one whom the Indians respected most because he knew their language, having lived among them four months on one occasion and for shorter periods at other times."[12] In a letter written by Domingo Ramón on July 26, 1716, he declared that St. Denis had been very helpful to him because of his knowledge of the habits and customs of the Tejas and of their language, a knowledge which he had acquired while living among them. He states that St. Denis spent "six months in the province on two different occasions."[13]

When the Ramón expedition arrived in the country of the Tejas it was noted that the Indians had cloth of good grade, beads, firearms, and trinkets of various kinds. Upon being asked where they secured all these things they said the French from Natchitoches brought them in square boats on the river and gave them to the Indians for horses and skins of animals.[14]

All evidences seem to point out clearly to the fact that this trade had been going on for years. Ramón declared he had noticed as many as 18 or 20 long French arquebuses, beads, trinkets, large knives, pocket knives, cloth of good grade, and hatchets, all of which the Indians obtained from the French in exchange for cattle and horses.[15] On August 29, 1707, Don Gregorio Salinas Varona, Governor of Santa María de Galve wrote a long letter to the viceroy of Mexico. In the letter he declares that he had just heard that on the 22nd of the said month of August the governor of Mobile had sent out an expedition consisting of twenty-five Canadians armed with rifles, one hundred Indians, and two pirogues loaded with merchandise to explore the approaches to the dominions of the king of Spain for the purpose of introducing merchandise

---

[10]This map is referred to by the *fiscal* in his report of August 20, 1715, ASFG 8:3; and again on pages 34, 39, and 41 of the same volume.

[11]"Resumen de los autos sobre noticias," 126–163.

[12]Ibid., 148.

[13]"Acuerdos de la Junta de Guerra y Hacienda que el CapitánRamón aprehenda los 4 franceses," Dec. 2, 1716, ASFG 8:170.

[14]"Resumen de los autos sobre noticias," 145 ad passim.

[15]"Acuerdos de la Junta de Guerra," 170.

and establishing trade with Nueva Vizcaya, Nuevo Reino de León, and Coahuila, which they called Nueva Estremadura.[16]

Immediately upon receipt of this information a council of war [Junta de Guerra] was held and it was decided that the viceroy should send out without delay instructions to the governors and commanders of these provinces to prevent by all means in their power the introduction of merchandise or the entrance of foreigners. They were duly authorized to use all available forces under their commands to watch all river and mountain passes, and to utilize the friendly Indians in keeping a close watch on the movements of the intruders. In case the merchandise had already been introduced before the orders were received, the governors, commanders, and all public officials were instructed to confiscate all such goods wherever they were found and to arrest all persons holding said goods or connected in any manner with their introduction.[17]

The viceroy was further requested to write to the governor of Louisiana and to inform him, without revealing the source, that information of the attempted establishment of trade with the various frontier provinces of New Spain had been received; that such trade was strictly prohibited by the king of Spain, and that in view of the circumstances the governor of Louisiana should warn all subjects of his Most Christian Majesty to abstain from such trade.

Not content with all this, the Junta recommended that immediate steps be taken to establish contact with the Tejas Indians and all their neighbors in order that they might be used to prevent the introduction of illicit trade into New Spain. It was this last suggestion that resulted in the Espinosa-Olivares-Aguirre expedition of 1709, which paved the way for the *entrada* of Ramón seven years later, and which, as stated before, was practically unknown until its recent publication.

In accord with a special council held on August 7, 1708, Captain Pedro de Aguirre, commander of Presidio Río Grande del Norte, was ordered by His Excellency, the Duke of Albuquerque, to escort Fathers Antonio de San Buenaventura Olivares and Isidro Espinosa, both friars of the Franciscan Order, as far as the San Marcos (the Colorado) in an effort to meet the Tejas Indians and their allies at this point. Accordingly, the expedition set out from San Juan Bautista on April 15, 1709. Fourteen soldiers and the captain accompanied the two Franciscans on their lonely quest for the Tejas. The little group crossed the Rio Grande and by the 8th had reached the Nueces. Traveling as rapidly as possible and inquiring along the way for news of the Tejas, the little group arrived in the present site of San Antonio on the 13th

---

16 Ibid., 164–165.

17 Ibid.

and named the San Pedro Springs. Six days later they reached their goal, the Colorado River, but much to their disappointment found no Tejas Indians awaiting them there as they had expected. After a day of fruitless searching for friendly Indians, they discovered a group of Yojuames. But let the pious Espinosa tell the story himself.

> Seeing that our efforts to reach the Arroyo of the Otates in the hope of meeting the Tejas had been fruitless, and knowing that the Indian leader of the Yojuanes, called Cantona, frequents the province of the Tejas with his followers, we inquired particularly about the said Indians, and asked if it was true that they had left their territory and had come to settle on the San Marcos River. To this they replied that the Asinai Indians, commonly called Tejas, were in their own country where they had always lived; that they had not moved to the place we inquired about; that only a few were in the habit of going in search of buffalo meat to the Colorado River and its neighborhood. Asked again, if they knew this to be the truth, they maintained what they had said and declared further that Bernardino, a Tejas Indian, who knew Spanish and was very crafty, having lived many years among the Spaniards, was the chief of all the Tejas, and this they knew well. All this caused us sorrow on the one hand, because we wanted to see the Tejas, and [joy] on the other hand, because it relieved us of the uncertainty under which we had labored concerning the whereabouts of the Tejas. The Indians said also that it was a three-day journey from the place where we were to the village of the Tejas. Not having planned to stay any longer, and the Captain of the military expedition not having instructions to go any farther, and having been told by all who knew him that the chief of the Tejas was very adverse to all matters of faith, never having been made to live like a Christian, and that he had escaped from the mission on the Rio Grande with some Indian women who had been there, we decided not to proceed any farther.
>
> Saturday afternoon we made a paper cross, which we painted with ink as best we could, and gave it to the Indian Cantona, who came with us. We commissioned him to take it to the governor of the Tejas and to tell how we had searched for them; that they should go to our mission on the Rio Grande since they knew where they were; and to show them the cane he had, that they might give credence to his words. This being done we started our return march to the Rio Grande.[18]

[18]Tous, "The Espinosa-Olivares-Aguirre Expedition of 1709."

Although the expedition failed to meet the Tejas Indians which it went out to contact for the expressed purpose of securing their good will and cooperation to check the activities of the French, nevertheless it was not a failure, for it made possible a few years later the Ramón expedition. The Tejas Indians, it must be borne in mind, were crafty and astute. They no doubt carried word of the visit of the missionaries and the small group of soldiers to their Louisiana friends. The news of the intention of the Spaniards to establish a mission among them only aroused the cupidity of the French, who saw in the establishment not a hindrance to their designs but an invaluable opportunity to introduce their merchandise farther into the interior by this means without so much danger. In short the projected settlement of East Texas would bring the Spanish frontier nearer to them and make it easier to establish trade.

The Spanish officials were well aware of this fact. When St. Denis made his declarations in Mexico the *fiscal* was not in the least convinced by the apparently guileless statements. There were too many discrepancies. It may be lightly thought that the French fooled the Spaniards on more than one occasion. This impression is erroneous. It was not because the Spaniards did not understand or realize the true import or intentions of the French that they did not stop the activities or take more aggressive measures. It was that they were powerless to act: first, because the king did not give them the authorization, nor even the moral support they deserved for their zeal in protecting his royal interests; and second, because they did not have the resources nor the man power to put into effect a more decisive policy.

Take for example the summary of the Texas situation made by the Fiscal, Doctor Velasco, in Mexico City on November 30, 1716. After giving a long and detailed resume of everything that had taken place since 1689, he draws up his conclusions and analyzes the reasons for the occupation of Texas, revealing with amazing clearness that he understood the motives for the activity of the French and the character of St. Denis.

"Today," he declares,

> in addition to the primary purpose for the establishment of the missions which is the conversion and civilization of the Indians of Texas, there exists a second and very important one of a temporal nature, the need for the friendship and good will of these Indians, who are under the jurisdiction of His Majesty, in order that with their aid the extent of the French conquest may be ascertained. The establishment of a presidio would serve as a defense for the province, it would impede the movements of the French from Mobile and Canada, and it would serve as a point of observation which would enable us to learn their inten-

> tions in time to check their advance. Should we fail to take these steps the French will no doubt extend their influence from Natchitoches to Coahuila and introduce their merchandise from that post to the province of Texas, having explored the country already and being acquainted with it as far as the Río Grande del Norte.

He then goes on to state that a quantity of goods had already been introduced at various times from Mobile where, according to St. Denis' statement there were more than two millions worth of cloth and other merchandise. The *fiscal* wisely observes that the distance from Mobile to Texas is only 280 leagues over the all land route and 320 over the water and land route; that the country abounds with wild fruits and game, all of which would make the cost of transportation of the goods much cheaper; and that since the population of Louisiana is small and the amount of merchandise far too great for their consumption, it is evident it was intended for introduction into New Spain.

He points out that St. Denis himself came to the Rio Grande for no other purpose, as shown by the letter sent by the governor of Santa María de Galve in 1713, giving notice of his departure from Mobile with six pirogues loaded with merchandise; that he and his companions must have disposed of this merchandise is likewise proved by another letter of the governor of Santa María de Galve, who on October 20, 1715, wrote the viceroy of Mexico that a group of twenty Frenchmen had returned to Mobile and publicly averred they had been to the Nuevo Reino de León and Coahuila from where they brought back large numbers of horses and cattle.

The *fiscal* argues with much logic that these two letters of the governor of Santa María de Galve explain some of the obscure points in the declaration of St. Denis. He points out that the date of the first letter coincides with that of the departure of St. Denis, while the date of the second would correspond to the time the twenty companions of St. Denis would require to return, as they did, from Texas to Mobile. Now, if St. Denis had traveled directly from the Texas to the Rio Grande, it could not have taken him nine months. It is clear then, thinks the Fiscal, that what actually took place was that St. Denis and his companions did stop among the Tejas for a while and with their aid perhaps reached the Rio Grande and disposed of most of their goods; that St. Denis then sent back his companions with the horses and cattle obtained in exchange, and presented himself with only two or three companions to the commander at San Juan Bautista after the departure of the rest.

"His statement," declares the *fiscal*,

> that he did not stop among the Tejas or ever lived among them is false, for it has been proved that he was among them at various times and

learned their language. The assertion that wild horses and cattle are numerous in the province of the Tejas and that these Indians live in pueblos is likewise false, as shown by documents and reliable sources in the office of the secretary of the viceroyalty, from all of which it appears that these Indians live separately and widely scattered.[19]

The solicitude of the French in asking that missionaries be sent to these Indians may well be the result of their desire for closer friendship with the soldiers that may be sent as an escort in order that through these closer relations the introduction of their merchandise may be facilitated. This assumption is founded first, on the fact that St. Denis or one of his companions [Medar Jalot] married the niece of the leader of the Texas expedition;[20] the other that St. Denis went to Mobile to bring back to Texas 18,000 pesos worth of merchandise which he had there.[21]

The attitude of the king in the whole matter is well illustrated by the following incident. On April 14, 1702, Martínez, who was temporarily in command of Pensacola, informed the Council of the Indies that on December 16, 1701, Iberville had appeared at Pensacola and requested permission to enter. The request was granted in view of the close relations then existing between the two crowns. Three days later Iberville informed Martínez he had orders from the king of France to occupy Mobile Bay "before the English should seize it." In vain did Martínez protest and entreat Iberville to defer carrying out his purpose until he could receive instructions from the viceroy

---

[19]The subsequent events of the occupation of East Texas bear out this statement. The Texas Indians could not be congregated and it was for this reason that Rivera advised the abandonment of the missions in 1728.

[20]Up to the present there has been no doubt as to the marriage of St. Denis with Manuela Ramón, sometimes referred to as María Villescas, daughter of a son of Diego Ramón, of the same name and brother of Domingo, the commander of the expedition in 1716. But Father Fr. Olivares says:

> Either Medar Jalot or St. Denis married at the presidio of Rio Grande a granddaughter of the Captain of the Presidio of Rio Grande, Diego Ramón, who is a niece of the actual commander of the twenty-five men of the expedition and although I do not doubt that one of the two married the granddaughter of Captain Ramón, I have not been able to determine with any certainty which of the two did. ("Resumen de los autos sobre noticias," 148.)

Two other witnesses are cited by the *fiscal* in support of his statement as to the doubt he had concerning who married the girl. It is the opinion of the writer that St. Denis did not marry Manuela Ramón at San Juan Bautista, but waited until he reached Natchitoches. The reasons for this opinion are that St. Denis was a nobleman; that he could not marry according to French law without the consent of the king or in his absence that of the governor; that the girl could accompany the expedition safely escorted by her uncle; that immediately upon the arrival in the Tejas area, St. Denis, Ramón and one other person proceeded to Mobile; and that after this visit, having obtained the consent of the governor, the marriage was in fact performed at Natchitoches. The writer has not all the facts to prove his deductions, but expects to get them.

[21]"Resumen de los autos sobre noticias," 150–153.

of New Spain. The French commander merely reiterated that his royal master's only desire was to "act for the best interest of both crowns."

Upon receipt of this information the Junta immediately held a meeting and on August 1, 1702, reported the whole matter to the king. They called his royal attention to the fact that the extension of the French settlements in the coast region was detrimental to the best interests of Spain, that on two previous occasions the attention of the king had been called to these encroachments; that until he made some decision in the matter the Junta was unable to apply the necessary remedy to preserve the integrity of the king's domain.[22]

The king did not appreciate the zeal of the Junta in pointing out the serious consequences of his procrastination. Such frankness shocked the sensitive nature of the monarch who, instead of thanking his well-meaning advisers, made the following annotation on the margin of the report:

> This notice is incomplete. Since the papers which the Junta says have not arrived are lacking, this representation is premature, and it is couched in such ill-advised terms that it has displeased me exceedingly, and caused me great surprise that ministers of such experience and high rank should have allowed it to reach my hands.[23]

Thus we see that the high officials of Spain, both at home and in America fully realized the dangers to the colonial empire from the French settlement of Louisiana and understood the nature of their activities, but the first received a reprimand for their zeal and the second were left powerless to apply the necessary remedies to check the advances and strengthen Spain's claim to Texas.

---

[22] "Consulta de la Junta de Guerra."

[23] Dunn, *Spanish and French Rivalry in the Gulf Coast Region*, 215.

Select Bibliography

I: Manuscript sources cited in the text.

Catholic Archives of Texas, Austin	CAT
Center for American History, University of Texas at Austin	UT
Texas State Archives, Austin	TSA

Archivo de la Biblioteca Pública del Estado de Jalisco. Photostatic copies of selected files at CAT and UT.

Archivo General de Indias: Audiencia de Guadalajara; Audiencia de México. Transcripts and photostatic copies of selected files may be consulted at CAT, TSA, and UT.

Archivo General y Público de la Nación de México: Ramo Historia; Ramo Provincias Internas. Transcripts of large portions of these collections may be consulted at CAT, TSA, and UT. Microfilms of the entirety of the two sections are available at UT.

Archivo de San Francisco el Grande, Biblioteca Nacional de México. Photostatic copies of selected files at CAT and UT.

Genaro García Collection, Benson Latin American Collection, University of Texas at Austin.

II. Works cited in the text.

Arricivita, Juan Domingo. *Crónica seráfica y apostólica del Colegio de Propaganda Fide de la Santa Cruz de Querétaro en la Nueva España.* Mexico, 1792.

Bancroft, Hubert Howe. *History of the North Mexican States and Texas*, 2 vols. San Francisco, 1886.

Barker, Eugene C. *Life of Stephen F. Austin, Founder of Texas, 1793–1836: A Chapter in the Westward Movement of the Anglo-American People.* Nashville, 1926. (Reprint, Austin, 1969.)

Benjamin, Gilbert G. *The Germans in Texas: A Study in Immigration.* Philadelphia, 1909. (Reprint, San Francisco, 1970; Austin, 1974.)

Biesele, Rudolph L. *History of the German Settlements in Texas, 1831–1861.* Austin, 1930. (Reprint, San Marcos, Texas, 1987.)

Bolton, Herbert E. "The Mission Records at San Antonio." *The Quarterly Texas State Historical Association* 10, 4 (April 1907): 297–308

———. "The Native Tribes about the East Texas Missions." *The Quarterly of the Texas State Historical Association* 11, 4 (April 1908): 249–76.

———. "The Spanish Occupation of Texas, 1519–1690" in *The Southwestern Historical Quarterly* 16, 1 (July 1912): 1–26.

———, ed. *Spanish Exploration in the Southwest, 1542–1706.* Original Narratives of Early American History Vol. 18. New York, 1916, reprinted 1925. (Reprint, New York, 1946, 1952, 1959, 1967.)

———. *Texas in the Middle Eighteenth Century: Studies in Spanish Colonial History and Administration*, The University of California Publications in History Vol. 3. Berkeley, 1915. (Reprint, Austin, 1970.)

Buckley, Eleanor Claire. "The Aguayo Expedition into Texas and Louisiana." *The Quarterly of the Texas State Historical Association* 15, 1 (July 1911): 1–65

Casís, Lilia M. trans."The 1690 Letter from Fray Massanet to Don Carlos de Sigüenza." *The Quarterly of the Texas State Historical Association* 2, 4 (April 1899): 253–312. (Reprinted in Bolton, ed. *Spanish Explorations in the Southwest.*)

Castañeda, Carlos E. "Earliest Catholic Activities in Texas." *The Catholic Historical Review* 17, 3 (Oct. 1931): 278–95. (Reprint, *Preliminary Studies of the Texas Catholic Historical Society* 1, 8 (Oct. 1931) and *Preparing the Way: Preliminary Studies of the Texas Catholic Historical Society I*, 1997.)

———, ed. *Morfi's History of Texas*, 2 pts. Albuquerque, 1935. (Reprint, New York, 1967.)

Dunn, William E. "Apache Relations in Texas, 1718–1750." *The Quarterly of the Texas State Historical Association* 14, 3 (Jan. 1911): 198–274.

———. *Spanish and French Rivalry in the Gulf Coast Region of the United States, 1678–1702*, Studies in Texas History No. 1. Austin, 1917.

Espinosa, Isidro Félix. *Chrónica apostólica, y seráphica de todos los colegios de Propaganda fide de esta Nueva-España.* Mexico, 1746.

————. *El peregrino septentrional atlante: delineado en la exemplarissima vida del venerable padre F. Antonio Margil de Jesús.* Mexico, 1737.

Forrestal, Peter P., trans. "The Solís Diary of 1767." *Preliminary Studies of the Texas Catholic Historical Society*, 1, 6 (March 1931). (Reprint, *Preparing the Way: Preliminary Studies of the Texas Catholic Historical Society I*, 1997.)

————. "The Venerable Padre Fray Antonio Margil de Jesús." *Mid-America*, 3, 4 (April 1932). (Reprint, *Preliminary Studies of the Texas Catholic Historical Society* 2, 2 (April 1932) and this volume.)

Hatcher, Mattie Austin. "The Expedition of Don Domingo Terán de los Ríos into Texas." *Preliminary Studies of the Texas Catholic Historical Society*, 2, 1 (Jan. 1932). (Reprinted in this volume.)

————. *The Opening* of *Texas to Foreign Settlement, 1801–1821.* University of Texas Bulletin No. 2714. Austin, 1927.

Hodge, Frederick Webb. *Handbook of American Indians North of Mexico.* Bureau of American Ethnology Bulletin 30, 2 pts. Washington, D.C., 1907.

Houston, Virginia H. Taylor. "Surveying in Texas." in *One League to Each Wind: Accounts of Early Surveying in Texas*, Sue Watkins, ed. Austin, 1964.

Informe que se dio al Excmo. Sr. Presidente de la República Mejicana sobre límites de la Provincia de Tejas . Zacatecas, 1828.

Keene, Ricardo Raynal. *Memoria presentada a S.M.C. el Señor Don Fernando VII sovre el asunto de fomentar la población y cultivo en los terrenos baldios en las provincias internas del reyno de México.* Madrid, 1815.

Kress, Margaret Kenney, trans. "Diary of a Visit of Inspection of the Texas Missions Made by Fray Gaspar José de Solís in the Year 1767–68." *Southwestern Historical Quarterly* 35, 1 (July 1931): 28–76.

López Aguado, Juan. *Voces que hicieron eco.* Mexico, 1726.

Margry, Pierre. *Memoires et Documents pour servir a l'histoire des origines francaises des pays d'outre-mer: Descouvertes et etablissements des Francais dans l'ouest et dans sud de l'Amerique Septentrionale.* 6 vols. Paris, 1876–1886.

Mexicana Beatificationis et canonizationis Ven. Servi Dei Antonii Margil a Jesu: De Tern perantia, XXX, 32. [Rome], n.d.

Mota Padilla, Matías. *Historia de la conquista de la provincia de la Nueva Galicia.* N.p., 1742. (Reprint, Mexico, 1871–72; Guadalajara 1920, 1973.)

Newcomb, W. W. *The Indians of Texas: From Prehistoric to Modern Times*. Austin, 1961.

Portillo, Esteban. *Apuntes para la historia de Coahuila y Tejas*. Saltillo, Mexico, 1886. (Reprint, Saltillo, Mexico, 1984.)

S. Esteban y Andrade, Francisco de. *Título glorioso del crucificado con Cristo y segunda azucena de la religión seráfica*. Mexico, 1729.

Sotomayor, José Francisco. *Historia del Apostólico Colegio de Nuestra Señora de Guadalupe de Zacatecas: desde su fundación hasta nuestros dias*, 2nd ed. Zacatecas, 1889.

Summarium beatificationis et canonizationis Ven. Servi Dei Antonii Margil a Jesu, no. 5, p. 50. sec. 48. N.p., n.d.

Tiling, Moritz. *History of the German Element in Texas from 1820–1850, and Historical Sketches of the German Texas Singers' League and Houston Turnverein from 1853–1913*. Houston, 1913.

Tous, Gabriel, trans. "The Espinosa-Olivares-Aguirre Expedition of 1709." *Preliminary Studies of the Texas Catholic Historical Society*, 1, 3 (March 1930). (Reprint, *Preparing the Way: Preliminary Studies of the Texas Catholic Historical Society I*, 1997.)

Vilaplana, Hermenegildo. *Vida portentosa del americano septentrional apóstol, el v. p. fr. Antonio Margil de Jesús, fundador, y ex-guardián de los colegios de la Santa Cruz de Querétaro, de Christo Crucifado de Guatemala, y de Nuestra Señora de Guadalupe de Zacatecas*. Madrid, 1775. (Reprint, Madrid, 1775; Querétaro, 1981.)

West, Elizabeth Howard, trans. "Bonilla's Brief Compendium of the History of Texas, 1772." *The Quarterly of the Texas State Historical Association* 8, 1 (July 1904): 3–78.

III: Other primary and secondary literature.

Alessio Robles, Vito. *Coahuila y Texas en la época colonial*. 2. ed. Mexico, 1978.

Almaráz, Félix D., Jr. *Crossroad of Empire: The Church and State on the Rio Grande Frontier of Coahuila and Texas, 1700–1821*. San Antonio, 1979.

————. "Harmony, Discord, and Compromise in Spanish Colonial Texas: The Río San Antonio Experience, 1691–1741. *New Mexico Historical Review* 67, 4 (Oct. 1992): 329–56.

Arricivita, Juan Domingo. *Apostolic Chronicle of Juan Domingo Arricivita : The Franciscan Mission Frontier in the Eighteenth Century in Arizona, Texas, and the Californias.* 2 vols. Trans. George P. Hammond and Agapito Rey, intro. and notes by W. Michael Mathes. Berkeley, 1996.

Benavides, Adán, Jr., comp. *Archival Investigations for Mission Nuestra Señora de los Dolores de los Ais, San Augustine County, Texas.* Texas Department of Transportation Environmental Affairs Division Archeological Studies Program Report No. 11. Austin, 1998.

Beers, Henry P. "Part II: The Records of Texas." *Spanish and Mexican Records of the American Southwest: A Bibliographical Guide to Archive and Manuscript Sources.* Tucson, 1979.

Bolton, Herbert E. The Location of La Salle's Colony on the Gulf of Mexico." *The Southwestern Historical Quarterly* 27, 3 (Jan. 1924): 171–89.

———, comp. *guide to Materials for the History of the United States in the Principal Archives of Mexico.* Reprint. New York, 1965.

Bugbee, Lester Gladstone. "The Real Saint-Denis." *The Quarterly of the Texas State Historical Association* 1, 4 (April 1898): 266–81.

Caldwell, Norman W. "Charles Juchereau de St. Denys: A French Pioneer in the Mississippi Valley." *Mississippi Valley Historical Review* 28, 4 (March 1942): 563–80.

Castañeda, Carlos E. *Our Catholic Heritage in Texas, 1519–1936.* 7 vols. Austin, 1936–58.

Cavazos Garza, Israel. *Dos Alonsos de León: el cronista y el descubridor.* Monterrey, 1984. (Reprint, Monterrey, 1994.)

———. *El general Alonso de León: descubridor de Texas.* Monterrey, 1993.

Celiz, Francisco. *Diary of the Alarcón Expedition into Texas, 1718–1719.* Quivira Society Publications Vol. 5. Los Angeles, 1935.

———. *Unas páginas traspapeladas de la historia de Coahuila y Texas; el derrotero de la entrada a Texas del gobernador de Coahuila, sargento mayor Martín de Alarcón.* Ed. Vito Alessio Robles. Mexico, 1933.

Chapa, Juan Bautista. *Historia de Nuevo León, con noticias sobre Coahuila, Tamaulipas, Texas y Nuevo Mexico.* Monterrey, Mexico, 1961. (Reprint, Monterrey, 1985, 1990.)

————. *Texas & Northeastern Mexico, 1630-1690.* Ed. and intro. William C. Foster, trans. Ned F. Brierley. Austin, 1997.

Chipman, Donald E. "Alonso de León: Pathfinder in East Texas, 1686–1690." *East Texas Historical Journal* 33, 1 (Oct. 1995): 3–17.

Cross, Ruth. *Soldier of Good Fortune, an Historical Novel.* Dallas, 1936.

D'abbadie Soto, Enrique. *Fray Damián de Massanet (del Colegio Apostólico de la Santa Cruz de Querétaro) y la conjura francesa.* Querétaro, 1994.

Deveau, Augustine Francis. "Fray Antonio Margil de Jesús, apostolic missionary." M.A. thesis, University of Texas at Austin, 1953.

Dunn, William E. "Spanish Reaction Against the French Advance Toward New Mexico, 1717-1727." *The Mississippi Valley Historical Review* 2, 3 (Dec. 1915): 348–62.

Eckhart, George B. "Spanish Missions of Texas 1680-1800." *Kiva* 32, 3 (1967): 73–95.

Epistolae ad sanctissimum in Christo patrem Pium sextum pont. opt. max. ac sacram Rituum congregtionem pro causa beatificationis & canonizationis ven. servi Dei Antonii Margil a Jesu, missionarii apostolici Ord. min. S. Francisci de observantia. Rome, 1792.

Espinosa, Isidro Félix de. *Nuevas empressas del peregrino americano septentrional atlante: descubiertas en lo que hizo quando vivía, y aun después de su muerte han manifestado el V.P.F. Antonio Margil de Jesús.* Mexico, 1747.

Foster, William C. *Spanish Expeditions into Texas, 1689–1768.* Austin, 1995.

Foster, William C. and Jack Jackson, eds., and Ned F. Brierley, trans. "The 1693 Expedition of Governor Salinas Varona to Sustain the Missionaries Among the Tejas Indians." *The Southwestern Historical Quarterly* 97, 2 (Oct. 1993): 264–311.

Gilmore, Kathleen. "La Salle's Fort St. Louis in Texas." *Bulletin of the Texas Archeological Society* 55 (1984): 61–72.

Gómez, Arthur R., ed. *Documentary Evidence for the Spanish Missions of Texas.* Spanish Borderlands Sourcebooks Vol. 22. New York, 1991.

Gómez Canedo, Lino. *Primeras exploraciones y poblamiento de Texas, 1686–1694.* Monterrey, 1968.

Gregory XVI. *Decretum. Mexicana beatificationis, et canonizationis ven. servi Dei, fr. Antonii Margil a Jesu, missionarii apostolici ordinis minorum sancti Francisci de observantia.* Rome, 1836.

Guerra, José. *Fecunda nube del cielo guadalupano, y mystica paloma del estrecho palomar de el Colegio apostólico de Nuestra Señora de Guadelupe: relación breve de la vida exemplar del V.P.F. Antonio Margil de Jesús . . . sermón, que predicó en la Iglesia de N.S.P.S. Francisco de la Ciudad de Zacatecas el R.P.F. Joseph Guerra . . . en las honras que celebró . . . el dicho Colegio apostólico el dia 25 de Septiembre de 1726.* Mexico, 1726.

Gusmán, José María. *Notizie della vita, virtu, doni e miracoli del ven. sevo di Dio F. Antonio Margil de Gesu, missionario apostolico, dell' ordine de' minori osservanti. Estratte dai processi compilati per la causa della sua beatificazione e canonizzazione, e date alla luce dal P. Fr. Giuseppe Maria Gusman.* Rome, 1836.

Habig, Marion A. "Mission San José y San Miguel de Aguayo, 1720–1824." *The Southwestern Historical Quarterly* 71, 4 (1968): 496–516.

————. *The Zacatecan Missionaries in Texas, 1716–1834.* Texas Historical Survey Committee, Office of the State Archeologist Reports No. 23. Austin, 1973.

Hackett, Charles W. "The Marquis of San Miguel de Aguayo and His Recovery of Texas from the French, 1719–1723." *The Southwestern Historical Quarterly* 49, 2 (Oct. 1945): 193–214.

————. *Pichardo's Treatise on the Limits of Louisiana and Texas.* 4 vols. Austin, 1931–46.

Hickerson, Nancy Parrott. *The Jumanos: Hunters and Traders of the South Plains.* Austin, 1994.

Hoerig, Karl A. "The Relationship Between German Immigrants and the Native Peoples in Western Texas." *The Southwestern Historical Quarterly* 97, 3 (1994): 423–51.

Hoffmann, Fritz L. "The Mezquía Diary of the Alarcón Expedition into Texas, 1718." *The Southwestern Historical Quarterly* 41, 4 (April 1938): 312–23.

Houston, Margaret Belle. "Josita Rides by Night: The Story of a Girl Who Raced with Death to Save Her Lover's Life." *Good Housekeeping* (Apr. 1928): 20–22, 152, 155–156, 158, 161–162, 164, 166.

Jackson, Jack. *Los Mesteños : Spanish Ranching in Texas, 1721–1821.* College Station, 1986.

Jackson, Jack, Robert S. Weddle, and Winston De Ville. *Mapping Texas and the Gulf Coast: The Contributions of Saint-Denis, Oliván, and Le Maire.* College Station, Texas, 1990.

John, Elizabeth A. H. *Storms Brewed in Other Men's Worlds: The Confrontation of Indians, Spanish, and French in the Southwest, 1540–1795.* College Station, Texas, 1975.

Jones, Alice Ilgenfritz. *The Chevalier de St. Denis.* Chicago, 1900.

Jordan, Gilbert J. "W. Steinert's View of Texas in 1849." *The Southwestern Historical Quarterly*" 80, 1–4 (July–April 1976–77): 57–78, 177–200, 283–301, 399–416; 81, 1 (1977): 45–72.

Jordan, Terry G. "A Religious Geography of the Hill Country Germans of Texas," in *Ethnicity on the Great Plains.* Lincoln, 1980.

Jordan, Terry G., ed., and Marlis Anderson Jordan, trans. "Letters of a German Pioneer in Texas." *The Southwestern Historical Quarterly* 69, 4 (April 1966): 463–72.

Joutel, Henri. *The La Salle Expedition to Texas: The Journal of Henri Joutel, 1684–1687.* Ed. and intro. William C. Foster, trans. Johanna S. Warren. Austin, 1998.

Kattner, Lauren Ann. "From Immigrant Settlement into Town: New Braunfels, Texas, 1845-1870." *Amerikastudien/American Studies* 36, 2 (1991): 155–77.

Kavanaugh, Thomas. *La obra misionera de fray Antonio Margil de Jesús; tesis que presenta el señor Thomas Kavanaugh para obtener el grado de maestro en artes en español.* Mexico, 1950.

Keeth, Kent. "Sankt Antonius: Germans in the Alamo City in the 1850's." *The Southwestern Historical Quarterly* 76, 2 (Oct. 1972): 183–202.

Lemée, Patricia R. "Tios y Tantes: Familial and Political Relationships of Natchitoches and the Spanish Colonial Frontier." *The Southwestern Historical Quarterly* 101, 3 (Jan. 1998): 341–58.

Leutenegger, Benedict. *Apostle of America, Fray Antonio Margil.* Chicago, 1956.

————. "East Texas and the Venerable Margil." *El Campanario* 2, 1 (1971).

McCloskey, Michael B. *The Formative Years of the Missionary College of Santa Cruz of Querétaro, 1683–1733.* Washington, D.C., 1955.

McCorkle, James L., Jr. "Los Adaes: Outpost of New Spain." *North Louisiana Historical Association Journal* 12, 4 (1981): 113–22.

McDonald, Dedra S., comp. and Kinga Perzynska, ed. *Guide to the Spanish and Mexican Manuscript Collection at the Catholic Archives of Texas.* Austin, 1994.

McGraw, A. Joachim, John W. Clark Jr., and Elizabeth A. Robbins, eds. *A Texas Legacy: The Old San Antonio Road and the Caminos Reales, a Tricentennial History, 1691–1991.* Austin, 1991.

Moore, William Dyer. *Southwestern Nights and Romance* [poem]. Dallas, 1936.

The New Handbook of Texas. Ed. Ron Tyler, et al. 6 vols. Austin, 1996.

NewKumet, Vynola Beaver and Howard L. Meredith. *Hasinai: A Traditional History of the Caddo Confederacy.* College Station, Texas, 1988.

O'Connor, Kathryn S. *The Presidio La Bahía del Espíritu Santo de Zúñiga, 1721–1846.* Austin, 1966.

Oberste, William H. *the Restless Friar: Venerable Fray Antonio Margil de Jesús, Missionary to the Americas—apostle of Texas.* Austin, 1970.

Omaechevarría, Ignacio. *Pedro Pérez de Mezquia, O. F. M., 1688–1764; maestro y precursor de fray Junípero Serra en las misiones.* Vitoria, Spain, 1963.

Orozco y Jiménez, Francisco. *Epistolae ad sanctissimum im Christo patrem Pium Sextum pont. opt. max. ac sacram rituum congregtionem pro causa beatificationis & canonizationis ven. servi Dei Antonii Margil a Jesu missionarii apostolici ord. min. S. Francisci de observantia iterum prelo mandavit exc.mus ac rev.mus. D.D. Franciscus Orozco et Jimenez.* Guadalaxarae, 1931.

Peña, Juan Antonio de la. *Aguayo Expedition into Texas, 1721: An annotated Translation of Five Versions of the Diary Kept by Br. Juan Antonio de la Peña.* Ed. and trans. Richard G. Santos. Austin, 1981.

Perttula, Timothy K. *The Caddo Nation: Archeological & Ethnohistoric Perspectives.* Austin, 1992.

Phares, Ross. *Cavalier in the Wilderness; the Story of the Explorer and Trader Louis Juchereau De St. Denis.* Baton Rouge, 1952. (Reprint, Glouceter, MA, 1970.)

Picazo i Muntaner, Antoni. "Presupuestos defensivos y económicos de la colonización de Texas." *Archivo Ibero-Americano* 53, 209–212 (1993): 315–23.

Poyo, Gerald E., ed. *Tejano Origins in Eighteenth-century San Antonio.* Austin, 1991.

Ramón, Regino F. *Historia general del estado de Coahuila.* 2 vols. Saltillo, Mexico, 1990.

Ricklis, Robert A. *The Karankawa Indians of Texas: An Ecological Study of Cultural Tradition and Change.* Austin, 1996.

Ríos, Eduardo Enrique. *Fray Margil de Jesús, apóstol de América.* Mexico, 1941. (Reprint, Mexico, 1959.)

———. *Life of Fray Antonio Margil, O. F. M.* Washington, 1959.

Sánchez G., Daniel. *Vida popular del V. fray Antonio Margil de Jesús, franciscano recoleto.* Cartago, Costa Rica, 1924

———. *Un gran apóstol de las Américas septentrional y central: el V.P. Fr. Antonio Margil de Jesús, franciscano.* Guatemala, 1917.

Schenck, Friedrich. "A Letter From Friedrich Schenck in Texas to His Mother in Germany, 1847." Trans. Edward Herzberg, intro. Glen E. Lich. *The Southwestern Historical Quarterly* 92, 1 (July 1988): 145–165.

Schuetz-Miller, Mardith K. *Excavation of a Section of the Acequia Madre in Bexar County, Texas and Archeological Investigations at Mission San José in April 1968.* Austin, 1970.

Shelby, Charmion Clair. "St. Denis's Declaration Concerning Texas in 1717." *The Southwestern Historical Quarterly* 26, 3 (Jan. 1923): 165–83.

———. "St. Denis' Second Expedition to the Rio Grande, 1716–1719." *The Southwestern Historical Quarterly* 27, 3 (Jan. 1924): 190–216.

Shook, Robert W. "German Migration to Texas, 1830–1850: Causes and Consequences." *Texana* 10, 3 (1972): 226–43.

Stallard, Kathryn, et al., eds. *Society of Southwest Archivists Guide to Archival and Manuscript Repositories.* N.p., 1993.

Struve, Walter. *Germans and Texans: Commerce, Migration, and Culture in the Days of the Lone Star Republic.* Austin, 1996.

Teja, Jesús F. de la. *San Antonio de Béxar: A Community on New Spain's Northern Frontier.* Albuquerque, 1995.

Tiscareno, Angel de los Dolores. *El colegio de Guadalupe.* Zacatecas, 1905.

Tunnel, Curtis. "A Cache of Cannons: La Salle's Colony in Texas." *The Southwestern Historical Quarterly* 102, 1 (July 1998): 19–43.

Weber, David J. *The Spanish Frontier in North America.* New Haven, 1992.

Weddle, Robert S. *The French Thorn: Rival Explorers in the Spanish Sea, 1682–1762.* College Station, Texas, 1991

————. *San Juan Bautista; Gateway to Spanish Texas.* Austin, 1968. (Reprint, Austin, 1991.)

————. *Wilderness Manhunt: the Spanish Search for La Salle.* Austin, 1973.

Wellman, Paul Iselin. *Ride the Red Earth, a Novel.* Garden City, N.Y., 1958.

Yáñez, Jaime. *Fray Antonio Margil de Jesús: un misionero santo e incansable.* Mexico, 1983.